Knead It!

35 Great Bread Recipes to Make at Home Today

Jane Barton Griffith

I·5
EST 2013
·PRESS·

Lead Editors: Jennifer Calvert and Jarelle S. Stein
Senior Editor: Amy Deputato
Art Director: Jerome Callens
Book Project Specialist: Karen Julian
Production Manager: Laurie Panaggio
Production Supervisor: Jessica Jaensch
Production Coordinator: Leah Rosalez
Indexer: Melody Englund

i-5 PUBLISHING, LLC™
Chief Executive Officer: Mark Harris
Chief Financial Officer: Nicole Fabian
Vice President, Chief Content Officer: June Kikuchi
General Manager, i5 Press: Christopher Reggio
Editorial Director, i5 Press: Andrew DePrisco
Art Director, i5 Press: Mary Ann Kahn
Digital General Manager: Melissa Kauffman
Production Director: Laurie Panaggio
Production Manager: Jessica Jaensch
Marketing Director: Lisa MacDonald

Library of Congress Cataloging-in-Publication Data
Griffith, Jane Barton, 1944-
  Knead it! : start making artisanal bread today / by Jane Barton Griffith.
    p. cm.
  Includes bibliographical references and index.
  ISBN 978-1-935484-29-5
  1. Bread. 2. Cooking (Bread) I. Title.
  TX769.G745 2012
  641.81'5--dc23
                  2012027730

i-5 Publishing, LLC™
3 Burroughs, Irvine, CA 92618
www.facebook.com/i5press
www.i5publishing.com

Printed and bound in China
14 15 16 17   1 3 5 7 9 8 6 4 2

Dedication

To the memory of my mother, fine baker and extraordinary person.

How I wish she had lived to see this book.

Acknowledgments

Thanks to my daughter, Maria, and son, Nicholas. My professional baking adventure was sparked by my daughter's loving insistence that I make a list of what I wanted to achieve in life and by my son's enthusiastic consumption of my baked goods and his encouragement that I share my skills and interests with a wider world.

Thank you also to master bakers Christie Timon, Solveig Tofte, Ned Atwater, and Jim Amaral, and to bakery business expert Abe Faber, for taking time for interviews in which you shared your baking journeys and recipes. Richard Bourdon deserves special credit for his passion and devotion to artisanal bread baking—for his role as mentor to Chad Robertson, Mac McConnell, Ned Atwater, myself, and many other bakers and for letting Mac and me use the bakery and ingredients to test bread.

Finally, thank you to the bread testers who baked, gave their time without remuneration, and shared suggestions so that the included recipes are worthy and reliable. Louis Hutchinson, Julie Johnson, Aaron Stuvland, Nanci Edwards and Virginia Rice: I enjoyed working with you all. A special thanks to museum administrator and friend Judy Gradwohl, who displayed her scientific training as she meticulously tested and recorded many recipes, invented the "oven-safe bowl within the large Dutch oven" method, and encouraged me over cups of coffee after our Sunday gym workouts.

Thank you.

"[Bread baking is] one of those almost hypnotic businesses, like a dance from some ancient ceremony. It leaves you filled with one of the world's sweetest smells... there is no chiropractic treatment, no yoga exercise, no hour of meditation in a music-throbbing chapel that will leave you emptier of bad thoughts than this homely ceremony of making bread."

—M. F. K. Fisher,
The Art of Eating

CONTENTS

Bread is an everyday food, but when you form it with your own hands from fresh, wholesome ingredients, it becomes much more than that.

INTRODUCTION

Flour, water, and fire: these basic elements are the essence of breads made by civilizations throughout history. For millennia, bread was a staple of most meals and was at the center of the ritual of daily life at home. Days began with the preparing and baking of bread and ended with the breaking of it among family members. The rhythm of the seasons dictated the planting and harvesting of the grains. Then came the Industrial Revolution in the mid-nineteenth century, and the mechanization of food production changed the role of bread in our lives. Bread lost its flavor, dietary value, and—with the disappearance of warm homemade bread—its role in sustaining community and bringing family and friends together.

Fortunately, for the past three decades, a small revolution has been taking place in bread baking and a serious movement of bakers dedicated to reviving the tradition of artisanal breads has emerged and multiplied. There is debate about the definition of *artisanal bread*, but it is commonly defined as bread that uses only pure ingredients (no preservatives, chemicals, pesticides, or genetically altered elements) and is made by bakers personally involved in every step of the process. Most artisanal bakers use natural leavening agents such as wild yeast sourdough starters or preferments to make the bread rise, and they bake with whole grains. If they use white flour as an ingredient, the flour is unbleached and often stone-ground. The results are healthy breads with integrity—complex taste, nice crumb (air holes), and great texture and crust.

When I worked at Berkshire Mountain Bakery—a brick nineteenth-century former paper mill on the banks of the Housatonic River in the Berkshires (western Massachusetts)—I found everything about the bakery to be seductive. Customers, especially in the winter, seemed mesmerized by the warmth and red glow from the ovens when bakers opened the doors and pulled out sourdough breads using long wooden peels. The customers would take long deep breaths to take in the warm air, smell the aroma of the baking bread, and listen to the sound of the steam being injected into the oven. They surely envisioned breaking the crusts and biting into one of the golden breads spectacularly lined up on metro shelving. Richard Bourdon, owner and master baker of Berkshire Mountain Bakery, has a twenty-five-year history of perfecting his sourdough breads, and his customers appreciate his efforts.

If you can buy artisanal bread locally from a place like Berkshire Mountain Bakery, that is great (see the back of the book for a list of some artisanal bakeries around the United States). But even better is the ability to bake your own bread at home on a regular basis. The mission of this book is to get you to that goal, to walk you through each simple step of making your own artisanal bread. There are so many reasons to embark on this bread-making journey.

Besides just tasting better, artisanal breads made of whole grains are more healthful. And making your own bread forces you to slow down and teaches you to be more mindful. In fact, the easy availability of prepared foods with their high salt, fat, and sugar content is a major factor in overeating. But the opportunity to be involved in food from its beginning (because you know the origins of your ingredients) to creating the

product you put on the table invariably leads to eating a better balanced diet. Baking your own bread will also reduce your carbon footprint and contribute to your personal impact on the environment. Perhaps above all is the strong sense of personal satisfaction and accomplishment (not to mention the positive effect of praise from those who taste your bread). It's close to an outer-body experience.

Through this book you will discover how to bring this basic food into your life and experience the value of making and sharing bread. Baking bread is an achievable and rewarding activity. Currently, you may sometimes spend a day baking certain special-occasion breads. But the ultimate purpose of this book is to help you discover the bread-baking methods and recipes that best suit your lifestyle and taste buds in order for you to incorporate bread into the regular rhythms of your life. Enjoy filling your kitchen with the delicious aroma of fresh bread by using these traditional recipes adapted for the modern kitchen.

A taste of fresh artisanal bread will transform the way you think about the world!

PART I:

The How-Tos

CHAPTER 1

Benefits of Artisanal Bread

When you eat artisanal bread, the complexity of flavor and texture makes it clear why so many people have taken to baking their own. Eating a piece of warm crusty homemade bread evokes a childlike pleasure in the flavor as well as a sense of concrete accomplishment. The latter is especially satisfying in a world where many of our transactions are electronic and our jobs are process-oriented without a tangible end product. Food is meant to satisfy the stomach and the soul, and baking and eating your own bread do both.

Artisanal bread is also enjoying a recent surge of interest based on the awareness that we need to pay more attention to what we eat. If you make your own bread, you can put critical nutrients into your body and, especially if you use whole grains, increase the positive effects of fiber on your health. You are even eating less and feeling better because whole grains are more satisfying. The very act of inviting friends to sit down with you and share your homemade bread is a valuable way of eating mindfully and bringing people together to strengthen human connections. Eating in a joyful manner can be your "dietary ally," according to Peter Kaminsky (see "Dietary Allies" on page 12).

Baking bread can have a positive impact on more than your personal health and the health of your family—by choosing sustainably harvested ingredients, such as wheat that is grown and milled locally, you can also have one on the health of the planet. A few years ago, some people might have dismissed the idea of using local sustainably grown food as a fad. That's

more difficult to do today, when even the White House has its own a vegetable garden. And if healthfulness and eco consciousness aren't enough to sway you, you can also save money by baking your own bread and support your local economy and food producers by buying the ingredients closer to home. Baking artisanal bread is an easily achievable, rewarding activity that benefits you as well as your environment.

Dietary Allies

There is a genuine alarm over the increase in obesity in the country, with a recent report predicting that within twenty years, 51 percent of Americans will be obese or morbidly obese. New York food writer Peter Kaminsky's new book, *Culinary Intelligence*, makes a case for "engaging pleasure as your dietary ally." Kaminsky told a *New York Times* reporter, "I didn't want to write a finger-wagging book because I don't think that motivates people to eat well." Instead, he promotes eating more "FPC" (flavor per calorie) food. "By amping up the taste, you can satisfy your cravings," he said, pointing to foods such as spelt, olives, and porcini mushrooms as "emissaries of FPC." Kaminsky even ends a lot of meals with a square of dark chocolate. So top your whole-grain breads with some dark chocolate and enjoy losing weight!

WHAT'S GOOD FOR YOU

Flour, water, and salt are the basic ingredients of bread. Because different flours have different qualities, it's important to begin this book by looking at the most common flours we use for baking and the differences between them. We'll also discuss a few of the heritage grains that are becoming popular and more readily available.

To understand the vast difference between the nutritional value of the bread you bake at home and the bread you buy at the grocery store, it helps to begin with a little history lesson. When it comes to bread and nutrition, the Industrial Revolution, which began in the mid nineteenth century, had some detrimental effects. The transformation of milling methods and the mechanization of baking equipment both led to the production of less nutritious bread.

THE TRANSFORMATION OF FLOUR

During the Industrial Revolution, the operators of baking equipment, frustrated at how dough stuck to and gummed up equipment, reduced the amount of water and created drier dough. Reducing the ratio of water to grains deprived the grains of the water needed to force them to

The Industrial Revolution changed the way flour was milled and removed much of its beneficial content. Today, artisanal bakers are changing things back and embracing healthier whole grains.

release their nutrients. Simply put, your body will receive more nutrients from grains baked in more, rather than less, water. Think of how you cook rice: if you don't add the proper amount of water, the rice will be dry and undercooked. The same is true in bread. An ample amount of water is necessary to allow the starch in the grains to properly gel. If grains don't gel, they don't release their nutrients. Sure, they cook, but you are not getting the full value of the grains when you consume them. Properly cooked grains are also more digestible and create more harmony in your stomach.

The Industrial Revolution also changed where and how milling was done. Over the millennia of

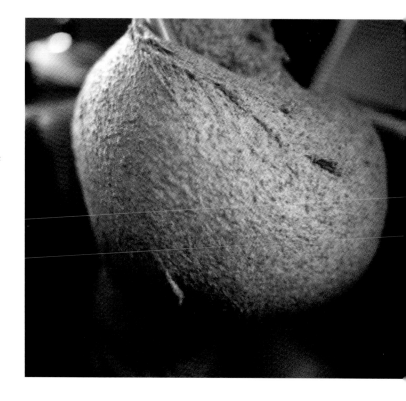

The wetness of dough made with the proper ratio of flour to water was an inconvenience to the mechanization of the bread-making process but is integral to the flavor and nutrition of homemade bread.

bread making before the late 1800s, milling grain was a local affair, with small mills grinding whole grains of wheat into flour for people in the nearby communities. Millers only produced as much flour as people could readily use in a limited time period because the fatty acids in the germ of milled wheat become rancid when exposed to oxygen for too long.

With the Industrial Revolution, the mechanization of milling made it possible to produce huge quantities of flour quickly and efficiently, and manufacturers wanted to transport this milled flour over longer distances to larger populations. To do that, they needed to find a solution to the problem of flour's becoming rancid in a relatively short period. What they found was that if the germ was eliminated from the wheat kernel, the flour that remained could be kept indefinitely. (Unfortunately, the germ contains most of the nutrients while the endosperm is mostly starch.) Manufacturers also proceeded to remove the hull, or bran, that produced flour's brownish tinge, which meant they ended up with whiter flour. Removing the bran, however, removed much of the nutrients and all of the fiber. What was left was the white endosperm that was milled into a fine flour of a fairly uniformly white color. Today, most flour is mass-produced from wheat grown with chemicals and pesticides and delivered to mills where huge stainless-steel rollers, generated by fossil fuel, mill the grain.

Wet and no-knead dough

Master baker Jim Lahey's no-knead bread recipe, published in a 2006 *New York Times* column, proved to be "one of those recipes that literally change the culinary scene with discussions on hundreds of blogs in dozens of languages around the world," in the words of author Paula Wolfert. Lahey's bread recipe was, in fact, a wet-dough recipe. Because wet dough is harder to knead, it is folded instead, so Lahey used the "no knead" label. (I wish it had been called the "wet dough" recipe to hark back to pre–Industrial Revolution bread, like Great Granny used to make.) You will learn to make wet dough and discover other secrets for producing the bread-baking methods that set the world on fire.

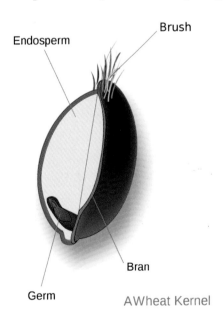

Endosperm
Brush
Germ
Bran
A Wheat Kernel

Manufacturers essentially began dissecting wheat and selling off its components separately to increase their profits. The endosperm, which was alone used to create white flour, is the least nutritious part of wheat.

Even in World War I, the government recognized the fact that bleaching leached from the flour nutrients that the army needed to fuel their troops.

Seeking to make flour even whiter and to speed up the aging of milled flour, companies began using bleaching in the early part of the twentieth century. Aging, as Harold McGee explains in his book *On Food and Cooking*, "affects the bonding characteristics of the gluten proteins in such a way that they form stronger, more elastic dough." Flour will age naturally, whitening and improving its baking qualities, but modern millers had little desire to store large amounts of flour for long periods of time and so took the bleach shortcut. Unfortunately, in addition to the questionable safety of the various bleaching products used, bleaching also destroys more nutrients in the flour. Eventually, as researchers realized that something had to be done to make flour more nutritious, manufacturers began to enrich flour, adding back some of the nutrients that had been lost.

Converting to Whole Grains

Converting to whole grains, or adding more whole grains to your diet, can make a huge difference. Why? Whole grains have fiber, which slows down the digestive process and causes food to spend more time in the digestive tract. This gives the body more time to absorb nutrients from the food. Most processed food and processed grains are "cheaters." They seem like food but they don't offer much of a health benefit. Simple carbohydrates, like those in highly processed white flour, cause blood sugars to spike quickly—making you feel energized—and then drop just as suddenly—resulting in low energy. Many people overeat to maintain the high from processed white flour and sugar. Whole grains, however, are complex carbohydrates, which are carbohydrates that the body "chews on" longer. This leaves you more satisfied and less hungry. One of the simplest ways to introduce whole grains into your diet is to bake your own bread. You are getting more bang for your buck, financially and (more importantly) health-wise.

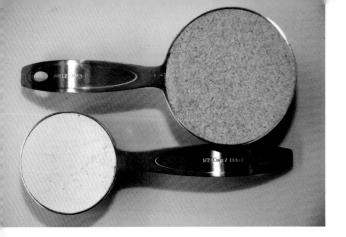

While white flour (bottom) is the most popular option for baking, whole-wheat flour (top), packed with more flavor and nutrition, is making a comeback.

WHEAT FLOURS

Most Americans think of flour as being made from wheat, so let's first look at the two categories of wheat flour that you will need to consider for bread baking: white and whole wheat. What we commonly refer to as *white flour* is basically wheat flour made from just the endosperm of the wheat kernel, rather than the whole kernel—the bran and the germ of the kernel having been stripped away in the manufacturing process, as mentioned previously (see the diagram of wheat kernel on page 14). White flour is not as healthy as that made from whole grains. Thankfully, heightened awareness of the connection between food and good health has actually prompted more Americans to eat more whole-grain products.

Whole-grain flour is nutritious because it retains its valuable nutrients as well as the fiber and the protein from the wheat's bran and germ. Manufacturers mill the whole grain, not just the white endosperm, to make whole-wheat flour.

WHEAT (WHITE) FLOUR

When it comes to wheat (white) flour, you can choose from two popular options: bread flour and regular unbleached flour. You might want to buy the stone-ground variety of wheat flour, which uses a process that preserves more nutrients (see "Advantages of Stone-Ground Flour" on page 18).

Bread flour has a high protein (gluten) content of 12 to 14 percent, which will cause the bread to rise well. This is the preferred flour for baking bread. *Regular unbleached flour* has a lower protein/gluten content of 10 to 12 percent, but it is perfectly adequate for making great bread. This flour is usually made by combining a hard red wheat with a softer

White flour is the flour many Americans grew up eating. Only in more recent years has it come under scrutiny for its comparable lack of nutritious value.

white wheat. You definitely want to buy unbleached flour because, as you just learned, bleaching it weakens gluten (the key to gaining a successful rise) and destroys nutrients. Although many white flours are enriched and fortified, the better brands of flour are grown and milled in ways that preserve what you need to make great bread.

WHOLE-WHEAT FLOUR

Whole-wheat flour is usually milled from hard red wheat, though with the advent of local wheat types, the strain may vary. In fact, don't be confused if you see whole-wheat white flour. This is a variety made with a strain of hard white spring wheat (more popular in the United Kingdom) that results in a slightly lighter, milder taste than bread made with whole red winter wheat. You can make a fairly light loaf of 100 percent whole-wheat flour, as long as the recipe includes enough water, you knead the dough long enough for the gluten to develop adequately, and you allow for a longer rise before shaping the dough.

Be cautious when you purchase whole-wheat flour because regulations allow bread to be labeled "whole wheat" even if it only contains a percentage of whole wheat. Plus, manufacturers sometimes add enough bran to darken the bread but advertise it as if the flour contains the bran and germ of each wheat berry.

Whole wheat keeps its nutritional content intact, so bread made with whole-wheat flour will be both healthful and delicious.

While stone milling may seem old-fashioned, there's a reason people have returned to using it. The process of grinding wheat this way preserves vital nutrients.

Advantages of Stone-Ground Flour

The stone-milling method slowly grinds the entire grain (bran, endosperm, and germ), preserving valuable nutrients that are lost in conventional high-speed high-heat milling methods. The process of slowly grinding grains without creating heat preserves vital nutrients. Another reason that stone-ground flours are better for you is that they must be sold while the germ is still fresh. All grains start to lose their nutrients as soon as they are milled, thus freshly milled grains have more nutrients.

Be sure to look for legitimate sources for stone-ground flours. (Government regulations in the United States allow manufacturers to label flour as "stone-ground" if the grain has only been put through a stone mill once and thereafter is ground by high-speed steel rollers.) Many good sources for stone-ground flours are available (see Resources at the back of this book).

Does the bread made from stone-ground grain taste better? Most people think so. Master baker Jeffrey Hamelman discusses the debate in his book *Bread: A Baker's Book of Techniques and Recipes* by summarizing a seminar he attended in France on the topic of stone-ground grains with "an august group of French bakers [with] strong opinions, backed up with impassioned voices, wagging fingers, and photos." Hamelman writes that "the conclusion . . . seemed to be that stone-ground flour produced bread with better flavor, while bread made with roller-milled flour had better volume."

NONWHEAT FLOURS

As the song proclaims "amber waves of grain," most Americans think of flour as being made only of wheat, but flour can be made from a variety of grains, nuts, and seeds. As we become more global, flours made from different grains are being introduced and recognized for their nutritional value. In addition, a growing movement calls for a return to what are termed *heritage* or *ancient grains*. Often, these grains are purer than wheat, which has been altered and crossbred many times. Recipes in this book include two ancient grains—spelt and KAMUT—as well as rye made from rye grass.

Society's awareness of ancient (or heritage) grains is increasing thanks to their health benefits and their availability through catalogs and in some stores. Large grocery chains and agricultural companies are becoming interested in these grains, as they see potential new markets for sales.

RYE

Rye grows well in poorer soils and cool climates and thus was widely used for flour by populations of eastern and northern Europe and Scandinavian countries. Like winter wheat, rye is planted in the fall; although green shoots appear, the plant lies dormant all winter. One interesting advantage is that cattle can feed off the green shoots in the fall without damaging the roots or inhibiting its rebirth in the spring. Come spring, the rye plants grow again and are ready for harvest during the summer.

Rye contains high levels of protein and fiber as well as valuable amounts of iron, calcium, zinc, and B and E vitamins. Rye's soluble fiber helps slow down the release of carbohydrates and sugars, so the consumer is satisfied longer than if he or she had eaten white flour. Some believe rye is a good source of prebiotics that help prevent cancer, type 2 diabetes, and heart disease. Because rye has little gluten, recipes that use all-rye flour tend to produce a heavy bread. I recommend that you use a ratio of 20 percent rye to 80 percent wheat (white) flour.

This hearty wheatlike grass creates equally hearty bread with benefits that include prebiotics for better health.

Home bakers are returning to spelt, an ancient grain, because of its unique flavor, health benefits, and easy digestibility.

SPELT

Thought to date back thousands of years to the Near East, spelt was the most common grain used in Europe during the Middle Ages. It did not arrive in the United States until the 1890s, however, and this proved to be an inauspicious time for its debut. The new machines of the Industrial Revolution could not mill spelt as easily as they could wheat because spelt has a tougher husk.

This outer hull has significant benefits, including that it allows for the development of a more delicate, water-soluble kernel, making it more easily absorbed by the body. The hard hull also helps in the retention of nutrients and prevents pollutants and insects from damaging the kernel. Those benefits, even had they been recognized at the time, would still have been outweighed by the difficulty in processing spelt. In addition, even though spelt was grown and used for bread in other countries, the US Department of Agriculture had a negative view of it. Their *Farmer's Bulletin* from July 1938, titled *Emmer and Spelt*, states: "Flour from emmer and spelt produces an undesirable dark, heavy bread; when flour is made, it is used mostly in mixtures with wheat flour. These crops are not suitable for the manufacture of bread-making flours in this country."

Zoom ahead half a century to the 1980s, when people begin to rediscover spelt—its popularity has grown steadily since then. People love the nutty flavor and appreciate the high protein and nutrition content. Spelt contains special carbohydrates that are an important factor in blood clotting and stimulating the body's immune system. It is also a superb fiber resource and has large amounts of B-complex vitamins. Spelt's total protein content is from 10 to 25 percent greater than the common varieties of commercial wheat, so bread made with spelt starter will have better crumb and volume.

Another reason for spelt's resurgence is that many people with gluten intolerances have turned to this more easily digestible grain. Some individuals who are unable to eat wheat can tolerate spelt, despite the fact that spelt is in the wheat family and contains gluten. I was first introduced to spelt by a friend who was diabetic and wheat-intolerant; she could tolerate spelt and it helped her maintain her weight.

KHORASAN (KAMUT)

Khorasan wheat is a brown grain that looks a bit like basmati rice; the grain is two to three times larger than that of traditional wheat. Scientists have determined that it originated thousands of years ago in the Near East, containing the toughness and diversity that many modern varieties of plants lack. Khorasan is thought to have survived through the centuries in small subsistence farming plots.

How the ancient grain found its way to the United States and became a viable crop makes quite a story. In 1949, a US airman on a trip to Egypt bought thirty-two wheat kernels from a local vendor who *claimed* they had been taken from an Egyptian tomb. The first airman gave them to another airman, who sent them to his father, a farmer in Montana. He grew and harvested this grain, which he called "King Tut's Grain." The farmer wasn't able to sell much of the grain, and it was only grown as a novelty over the next few years. Then, in 1977, a young organic farmer, Bob Quinn, came across a small quantity of the khorasan seeds at a local fair in Montana and spent ten years propagating the kernels. The health food market showed an interest in this new-old grain, and in 1990, the grain was registered and trademarked under the name KAMUT, an ancient Egyptian word meaning "Soul of the Earth."

KAMUT is also high in lipids, amino acids, zinc, vitamins B and E, and magnesium. Some claim the grain also has immune-boosting and anti-inflammatory properties. KAMUT has a high gluten content and less fiber than wheat. I consider the KAMUT bread made and sold at Tartine, Chad Robertson's bakery in San Francisco, to be one of the best artisanal, heritage-grain breads offered in the United States at this time.

The ancient grain khorasan, now found under the trademarked name KAMUT, is certified as organic in the United States because it is grown without the use of pesticides or fertilizers.

WHAT'S GOOD FOR THE COMMUNITY AND FOR THE EARTH

Baking artisanal breads involves more than questions about what type of flour to use. Hand in hand with the choice of flour come the questions of where to buy that flour and where that flour is grown and even how it is milled. Once again, we are turning back to recognize the value of methods we have discarded.

What factors brought about this change—or return—to growing wheat locally? Among them have been rising fuel costs, the diversion of former wheat lands to subsidized ethanol (corn) production, and rising demand for grain in China and India. At first, the demand for locally grown wheat was mainly from farmers who needed organic sources of feed for cattle raised to conform to organic standards. Now both commercial and home bakers are seeking local wheat sources because they realize that buying locally is good for the environment and supports local communities, not to mention that locally grown wheat is usually more nutritious and flavorful. Unlike other wheat, local wheat hasn't been overbred to suit every climate and purpose.

On the whole, society is already trending toward buying fresh goods locally, a habit that's healthy both physically and financially. Home bakers are extending this trend to locally and sustainably grown wheat.

At first, wheat was mainly grown locally for animal feed, often for organically raised cows.

LOCAL WHEAT

At one time, the Connecticut River Valley stretching through Connecticut and Massachusetts was the breadbasket of New England, where hardy people grew their own wheat despite the diseases and pests spurred on by a rainy climate and a rocky terrain that made harvesting wheat difficult. As the country expanded and transportation systems made it possible to ship grains over long distances, more and more wheat was grown in the Midwest and the West because of favorable climates and flat terrains (in places) that facilitate quick harvesting. Over the twentieth century, wheat crops disappeared not only from New England but also from small farms throughout the country; most wheat came to be grown on large midwestern and western farms.

Although the majority of wheat is still produced on these large farms today, an increasing number of small farmers in states from Maine to New Mexico are also growing and milling wheat. Most of these farmers are using organic or sustainable methods. In the western part of the country, the local wheat movement took root in 1995 in New Mexico, when a handful of farmers—some new to agriculture—asked the state's Department of Agriculture for help. Officials worked with them to plant fields in a region where wheat had not grown for half a century, and the Sangre de Cristo Cooperative was born. Almost two decades later, the cooperative is an unqualified success. The movement has also expanded to multiple regional organizations such as the Northeast Organic Wheat Project and the Northern Grain Growers Association, where ideas are exchanged, organic seeds are saved and shared, and growers promote the improvement of new wheat varieties for their locale.

Buying flour or bread made from locally grown and milled wheat supports your local economy, the environment, and your personal health.

But it isn't as simple as planting wheat, as bakery owners Cheryl Maffei and Jonathan Stevens of the Hungry Ghost Bakery in Northampton, Massachusetts, discovered. In the process of encouraging one hundred of their customers to grow wheat, the enthusiastic bakers and bakery supporters learned that they couldn't even purchase decent wheat varieties that could flourish and resist disease in their locale. Plus, the facilities for storing and milling wheat had vanished and the closest mills were too far away to conveniently mill flour for their bakery. The Massachusetts bakery and its customers are continuing to advocate for local wheat, and Maffei and Stevens have persuaded their state university to start a research project to determine the best wheat strains for a future planting.

In some parts of the country, the federal government is offering assistance. In 2009, under an initiative called *Know Your Farmer, Know Your Food*, the US Department of Agriculture provided a portion of $19 million to the University of Maine to investigate and identify wheat strains that would increase Maine farmers' capacity to produce high-quality organic bread wheat. The USDA has also provided grants to the Northeast Organic Wheat Project and Northeast Sustainable Agriculture Research and Education (NESARE) to conduct wheat trials in Maine, Massachusetts, New York, and Vermont.

In April 2010, I interviewed Jim Amaral, founder of Maine-based Borealis Breads and a major proponent of local wheat. He spoke of his efforts to encourage both local farmers and millers to produce the quality flour he needs to fulfill his goal of making all of his baking products from

Maine-grown wheat. When another major Maine baker and I were discussing Maine wheat, he complained that his bakery couldn't buy enough local wheat, partially because Jim was purchasing it all. The demand for local wheat, at least in parts of New England, far outstrips the supply.

Farmers, millers, and bakers held the Fourth Annual Kneading Conference in Skowhegan, Maine, in July 2010 to discuss the local wheat movement—or in their words, "the quiet revolution." An attendee of the conference, Michael Scholz of the Albion Bread Company in Albion, Maine, started baking bread with local flour in 2004 and selling it at a farmers' market. "I never have enough," he told a *New York Times* reporter. "I have people in tears. One eighty-year-old lady screamed at me: 'Who took the last five baguettes? You louse, you louse!'"

It turns out, people can't get enough of home-baked bread made from wholesome local ingredients.

Stone Milling

Once again, we are beginning to recognize the value of methods we have discarded, such as traditional milling methods where grains are crushed between two large turning stones. Some traditional mills are being restored and put into use, as wheat that is grown locally needs to be milled nearby for the term *local* to make any sense. Other mills are also using this traditional method. The increased use of stone-ground wheat is not a return to horse-and-buggy days, however. Contemporary mills in the United States use methods powered with electricity rather than the former methods that used water or animals. At the same time, they are providing local jobs and offering a healthy food product. Some bakers mill flour even closer to home—in their own bakeries. Among them is Richard Bourdon, who mills his flours between two millstones powered by electricity right in his Berkshire Mountain Bakery.

CONCERNS ABOUT LOCAL WHEAT

Farmers must overcome several major hurdles to growing grains locally. Agribusiness grows wheat for consistency and yield, while the supporters of locally grown wheat focus on the wheat's taste and nutritional value. *Inconsistent* is, in fact, the adjective most frequently used to criticize locally grown wheat. The bread will not always perform equally due to variations in the wheat and milling, and American consumers demand uniform products. Some commercial bakers claim they cannot afford to take the risk of baking with local wheat that may produce an inconsistent product. In a 2008 *New York Times* article, "Flour That Has the Flavor of Home," Amy Scherber of Amy's Bakery in New York City spoke about the impracticalities involved in asking her bakers to deal with local flour's quirks and nuances. One mishandled batch, she explained, could translate into hundreds of pounds of dough headed for the dumpster.

Local wheat has not been homogenized and therefore may create an inconsistent product, unlike those produced by factories that purchase wheat from large agribusinesses. But small bakeries and home bakers feel this lack of uniformity is an advantage of home-baked bread.

Alton Earnhart, a small wheat producer and owner of Lightning Tree Farm in New York's Hudson Valley, clearly identifies the dichotomy with the locally grown wheat movement. He questions whether greater demand for local wheat will require more standardization. In the same newspaper article, Earnhart said, "The idea that we have to get it so sophisticated that everything is perfect kind of defeats what I think made this unique when we started out." Before local and in-season foods can become more universally accepted, we as consumers must adjust our expectations and allow for some variations in our locally grown products and produce. As home bakers and consumers support the local-food movement, commercial bakers will adjust to the market demand and adapt their bread baking to make delicious breads from local wheat.

We need to relearn the meaning of the term *balance*. As agribusiness increased yields and introduced chemicals and genetically altered seeds, the total nature of the industry shifted. It caused the loss of a culture and nutrition while promoting homogenization and simplification. According to author Gary Paul Nabhan, in his book *Where Our Food Comes From*, agribusiness has focused on growing limited types of food with limited methods in a landscape that has been extensively simplified and even made "regularly shaped to enable machinery to be applied copiously without the inconvenience of taking nature's messy complexity into account."

When you buy locally grown grain for your bread, you are participating in the process, determining who profits and how grains will be grown in the future. The Russian botanist Nikolai Vavilov was one of the first people to recognize and publicly profess that our foods have been shaped by past generations and that correlations exist between the cultural diversity in a landscape and the diversity of its agriculture and crop varieties. As I wrote this book, I thought about how my ancestors and the lands where they lived have influenced my love of New England Anadama bread and northern European-style rye breads. I hope that baking bread will evoke a sense of your own heritage and of preserving the environment for future generations.

Old Is New

People once knew what strains of grain would best resist the potential ravages of weather and disease in their regions, but that knowledge was lost when farmers stopped growing wheat locally. That means we must start over. Fortunately, we're getting some valuable help from the records left behind by seed pioneers and farmers. A century ago, Quaker Cyrus Pringle amassed a large collection of seeds from places throughout the United States and Mexico, as well as from seed exchanges with Europeans. The seeds collected by Pringle now reside at the Smithsonian Institution and Harvard University, part of the Pringle Herbarium, which today houses more than 20,000 samples. According to the Pringle Herbarium's website, "We have found that heritage wheat yields are higher in organic systems than the best-yielding modern wheat currently grown in Vermont." The Vermont Red Hen Bakery has even named one of their breads the Cyrus Pringle, a "one-pound boule made entirely with Vermont-grown wheat."

Another invaluable source has been an 1885 diary entry by a South Stafford, Vermont, farmer about a particularly successful strain of Hungarian wheat. Vermont researchers were able to acquire samples of the same seed from the Hungarian Cereal Genebank. In a 2010 article about the research, "Vermont's Heritage Wheat," printed in *Vermont's Local Banquet*, scientist Eli Rogosa reported that Hungarian yielded among the highest in our Vermont trials last year, with robust stalks and sturdy stands of fat, golden seed. It is beloved in Hungary for high baking quality." One step at a time, researchers, farmers, and consumers are exploring ways to grow local grains.

NO-TILL FARMING

A great debate is taking place about the way wheat and other crops are grown. Some farmers and scientists are studying and experimenting with methods that will be better for producers, consumers, and the earth itself. Traditional methods of farming can be hard on the land, leading to soil erosion, loss of water and nutrients, and further pollution of our air and surrounding environment. Farmers release huge amounts of carbon dioxide—the major greenhouse gas—just by plowing their fields. It's pretty simple: Good soil is dark and contains humus, which in turn contains organic carbon, built up from generations of decomposed crops. Tilling exposes the humus to sun and oxygen, which begin to destroy the microbes in the soil, eating them and "breathing out" carbon dioxide.

No-till (sometimes called *zero tillage*) methods of farming are gaining popularity. No-till farming reduces soil erosion, enriches the earth with old plants that are left to decompose, reduces gas emissions, and saves the lives of earthworms. OK, the idea of saving earthworms may not tug on your heart strings, but these insects and the other creatures that flourish in no-tillage systems are directly responsible for the benefits to the earth of this system of planting.

With the no-tilling method, a machine rotates a wheel across the field, poking holes in the ground into which seeds are released. The lack of disturbance to the land reduces soil erosion, and the carbon dioxide stored in the soil increases with each year the wheat plants are allowed to decompose, benefitting future crops. If the wheat is planted at high altitudes, there is an additional advantage: weeds aren't able to survive when the grain is grown high above sea level,

No-till farming avoids the use of large plows, which release greenhouse gases. Instead, a seeder creates divots in the earth into which it places seeds. After farmers harvest the wheat, the stalks are allowed to decompose in place. This eliminates the need for disturbing the earth to remove them.

Parts of Montana are perfectly suited by their location and climate to growing wheat using sustainable methods.

eliminating the need for herbicides or pesticides. In areas where rain and soil are rich feed for weeds, farmers and researchers are exploring other solutions. One of the most enthusiastic proponents of no-till organic wheat is Wheat Montana in Three Forks, Montana. Using no-till grains makes sense to master baker Richard Bourdon. Bourdon is a major supporter of the local sustainable agriculture movement called Berkshire Grown, a vigorous coalition of local food producers in the Berkshires of western Massachusetts. He began buying a no-till grain from Wheat Montana in 2010. Although buying wheat from Montana may seem to conflict with Bourdon's dedication to buying local, he believes it makes more sense to buy wheat from regions where the climate best suits its production (in this case, Montana), and where more sustainable agriculture methods can be used, than to buy wheat from a more hostile local environment, where herbicides will probably be required. Bourdon is waiting for local strains of wheat to be reintroduced to the Berkshires and grown—affordably—without chemicals. Then he will switch to buying wheat locally, as he does all his other bread-baking ingredients.

No-till farming offers a new option for growing wheat on a major scale with more sustainable methods. If you can buy organic or sustainably grown local and organic no-till grain, you will be giving a gift to yourself and to the planet.

CHAPTER 2

Scaling, Proofing, and Shaping

This chapter and the next will guide you through the major steps involved in bread making, explain the techniques involved, and reveal some priceless master baker secrets that you will rely upon for years to come. We'll also talk about the reasons for choosing certain techniques over others, such as why it's better to fold your dough than punch it (no matter how bad your day has been) when the time comes to degas (remove air bubbles from) the dough. In addition, you'll find boxes titled "Tools & Equipment" that list and discuss what you'll need during each step of the process.

In this chapter, I'll take you from "ready, set, go" to folding the dough and allowing it to proof through the final shaping stages before popping the dough in the oven. In the shaping section, you'll learn how to create basic bread shapes as well as some intricate variations, including the ubiquitous baguette and its festive wheat-stalk-shaped cousin, the *épi de blé*.

STEP 1: *MISE EN PLACE*

The French phrase *mise en place* means "everything in its place." Used in restaurants and culinary schools to signify that one has all necessary ingredients and equipment at hand, *mise en place* is a good way to begin your transformational journey to baking bread. No matter how excited I am to get started on a baking project, slowing down and making sure I am organized and ready to concentrate on the task, mentally and physically, is essential. To prepare yourself

Searching your cupboards for a necessary tool or ingredient is a hassle you don't need in the middle of a recipe.

for baking, begin by carefully reading the recipe and noting the stages and time frames for each phase. Adjust your work or other projects to accommodate baking or vice versa. If you're not sure you're going to have enough time today, then pick another day when you won't be rushed, especially if you're new to baking artisanal bread or you're trying out a new recipe. If today is the day, then gather up your ingredients and equipment and arrange them within easy reach. Now, with everything in order—*mise en place*—you can launch into making your very own bread.

The Logic of *Mise en Place*

When you pack your suitcase for a vacation, you put all the "ingredients" in it that you will need to "execute" your trip when you arrive—a bathing suit for that swim in tropical waters, shoes to match a dress or suit for a dinner outing. The same mentality applies to cooking or baking. Have you ever looked in a restaurant kitchen and noticed the bowls of presliced vegetables or chopped herbs in small dishes? Everything is ready so that once the chef begins, the steps toward perfection of the final dish flow smoothly.

Follow the examples of master bakers and great chefs by thinking ahead and having all ingredients and tools handy. Timing is critical in bread making, and taking *mise en place* seriously will help you prevent mishaps, such as failing to have a preheated baking container ready when you want to put the dough into the oven.

STEP 2: SCALING (MEASURING)

The next step in the process of preparing to bake bread is to weigh your ingredients. While you may be used to using measuring cups and spoons, the best tool for measuring ingredients is a scale. A "cup" of flour can vary depending on how densely you pack the flour, the size of the cup (because different manufacturers' measuring cups can vary slightly), and whether you scrape across the top of the cup or tap the flour down into it to finish measuring. Bakers agree that good bread depends on precise measurements, and measurements taken without a scale are too unpredictable. In addition, an important aspect of this book is to emphasize the benefits of bread with a high percentage of water. By weighing your ingredients, you will have better control over the water-to-flour ratio.

Although an old-fashioned scale is a charming addition to the kitchen, a digital scale will prove far more useful.

I was slow converting to scaling ingredients, but now I wouldn't work any other way. Once you begin weighing ingredients on a scale, you'll appreciate the advantages (just as professional bakers do). Many great authors of baking cookbooks offer their recipes in weights alone. All the recipes in this book are presented in grams, but equivalents are provided for those who haven't yet converted to weighing ingredients.

Digital scales have a tare button that takes the scale back to zero. Once you place the empty bowl on the scale, pressing the button will let you "zero out" the scale. You can repeat this process after adding and weighing each ingredient.

1. Place your mixing bowl on a digital scale.

2. Press the tare button on the scale to take the weight back to zero.

3. Weigh your first ingredient (usually flour) and then press the button again.

4. Continue to add ingredients to their correct weight, and always remember to go back to zero before putting in the next ingredient.

Tip: When you first start to use a scale, I suggest you measure each ingredient separately before adding them, one by one, to the bowl. That way, you're less likely to put an excessive amount of some ingredient into the bowl, which can be a hassle to remedy. With practice, though, you will be able to add one ingredient, tare/zero the scale out again, and then add another ingredient carefully without having to use separate bowls. In fact, this is one of the big advantages of using a scale—fewer dishes to wash.

Scales

Several types of scales are available, from balance scales to compression scales, but I recommend going straight to a digital scale because of its ease and accuracy. You can buy scales in most specialty kitchen shops or on the Internet. I prefer scales that are big enough that the bowl on the platform does not hide the digital screen. I've used some scales that forced me to crook my head and neck sideways to look under the bowl to read the measurements.

A good bargain site for scales is www.saveonscales.com. Primo brand scales are available for around thirty dollars and even come in red. If you want a higher quality or bigger scale, you can easily spend between fifty and a hundred dollars.

STEP 3: MIXING

The act of mixing ingredients while making bread is more critical than you might realize. It's not like whipping a brownie mix together, but it's not scary either. You will be mixing together flour, water, yeast, salt, and possibly other ingredients, such as seeds and nuts. The two most significant acts in mixing are ensuring that the water you use is the proper temperature and kneading the dough until the correct amount of gluten develops.

CHECKING WATER TEMPERATURE

Be sure to watch your water temperature (and even your dough temperature as you get more advanced). Water that is too hot can slow or kill the yeast and water that is not warm enough will not be conducive to the yeast's growing. An ideal water temperature for most bread baking is 85 to 95 degrees Fahrenheit; yeast thrives best in this range.

The easiest way to check water temperature is with an instant-read thermometer. If you don't have one, now is the time to buy one. While working at Berkshire Mountain Bakery in Massachusetts with master baker Richard Bourdon, I discovered that I had been using water that was a wee bit too cool for years, which had undoubtedly been affecting the quality of my sourdough breads by compromising the yeast.

While the concepts of mixing and kneading the dough may seem simple, you'll need to learn certain techniques to ensure that your bread turns out as you want it to.

Mixing Bowls and Scrapers

Having the right types and sizes of mixing bowls makes all the difference in how you work. Be sure to find a large ceramic, glass, or metal bowl, big enough to hold the total amount of flour and water for your bread-making plans.

The bowl should be a comfortable size for you. I find that the firmness of the bowl on the counter and curve of the inside of the bowl are important to my confidence as I work with the bread. I live in a historic farmhouse, and my bowls are mostly a collection of antique ceramic bowls, which are heavy. They look great, but once I started to bake bread more seriously, I switched to large metal bowls, which are lighter and easier to rinse out and wash. Using a light metal bowl makes a huge difference in the speed of my bread baking, so I recommend you consider metal bowls too.

You will also want several medium bowls to weigh the various flours or sourdough starter as well as a couple of very small bowls for weighing salt and yeast until you are secure with scaling all the ingredients together in one bowl. While you are at it, pick up a bowl scraper. This scraper comes with a gentle curve to one side, which makes it perfect for scraping the inside of a bowl. You'll find lots of uses for this tool, which is more comfortable to handle than a spatula.

Instant-Read Thermometer

To bake great bread, you'll need to purchase an instant-read waterproof "probe" food thermometer. The water and dough will need to be certain temperatures to ensure the best result, and the temperature of the baking loaf determines whether it has finished baking. (Don't believe the myth that you can tell when a loaf has finished baking by tapping on the bottom to see if it sounds hollow.) You don't need a super fancy instant-read thermometer—you just need one that can tell you the correct temperature.

You'll find two main types of thermometers: 1) a one-piece probe that you stick directly into the object you want to read, and 2) a probe that is attached via a wire to a box where you can see the temperature readout. I recommend buying the simpler stick thermometer because you can use it with one hand and you don't have to worry about the wire getting in the way of things.

Baking is the easy part. Creating the dough that will result in that perfect loaf of homemade bread is trying at first, but you'll get the hang of it with practice.

MIXING TECHNIQUES

The goal in mixing together water, flour, and yeast is to form gluten and get the random gluten molecules to align themselves in straight lines. These aligned gluten lines will then trap carbon dioxide gases that form as the yeast ferments, causing the bread to rise with volume and lightness. There is an even more complicated scientific explanation of what goes on during the mixing process, but if you focus on developing elasticity and consistency in your dough, you will be fine. The mixing of dough is complete when the dough has developed the right amount of gluten and can pass the windowpane test (see the sidebar "Gluten Windowpane Test"). Following are three mixing techniques.

Use your hands in an overlapping motion to mix the ingredients together, taking the ingredients from the bottom and mixing them with those at the top until they appear to be well blended. Now, with the dough still in the mixing bowl, you can start the pinching method:

1. Place your wet hands on the dough, thumb on one side and four fingers on the other side.

2. Pinch the dough in half.

3. Rotate the bowl and pinch the dough in the opposite direction.

Soon, the bread will develop the desired elasticity and you can use the windowpane test to see if it is ready. The pinching method is best for the recipes in this book because most dough will be wet and often quite sticky. Dough in a mixing bowl is easier to work with. If you keep your hands wet, you can manipulate the dough fairly effortlessly until the gluten develops. In the other two techniques, the wet dough will want to cling to your work surface or whisk, which leads to the tendency to add more flour to the dough.

Gluten Windowpane Test

No matter which of the mixing methods you have used, try the windowpane test to see if you have achieved the right amount of elasticity and cohesion in your dough.

1. Take a portion of dough, holding either side of the dough between your thumbs and first fingers with thumbs facing you.

2. Stretch out the dough, making a rectangular shape.

3. If the dough doesn't tear and you are able to see light through the windowpane you're creating, the dough is ready for the next stage.

Dough can sometimes be too sticky to effectively work with on a flat surface. Keeping your ingredients in the bowl and wetting your hands can help you avoid this problem.

KNEADING METHOD

Use your hands to mix the ingredients together as described in the pinching method. In the kneading method, however, you will slide the dough out onto a smooth workspace, such as a wooden cutting block or stone slab.

Kneading was the mixing method most commonly associated with baking bread before the pinching method gained popularity. One advantage of the traditional kneading method is that it can be a stress reliever.

1. Put the dough in front of you and place both hands on top of it.
2. Push down with the heels of your palms and push the dough away under your hands.
3. Roll the top of the dough over the portion you have just kneaded.
4. Turn the dough around and knead in the opposite direction.
5. Continue until the dough fully develops its gluten and can pass the windowpane test.

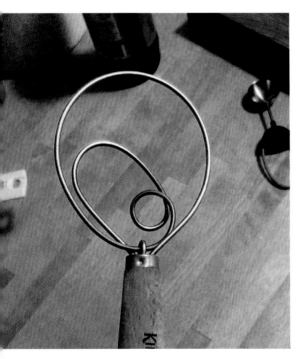

A Danish whisk is a good investment if you plan on making bread often.

WHISK METHOD

The third method for integrating ingredients and preparing the dough is to utilize a strong whisk, such as a Danish whisk. A thin wire whisk won't work because the dough will cling to the wire and you won't be able to mix the ingredients. The wire on a Danish whisk is firm, not flexible, and the wooden handle is strong. I've known people to rave about it as a wrist saver, saying they feel the whisk is an extension of their arm.

1. Starting at the edge of the dough, move the whisk in a circular motion around the bowl.
2. At the same time, lift up the dough and fold it over to move dough from the bottom to the top.
3. Continue until the dough fully develops its gluten and can pass the windowpane test.

STEP 4: FIRST PROOF

Dough, before it is baked, must be allowed to *proof* for a period of time. Some baking books will refer to this phase as the time to let the dough *rest* or *rise*. *Proof*, *rest*, and *rise* all refer to the same phenomenon. You want to let your bread proof in order to give the yeast time to do its magic. It will undergo various chemical changes that cause the dough to ferment (develop taste) and rise (capture carbon dioxide bubbles that make for a good structure, called *crumb*).

Although you don't have to understand the exact chemistry of what's occurring, it's important to know that fermentation is a balance among yeast, temperature, and time. During the fermentation stage, the yeast feeds on the natural sugars in the flour and creates the by-products of carbon dioxide and alcohol. Then, during the baking process, those carbon dioxide gases get caught in the strands of gluten that you have developed in your dough through kneading and make air pockets that give the bread a light and airy texture. The alcohol evaporates during the baking process, but it has already played its major role—affecting the taste of your bread.

For this first stage of proofing/fermenting, the dough can be left in the mixing bowl covered by a damp dishtowel. Recipes instruct you to allow the bread to rise in a warm location. Ideally,

All you need to do during proofing is place a covered bowl of dough in a warm location—the yeast in the dough will take it from there.

this is a space that is between 72 and 80 degrees Fahrenheit. You will find your own unique way of creating that warm space. Because my farmhouse is drafty and never reaches 72 degrees in the winter, I use a little space heater in a small bathroom. In the summer, I have the opposite problem—the temperature can be over 80 degrees with humidity. The testers of the breads in this book each had their own way of solving the issue, from using the top of a refrigerator or microwave to balancing proofing loaves on a radiator.

Traditionally, artisan bread proofs for three different periods of time. The first proof comes immediately after you have mixed the bread, the second proof follows the steps of dividing and preshaping the dough, and the last proof should begin when you have given the loaves their final shape. Each stage must be respected or your dough won't produce the results you desire.

Taking Time for Taste

Yeast that is allowed to proof for the time designated in a recipe develops flavor. Allowing bread to proof several times adds complexity to the taste and tang to the flavor. You may come across quick breads, which use a large percentage of yeast to make the breads rise rapidly and to shorten the whole baking process. These recipes often call for the addition of eggs, butter, oil, fruits, and nuts because the dough hasn't had enough time to develop its flavor.

CHECKING THE PROOFING

Testing your dough during each phase of proofing is a learning process. The recipes in this book will tell you how long into this first proofing period you should test the dough. Yet this is also your opportunity to begin developing your awareness of the stages of the dough's development and to learn when dough has finished proofing by examining its elasticity, texture, and smell. At the end of the recipe's time period, touch the dough. It should feel springy and have some resistance or body (not be too soft or floppy), and you should be able to smell a slightly acidic or vinegary odor. Your fingers will soon be sensitive to touching the dough to test whether the dough springs back with the proper amount of tension. Another way to test whether the bread has proofed properly is to stick a finger into the dough. If the indentation remains, and does not fill up with dough, the dough is ready. You need to become aware of how perfectly proofed bread feels to avoid these two pitfalls:

Underproofing: If bread hasn't had enough time to rise, it will be tight and spring back too quickly. Finding that delicate balance between bread with too much bounce and one that has already lost its spring is one of the challenges of learning to bake superb bread.

Overproofing: Occasionally, at first, you may overproof your dough by letting the dough rise too long. In this case, bubbles will have developed (and sometimes popped and collapsed). You can test for overproofing if, when you poke your finger into the dough, the impression made by your finger fills with dough. Overproofed bread usually won't rise much during baking because it has already gone through the stage of rising and collapsing.

Checking the proofing every so often is important; under- or overproofing the dough can both create baked results that are less than desirable.

Place a cup of just-boiled water in the microwave with proofing loaves, and you have a homemade proof box.

ASSISTING PROOFING

Commercial bakers have proof chambers—usually walk-in rooms—that encourage the dough's fermentation by controlling temperature and humidity. The warm temperatures increase the activity of the yeast, resulting in more carbon dioxide production and a higher rise. You shouldn't really need a proofing device at home. Instead, you can adjust your baking times to the heat and humidity of the space where you are baking.

However, if the place you are baking in is very cool, you want more predictability over the time frames involved in your bread baking; or if you are in a rush, you will want to have a proof box, which you can probably create from objects you already have on hand. Here are some examples from a few friends of mine:

- ❖ Surround the bowl containing the dough with several containers of hot water and then cover everything with a large plastic storage container.
- ❖ Put a couple of hot towels in the bottom of a clothes dryer, set the bowl of dough on the towels, and close the dryer door.
- ❖ Place a cup of just-boiled water and the dough in a microwave.
- ❖ Drape heavy, coarse, slightly floured fabric in a bowl, then place the dough on top of the fabric, and cover the bowl with another piece of heavy fabric to trap in some of the warm air generated by the dough.

RETARDING THE DOUGH

Retarding the dough is the opposite of proofing: you slow the rising process by placing the dough in a refrigerated location and lowering its temperature. Commercial bakers have controlled temperature spaces designated to retard the dough, but your kitchen refrigerator can become your very own retarding vehicle. (**Tip**: When you are retarding dough in your home refrigerator, be sure to cover the bread so that the dough doesn't dry out and form a crust.)

Slowing the fermentation process encourages the development of certain complex flavors—specifically, dough that is retarded has a slightly sour taste. Chapter 4 will teach you how to make bread using a slow-fermenting method. Jim Lahey's book on no-knead bread recommends an overnight retardation of the dough; this process brilliantly produces bread with a sour taste without the need to use a sourdough starter.

STEP 5: FOLDING (DEGASSING)

After the first proofing stage, you will need to fold the bread. For this you will need a flat surface such as a linoleum countertop, a wooden cutting board, or a marble slab. Whatever you choose should be lightly dusted with flour to prevent the dough from sticking to it. Folding bread with what are called *letter* or *circle* folds is a way of increasing the dough's strength by aligning the gluten strands. Folding the dough also removes excess carbon dioxide that has built up in the bread. Because too much carbon dioxide eventually will interfere with the yeast activity, you'll need to perform folds periodically (as called for in the recipe).

When I baked with my mother, she used to "punch down" her breads to degas them. Punching down the dough accomplishes only the single goal of degassing it, but folding both degasses the dough and builds strength in the gluten.

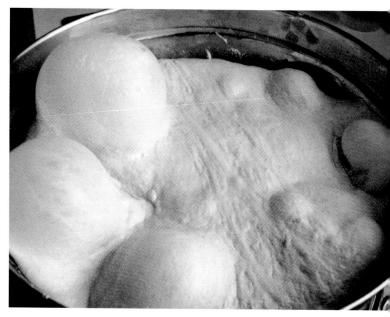

After proofing, dough may need to be folded to work out some of the bubbles created by fermentation.

LETTER FOLDING TECHNIQUE

The letter-fold method acquires its name from its imitation of the way a letter is folded into thirds to fit into a business-size envelope.

1. Lay the dough flat on the work surface with any odd scraps of dough on top.
2. With quick hand motions, gently pat the dough into a small rectangle with the longer side lying in a horizontal line (east-west) to you and the short ends perpendicular (north-south) to you.
3. Starting either from the right or left side, pick up one side of the dough and fold the piece so that the edge you picked up is in the center.
4. Repeat the same action with the other side of the dough so that its edge rests now at the other edge.
5. Now rotate the dough and have the longer side of the rectangle at a perpendicular angle (north-south) to you.
6. Take the top of the dough and fold it over, placing its edge in the middle of the rectangle.

7. Pick up the bottom of the dough and fold it over the other fold.

You have now completed the full letter fold: side-to-side folds and then top and bottom folds. That's a total of four folds. Sometimes you may only do a partial fold (two folds), or a recipe may call for eight folds. With experience and feel, you will know how many folds your dough requires.

CIRCULAR FOLDING TECHNIQUE

Lay the dough flat on the work surface and imagine the hands of a clock on it. You will follow the instructions below by lifting up the edges of the dough at each quarter marking, one after the other.

1. Flatten the dough gently into a circular shape.
2. Start at the twelve o'clock mark. Holding the side of the dough between your thumb and first finger, lift it up and press it into the center.
3. Move to the three o'clock mark and gather a second section of dough and press it into the center.
4. Continue with folds at the six and nine o'clock positions until you have formed a small ball of dough.
5. In either a forward or circular motion, drag or roll the dough, always tucking in the bottom to create a tension on the surface of the dough and form it into a more cohesive shape.

The letter fold method should come pretty naturally to anyone familiar with "snail mail."

STEP 6: DIVIDING

After you have finished folding the dough, it is ready to be divided, which means portioning the dough into the number of pieces you plan to shape into loaves of bread. The most common tool used for dividing dough is a bench scraper. When you divide the dough, you don't want to pull or yank it. Tearing the dough breaks the threads of gluten, creating weak areas, particularly because the gluten strings are supporting those nice fat air bubbles that are inflating the dough. By using a wide bench scraper, you can minimize the number of cuts and potential breaks in the dough.

1. Place the dough in front of you on your work surface.

2. Hold the bench scraper in your hand and, using a quick vertical movement, cut straight down into the dough, applying pressure and making a clean cut through the wet dough.

   Tip: If you put the bench scraper in water before using it, you can more easily cut through wet dough and avoid adding excessive flour. I love bench scrapers for dividing bread and cleaning the work surface. Flour that has been mixed with water can make for a pretty gummy surface, but with a scraper, you can clean it up in no time. I work on a marble slab and this tool can scrape the marble spotless.

Using a bench scraper is the easiest way to divide the dough into the number of loaves you're going to bake.

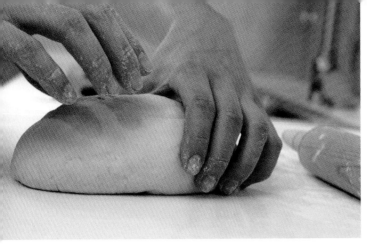

At this point in the process, you are creating a slight surface tension, a netting under which the bread can ferment. The netting assists the dough by directing its rise into the shape you want, rather than letting your dough flatten.

STEP 7: PRESHAPING

Rounding or rolling the dough into a preliminary shape aids in the development of gluten (which gives your bread structure) and in the surface tension needed to form a good shape for your final loaf. Preshaping is actually a simplified version of the methods described in the sections on final shaping. At the preshaping stage, you make a few manipulations with your hands, while the final shaping requires a bit more work to develop a taut skin on the dough and get the ball or oval into a more defined form. So give shaping a go this first time around. If you have any problems visualizing the steps, you can find a number of helpful videos on the Internet.

1. Place your unshaped piece of dough on the work surface.
2. Using a flat hand with your palm and fingers outstretched, press gently down on the dough to force out any air pockets.
3. While the dough is still resting on the work surface, pull the edges of the dough up and into the center and pinch them together.
4. Turn the dough over so that the seam you've created is against the work surface.
5. Now cup the dough with your thumbs toward the top and your pinky finger toward the bottom, and rotate the dough in a circular fashion—tucking the bottom underneath using the edges of your hands as you go—until you create the desired surface tension. You should now have a nice taut ball of dough.

STEP 8: SECOND PROOFING/ FERMENTING PERIOD

After you preshape the dough, it needs to proof again. Place the preshaped dough into an oiled bowl or onto a greased cookie sheet and place it in a warm location where the dough can rise for the time indicated in the recipe. (**Tip**: If the dough is wet, slide a bench scraper under it to help lift it.) Because the yeast has been growing and gaining strength, each successive proofing phase will be shorter. Again, follow the amount of time called for in the bread recipe to know when the dough has proofed long enough. Try the trick of poking the dough to see whether the indentation holds (ready) or fills (not ready). The dough will look stronger, and the slightly vinegary smell will be more pronounced.

STEP 9: FINAL SHAPING/LOAF PANNING

Now it is time to create the final shape for the type of bread you want. There are as many shapes of bread as there are nations of bread bakers through the ages. (For the purposes of this book, I'll just cover the basics.) The joy of baking your own bread is that you can customize the division and shape to suit your own practical needs and aesthetic preferences. For example, a single person might bake three smaller (freezable) loaves while a family might require one large loaf.

Before you begin with any shape, dust half of your work surface lightly with flour. You want the dough to grip the work surface and provide some traction as you turn it, so only dip into the flour when you need to. Again, if you have any problems visualizing the steps, the Internet is a great resource for helpful how-to videos.

ROUND (BOULE)

Boule (French for "ball") has been universally adopted to describe a round shape that is traditionally about 12 to 14 inches wide with a slightly crested top and flat bottom. The name refers to the shape and not the composition of the bread, so boules can be made with commercial or wild yeast, can come in a variety of flours, and can even include seeds or fruit.

To shape your boule:

1. Place the dough on the work surface with the sticky side (the bottom of dough that has been resting in a bowl during the proofing stage) facing you and the smooth side face down on the surface.

2. Gently press the dough with your palm and fingers once or twice. This action will remove some of the gas bubbles in the dough.

3. Gather up the edges of the dough into the center to form a ball and pinch to seal them.

4. Turn the dough over with the pinched side down on the work surface. At this point, you can continue in a couple of different ways. In either option, the goal is to create surface tension—almost like netting over the dough—that will keep the dough in a round shape and prevent it from falling into a flat cushion.

1. Cup the dough with both hands and pull the dough toward you.

2. With each pull, place your pinky finger near the bottom of the dough ball and keep tucking and smoothing the bottom inward, making the dough a rounder ball with each movement.

3. After each action, return the dough to the top of your work surface and repeat the pulling motion.

OPTION B

1. Cup the dough and rotate it under your hands in a circular motion.

2. As you pick up your hands with each rotation, replace them a bit to the left of your previous turn, creating a rounder ball with each movement.

LONG CYLINDER (BAGUETTE)

The long cylindrical baguette (literally "wand" in French) epitomizes French bread for many people. Who can resist the allure of a French woman with a baguette under her arm or protruding from a shopping basket? Although the baguette shape appears in French history as far back as the seventeenth century, the baguette became particularly popular after 1920, when French laws prohibited bakers from operating before 4:00 a.m. Labor laws had been instituted to protect bakers from the long and harsh hours they had previously worked. Larger, thicker breads take a long time to proof and bake. The thin, long shape of the baguette and its abbreviated proofing time allowed bakers to produce bread in time to provide it for breakfast.

With their reverence for food, the French created regulations to dictate that baguettes labeled as "traditional" or "artisanal" contain only flour (types and amounts also regulated), water, yeast, and salt, with absolutely no additives or wild yeast (to make a sour dough). Thus baguettes, though wonderfully fresh and crispy when they emerge from the oven, become stale within a day and are therefore baked daily in France.

The baguettes may look like an easy shape, but it is actually a bit tricky. The process for forming a baguette can be divided into three steps: basic shaping, thumbing, and rolling.

STEP 1: BASIC SHAPING

1. Place the dough on your work surface with the bottom, or seam side, up and facing you.

2. Degas the dough by pressing out any air pockets using a flat hand.

3. Again using a flat hand, press out the dough until you form a rectangle with the long side parallel with you (east-west to your body), and the short end perpendicular (north-south) to you.

4. Pick up the far long side of the dough and fold it over to the center of the rectangle.

5. Turn the dough around and repeat the same action—folding the far side of the dough onto itself with its edge now in the center of the dough, slightly on top of your previous fold.

STEP 2: THUMBING

Your goal will be—in three gestures—to form the dough into a cylindrical shape. The trick is to perform these actions gently so as not to tear or break the gluten threads or overwork the dough while keeping the baguette shape round.

1. Starting on the right end of the dough, place the thumb of your left hand in the center of the dough with your fingers curved around the top and buried behind it. Roll the top of the dough over your thumb using the fingers of the same hand. Press down ever so gently on the dough as you finish the fold.

2. Follow your left hand closely with your right hand, using the palm of your right hand to press down on the edge of the dough and creating a gentle seam about 1 inch from the bottom edge of the dough.

3. Repeat steps 1 and 2 as you move along the dough from right to left.

4. Rotate your dough so that the opposite edge is facing you.

5. Repeat steps 1 through 3, this time bringing the top edge of the dough all the way down to your work surface. You should now have a cylinder with a sealed seam.

STEP 3: ROLLING

You have formed the general cylinder shape of your baguette. Now you will perform an action that will lengthen and create the baguette's final shape.

1. Start with your hands cupped over the cylinder shape so that the heel of your hand and your fingertips are touching the work surface. Roll your hands over the dough in a gentle rocking motion, continuously working from the center to the ends of the dough.

2. When you have formed a uniform cylinder with tapered ends, move the baguette to the surface where you plan to let the dough rise, placing it there seam-side down.

Tip: Try to apply uniform pressure to the dough, and do not force or stretch the dough. As you become more experienced, you will learn the feel of your dough and adjust your rolling technique accordingly. Sometimes you will sense that the dough needs to rest and be allowed to retract a bit between some of your rolling actions. When you have a good relationship with your baguette dough, the dough will give you a better rise (you've left the right amount of air in the dough) and a nice surface (you formed a good surface tension with your rolling actions but did not overwork the dough so that it tore).

Ficelle

The French translation of *ficelle* is "string," and the shape of bread named for it looks like a thin string of cylindrical dough, slimmer than a baguette. Here is how to create a ficelle:

1. Start with a small piece of dough, smaller than what you use to form your baguettes.

2. Use the same shaping techniques as those for a baguette.

Remember that a ficelle will require fewer cuts to score the dough and will bake in a bit less time than a baguette. I'm sure you will love the crunchiness of a ficelle.

OVAL (BÂTARD)

Unlike the round boule and the wandlike baguette, the bâtard did not get its name from its shape (described as a football, torpedo, or cigar by some; an elongated oval here). No, this innocent loaf earned its unflattering moniker—literally, "bastard"—from culinary bullies who considered it no better than a short, fat bastardized version of the long, sleek baguette. Fortunately, the bâtard has become a popular form in many countries.

To shape your bâtard:

1. Place the preshaped dough on your work surface with the bottom, or seam side, up and facing you.

2. Degas the dough by pressing out any air pockets using a flat hand.

3. Flatten the dough into a rectangular shape, again using the flat of your hand.

4. Place the longer side of the rectangle perpendicular (north-south) to you.

5. Fold the top third of the dough onto itself.

6. Fold in the top corners of the folded portion toward the center. (Doing this always reminds me of doing an origami fold.)

7. Take the point created by the two folds and roll it over the top of the dough. Press it into the dough at the center of the piece and seal it with your thumbs.

8. Take the portion you have just folded over, and fold it over again to about three-quarters of the way down so that only a quarter of the dough remains. Seal the edge by rolling your thumbs into the dough.

9. Again, fold over the dough to cover the last remaining portion of it. Use the heel of your hand to seal the seam, moving it down the cylinder shape and pressing in gently. (You may hear some air bubbles popping at this point.)

10. Turn over the cylinder shape with the seam down, against the work surface. Similar to what you did with the baguette, place your hands over the top of the dough. Begin rocking the dough

back and forth as you work your hands from the center to the ends, putting slightly more pressure on the ends to taper them a bit. You can form a more blunt-nose-dolphin shape at the ends or taper them into sharper points (producing a crunchy, crusty end)—whatever you prefer.

The Harvest Bread: Épi de Blé

The épi de blé is the basic cylindrical baguette-shaped bread transformed into the shape of a shaft of wheat, with its kernels of wheat alternating to each side. This festive bread form is traditionally served in the fall to celebrate the harvest, but feel free to bake it at any time of the year.

Begin by making a long thin cylinder—it can be whatever width that you would like, usually a cylinder shape slightly smaller than a traditional baguette works best. The shape should be slightly longer than a baguette because the shaping technique will shorten the length.

1. Starting a few inches from one end of the dough and holding scissors at a 30 degree angle just above it, make your first cut into the top of the dough. Do not cut too deep or your center stem will be too weak to hold and will break into two or more pieces. However, you will want to make the cuts deep enough to create a graceful shape with the kernels of wheat fanning out from the stem.

2. Holding the oval portion you have snipped with the scissors, extend it to the side of the rest of the cylinder.

3. Move a few inches down from your last cut and repeat steps 1 and 2, but extend this kernel to the opposite side of the first.

4. Repeat the snipping and fanning motion until you have reached the end of the cylinder and the shape resembles kernels alternating along a stem all the way down the cylinder.

RECTANGULAR LOAF

You will want to become proficient with this shape if you plan to bake bread in loaf pans. Although some people think of artisanal breads as free-form breads, pan loaves are included if they are made by hand. This shape is obviously ideal if you want slices of toast with breakfast or sandwich bread for lunch. The actions to create a rectangular shape for a loaf pan are similar to the ones used for the oval, but you stop before you taper the ends.

1. Place the preshaped dough on your work surface with the bottom, or seam, up and facing you.

2. Degas the dough by pressing out any air pockets using a flat hand.

3. Flatten the dough into a rectangular shape, again using the flat of your hand.

4. Place the longer side of the rectangle perpendicular (north-south) to you.

5. Pick up the end farthest from you and fold it over onto a quarter of the dough.

6. Now, with your thumbs placed on the edge of the piece you have just rolled over, press down with your thumbs and use your other fingers to roll the dough onto itself. This is a sort of continual jerking action—a press, then a roll. When the dough is rolled about three-quarters of the way down the original rectangular shaped form, stop.

7. Pick up the end closest to you and roll it over the cylinder you have just created with your rolling actions. Press the edge of the dough to seal it. You should now have a big fat roll in front of you.

8. Roll the cylinder over so that the seam is on the bottom. If the ends of your loaf are too irregular, you can fold them over and tuck them under the bottom of the loaf.

9. Place your nice plump loaf in the pan and let it rise until it is ready to be baked.

BRAIDED BREAD

Several types of breads are braided, from the traditional Jewish Sabbath bread (challah) to Danish breads created with one braided circle placed on top of another larger braided circle. Braided braids make a special aesthetic presentation and are wonderful for celebrations.

Your breads will have a more uniform rise if each strand of the braid is the same width. As a child, I used to roll Italian bread sticks for my mother by starting in the middle of the dough and rolling my hands to the ends over and over. Now, after all these years, I have learned a method that delivers better results: first, let the dough rest for a while, and then place your hands on the irregular area and work just that location. This technique works better than repeatedly trying to even the strand from the center to the ends.

1. Start with a small round or oval shape that is well rested/proofed. The dough needs to be very relaxed so that it can be extended and does not keep contracting.

2. Place your fingers in the center of the dough and begin to roll it back and forth. Keep your hands in the center while you roll the dough four to five times.

    Tip: Don't press too hard or the dough will twist between the center portion and the higher, more bulbous sections at the end.

3. Place your left hand on the left bulbous end of the strand, and your right hand on the bulbous part at the other end. Perform the same rolling actions four or five times—as you did in the

The traditional Jewish challah bread uses six strands in its braid.

When you're first starting out, keep your braid simple. The fewer the strands, the easier the braid. This four-strand braid is a great place to start.

center of the cylinder—with your hands held flat on top of the dough. With each rolling action, move your hands toward the ends to elongate the piece.

4. Once the dough is of a uniform shape, move your hands back to the center and rock the entire width of the strand back and forth, moving your hands from the center to the ends to smooth out and elongate the shape.

When your strands are ready, you might want to lightly roll each in a tiny bit of flour. This coating of flour will help each strand retain its distinctive form and not blend into the braid. In the spirit of keeping things simple, below are instructions for a four-strand braid. If you would like to use more strands—for example, for the traditional six-strand Jewish challah bread—search the Internet for relevant instructional videos. Before you begin, I want you to learn the mantra *braid, braid, under*. This is the action you will be taking as you braid the four strands of dough together.

1. Connect the four strands by moistening their tips and pressing them together. The dough will be attached at the top with the four strands splayed out, facing you.

2. Think *braid*. Imagine that each strand is labeled 1 through 4, from left to right. Lift up the one farthest to the right (number 4) and place it over the one at its immediate left (number 3).

3. Think *braid* again. Lift up the third strand from the right (number 2) and place it over the number 3 strand. Now you have three strands engaged in the braiding process with a lone strand off to the left (number 1).

4. Think *under*. Slip strand number 1 under number 2.

5. Repeat this same "braid, braid, under" motion until you have completely woven the strands together. Each time you perform this motion, you will come back to the same pattern with three strands to the right engaged in the braiding steps and a lone strand to the left, which you will keep incorporating with the *under* step.

CHAPTER 3

Final Proofing, Scoring, and Baking

You have kneaded, proofed, folded, divided, preshaped, proofed again, and shaped your dough. Now you have, perhaps, a sourdough bâtard, a wheat boule, or a whole-wheat rectangular loaf ready for the final steps of the process. Those will include a third proofing period, scoring the bread, transferring the bread (carefully) into the oven, the actual baking (at last), and cooling the bread. While discussing each of these steps, the techniques involved, and the reasons behind them, we'll also take a look at some of your options for containers and tools to use in each step. The smell of bread baking and the taste of it when it's fresh are the great joys of home bread making.

STEP 10: THIRD PROOFING PERIOD

Most dough requires three periods of rest for the gluten to strengthen and for the chemical reactions happening inside the dough to develop flavor and cause the bread to rise. The earlier section on retarding the dough (see previous chapter) outlines the importance of, and issues relating to, fermenting dough.

This third proofing period will be shorter than the previous two as your dough is stronger and will rise faster. What also distinguishes this proofing period is that you are working with dough that has already been shaped. Once it finishes rising, it is ready to be transferred into the oven.

Although your dough can proof on a lightly floured work surface without a proofing container, most dough benefits from support as it rises. High-hydration dough in particular (such as that in this book's recipes) needs some support as it proofs. The dough also benefits from having a textured surface to climb up. You'll find many different kinds of bowls and baskets that are especially suited for proofing—such as bannetons

Now let's look at the boule, bâtard, baguette, and loaf-shaped breads and how each should be proofed in its final stage.

PROOFING BOULE AND BÂTARD BREADS

During the final proofing phase, you can use baskets made of woven grasses, plastic, or silicone as well as regular glass bowls to support your dough. You will want to coat the plastic or silicon bowls with oil and dust the baskets with flour. The top of the line in proofing devices are linen-lined or plain willow baskets in round, bâtard, or loaf shapes, but you can substitute colanders, sieves, or

any woven baskets with a smooth round interior surface that you have greased or lightly dusted with flour (depending on the material). You don't need to buy fancy grass or willow-reed baskets from baking-supply stores. You just need a container of the right size.

If you do decide to buy bread-proofing baskets, you will find a style that is lined with a type of heavy linen. They are sturdy and easy to handle, and the cloth prevents the dough from sticking to the sides of the baskets. These baskets are used to both provide the loaf with shape and wick moisture from the crust. My favorite baskets are French proofing baskets made of reeds or willow branches (called bannetons—see page 60 for more information), with or without a heavy cloth lining. The banneton baskets without the fabric liner will leave a snail-shell imprint on your dough (which I find irresistible).

These spiral baskets, called bannetons, help the dough rise by giving it a textured surface to climb and a round form to support its sides.

Bannetons not only provide the texture needed to help dough rise, they also transfer their spiral pattern to the dough for added visual interest.

Be sure that the container is twice the size of the dough to allow for proper expansion. If your baskets are of different sizes, remember to divide the dough appropriately. For most of the formulas in this book, a container that is 8 inches across and 5 inches deep will make a good form for proofing half the formula (so you'd need two baskets of this size for the recipe). **Tip:** You can also make your own fabric-lined baskets. Cut and sew heavy coarsely woven unbleached, undyed linen into a liner for a basket.

To use a woven basket for proofing:

1. Lightly dust the basket with flour. You can use regular white flour or the more delicate, finely milled rice flour (easily purchased in most Asian grocery stores). You could also opt to sprinkle bran into the basket and shake out the excess—just sift whole-wheat flour to separate the bran or buy regular bran in a store. I think that bran adds a pleasant texture and taste.
2. Place your round dough in the basket, with the seam on the bottom.
3. Cover the top of the dough with a damp dishtowel to prevent air from forming a hard crust.
4. Let the bread rise as the formula requires.

To use a plastic basket or glass bowl for proofing:

1. Lightly wipe the sides with oil.
2. Place your round dough in the basket, with the seam on the bottom.
3. Cover the top of the loaf with a damp dishtowel to prevent the air from forming a hard crust on it.
4. Let the bread rise as the formula requires.

Bannetons

Banneton is the French name and *brotform* the German name for traditional baskets made of a thick round fiber—a cane reed or willow-tree branch that has been scraped, prepared, soaked, and then formed into a circular or rectangular shape. The coiling pattern leaves a delicate impression on the surface of the bread—indentations in the shape of a spiraling seashell—when you transfer the dough, right side up, onto the baking surface.

You can order bannetons from baker's catalogs and online retailers. Shop around; these baskets are expensive and prices can vary greatly depending on the source. True banneton baskets do not have fabric linings, although some sources confuse the term with wicker baskets lined with fabric and sell them under the same name.

PROOFING BAGUETTES

There are two ways to help baguettes rise: with the support of a heavy linen fabric or with the support of a metal baking device specially made for baguettes (semicircle forms into which you place each piece of dough for proofing as well as baking). The traditional linen fabric used to support baguettes in the final proofing stage is called a couche. You can buy a couche or make one yourself. It should be as wide as the longest baguette you ever plan to make and long enough for as

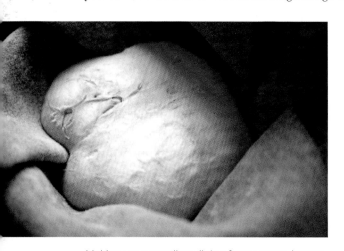

Making your own linen lining from coarse, heavy linen and securing it in place inside a woven basket is one way to add the necessary texture without spending a fortune on specialty items.

many baguettes as you might make. A heavy piece of linen that is 4 feet wide by 6 feet long is a good start for a home baker.

Because of the buildup of flour on the couche as well as its heavy texture, dough does not stick to it. The fabric is deliberately left unwashed; you just dust it off. It only gets better with time as the yeast and flour seep into the weft and warp. To use the couche, you will create what I think of as waves between each bread form. The peaks of the waves separate each baguette while the sides of the waves help keep the bread from spreading out.

The waves created by the couche separate the baguettes while giving them a rough surface to cling to as they rise.

To use the couche for proofing:

1. Take the shaped baguette and place it seam-side down on the couche at the left end of the fabric, north-south to your body.

2. With a first finger on either side of the long edge of the couche to the right of the dough, pull the fabric up to the height of the baguette to create a barrier, or wave, between it and the next one you will lay down. The fabric that's against the baguette will support it, and the flat bit of fabric next to the wave is ready for the next baguette.

3. You will now work your way down the fabric, laying down one cylinder of dough after another and pulling up pieces of fabric between them. Continue this same action until your baguette forms are all placed on the couche. Let the dough rise for its final proof before baking.

PROOFING LOAF BREADS

You can begin making loaves of bread in whatever loaf-shaped bread pan you have around. Eventually you may want to acquire cast iron or heavy-gauge aluminum pans. These two types of pans are far superior to the thin aluminum or glass ones, neither of which holds much heat.

Loaf pans vary in size depending on the manufacturer. The most common size for a bread pan is 9 inches by 5 inches and holds 8 cups (roughly a 1-pound loaf of bread). A smaller version is 8 inches by 4 inches and holds 6 cups. Both of these sizes are perfect for making two loaves of most of the bread in this book. Take whatever size pan you have, fill it three-quarters full with dough, and let the dough rise above the edge of the pan. While in the oven, the dough will rise even more to form a nice crown.

To use the bread pan for proofing:

1. Place into the loaf pan the fat spiral loaf you formed in your final shaping phase, seam on the bottom.

2. Cover the top of the loaf with a damp dishtowel to prevent air from forming a hard crust.

3. Let the bread rise as the formula requires.

One of the great things about proofing loaves of bread in their pans is that you don't have to take the extra step of transferring the dough. You can just pop the pan into the oven.

Aesthetically pleasing too, scoring the bread is necessary for the proper rising of the bread.

STEP 11: SCORING THE BREAD

Once the bread has fully proofed and the oven is hot, you'll need to make small cuts in the top of the bread, an action called *scoring*. Most free-form round, oval, and cylinder loaves are scored; pan loaves are not. Scoring is a way to add a pleasant visual presentation to your bread. You can follow the age-old scoring patterns and find comfort in the fact that someone before you fit the function (scoring) to the form. Or, you might be adventurous and strive to find your own signature way of scoring the bread.

Besides the aesthetic touch scoring adds to your bread, cutting into the top of a loaf before you bake it serves several functions. A final rise of your bread occurs in the oven and is called *oven spring*. As the bread expands, it will find the areas of greatest weakness in a loaf and direct the rise to these places—unless you create other "weaknesses" or openings for the bread to find. By cutting into the dough, you are controlling the rise of the loaf. Without these cuts, your bread might swell sideways or lift at points where the skin of the bread is weak.

The best approach to scoring is to make a quick decisive action, a bit like you do when you pull off a bandage—without hesitating.

While you'll find several scoring techniques in this book, you're always welcome to experiment with designs of your own.

Scoring Tools

The major tools for scoring bread fall into four categories: straight razor fastened into a holder, lame, serrated knife, and curved-edged tool. Everyone has a favorite and you can read lots of blog talk about each one. The most important criterion is that the tool be a sharp instrument that is safe and comfortable for you to handle.

Straight-edge razor: Straight-edge tools are used to make vertical cuts—ones that go directly into the dough. You are cutting directly down into the dough as you would when cutting a piece of pie. Cuts created by a straight blade are usually deeper than those from a curved blade. My preference is a straight razor held in a simple holder. Many professional bakers use razors mounted on those wooden coffee-stirring sticks. It's an ideal, simple tool—light and easy to handle. As soon as the blade gets dull, use the other side or change it. Straight razors are available at most hardware stores, sometimes in the same section as wallpapering tools.

Lame: A lame, made of plastic with a sharp metal edge, is a tool specifically made for scoring bread. I do not find lames particularly easy to handle; they are hard to sharpen and are more expensive to replace than a razor when you lose one.

Serrated knife: Serrated knives vary in the proportion and size of their serrations, or teeth, as well as in their overall size. Look for one that has sharp edges and is comfortable in your hand.

Curved-edge tools: These tools are designed to cut into dough at a slight angle (as in cutting into a baguette) to form a little bit of an overhang, called a *lip*, on the cut's opening. You use more of a shaving motion with the curved tool. Cuts made by a curved blade are usually about ¼ inch deep, but you can make them a little deeper if you bake oversize loaves.

Some bakers choose to go the medical route: they manage to get scalpels from medical supply stores or from friends in the profession. These scalpel-wielding bakers say the tools make great cuts.

1. Have the scoring pattern composed in your mind.
2. Hold your hand steady with a stiff wrist in a position that is at the proper angle and distance from the dough.
3. Swiftly and firmly score the dough.

Tip: Attractive cuts are uniform. Keep the cuts the same distance from each other, the same length, and the same depth into the dough. Speaking of depth, when you score, make a shallow cut—never more than ¼ inch. If you score too deeply, the bread will flatten out.

ROUND LOAVES: CROSSHATCHING

1. Using a straight blade, make two evenly spaced cuts across the dough.
2. Turn the loaf 90 degrees.
3. Score the bread with two evenly spaced horizontal lines that intersect the first lines at right angles to create a tic-tac-toe design (#).

Note: You can also make the cuts at an angle to create diagonal crosshatching.

ROUND LOAVES: BIG X

1. Using a curved blade, make your first cut diagonally across the top of the dough, from one upper corner to the opposite lower corner.
2. Your second cut should intersect the first at an angle to form a strong X design.

ROUND LOAVES: SQUARE

Using a straight blade, cut a square on the top of the loaf, allowing your scoring tool to go as deep as the top one-third of the dough. The square will rise to create a sort of hat on top of the loaf.

OVAL LOAVES: END-TO-END

1. Hold a curved blade with the concave side facing you.

2. Starting at the top of the loaf, make the first cut horizontally across the crest of the loaf. Make several more cuts equally spaced down the loaf. Play with the proportions. You will want strong lines but also need to leave some uncut sections at the top and bottom of the loaf.

OVAL LOAVES: SINGLE CUT

Cut a single line down the longest portion of the bread.

BAGUETTE

Using a curved blade, make several shallow cuts at a 45 degree angle to an imaginary line going from tip to toe of the baguette. Too many bakers score baguettes parallel with the width (making for a dumpy looking baguette) when the cuts should be at a 45 degree angle to their length. This type of cut allows the dough to expand while giving the bread a sleek look.

A baking stone is an ideal tool for baking. As the stone absorbs and radiates back heat, it creates a crisp crust, especially on the bottom of the loaf.

STEP 12: TRANSFERRING THE DOUGH

When your dough has finished proofing, you will need to figure out how to get it into the oven. Here are two basic methods depending on whether you are using a Dutch oven or a baking stone for baking. I've also included the method for transferring a baguette to a baking stone.

TO A DUTCH OVEN

Transferring dough from a proofing basket or a lightly floured work surface into a Dutch oven becomes easier with practice (see page 71 for more information on Dutch ovens). First, remove the hot baking container from the oven, and sprinkle the bottom with coarse cornmeal. This is an optional step, but it helps keep the dough from sticking to the bottom of the container. Then follow the steps below.

To transfer dough from a basket or bowl shape:

1. Wet your hands and run your fingers around the edge of the basket in a gathering motion to loosen the dough from the sides.
2. Spread out your fingers and place them lightly on top of the dough, ready to support it.
3. Slowly turn the basket over while your hand simultaneously supports the dough and then slides out from underneath it, allowing the bread to drop into the Dutch oven.

To transfer dough from a work surface:

1. If the dough has proofed on a lightly floured work surface, gather it as gently as possible.
2. Put it in the Dutch oven carefully. Do not drop it in; let the dough slide off your fingers. For a larger form, you may want to use a bench scraper to help support the dough from underneath. **Note:** On your first attempts, the dough may land a bit lopsided in the Dutch oven. Don't

Remember that you can put parchment paper right into the oven with the dough, so it's a handy surface on which to proof your dough.

worry—lopsided loaves still taste great! It's better to leave the loaf alone than to damage gluten buildup by trying to straighten it out. Usually the dough straightens out as it rises during the baking process.

Parchment Paper

TOOLS & EQUIPMENT

Most larger grocery stores carry parchment paper, sold in rolls like aluminum foil. It's always a little tricky to cut these rolls. If you use parchment paper frequently, buy it from a baking-supply store or through a baking catalog— the paper is sold as flat sheets to fit most baking pans. The best feature of these parchment sheets is that they are easy to cut and they lie flat on the cooking sheet without turning up at the edges.

If you are using the baking-stone method for baking, you'll let your shaped bread proof on top of parchment, resting on a rimless cookie sheet. Because parchment paper doesn't burn, you can slip your proofed dough directly into the oven, paper and all.

TO A BAKING STONE

One of the simplest transfers you'll make is when you've proofed your dough on a rimless cookie sheet covered with parchment paper and are planning to bake on a baking stone. A baker's peel adds to the ease of this move.

When the bread is fully proofed, transfer the dough—still on its parchment—onto a baker's peel (see the sidebar on page 68). Then use the baker's peel to slide the dough and parchment paper onto the preheated baking stone in the oven.

To transfer dough from a cookie sheet:
1. Move the cookie sheet close to the oven.
2. Open the oven and slide the loaves, while still on the parchment paper, onto the preheated baking stone. (Remember, parchment paper won't burn in the oven.)
3. Add water to create steam (see page 70 for more information), and close the oven door.

To transfer dough using a peel:

1. Open the oven door.
2. With a slight forward jerking motion, slip the peel under the bread and parchment paper on your work surface.
3. Hold the peel level with and slightly overlapping the baking stone.
4. With another jerking motion, pull the peel back and leave the bread and parchment paper on baking stone.

Baguettes, always baked on a baking stone, require their own technique for being transferred into the oven. You will need to use a stiff wooden board called a flipping board or transfer peel, which is a rectangular form as long as a baguette and usually about 4 to 5 inches wide. You can purchase one from baking catalogs or make your own version from stiff cardboard.

To transfer baguettes:

1. Line up the flipping board next to the baguette.
2. Lift one side of the linen or couche and gently roll the baguette onto the flipping board.
3. Gently roll the baguette from the flipping board onto the preheated baking stone.

TOOLS & EQUIPMENT

Baker's Peel

The baker's peel, except for being a bit narrower, is nearly the same tool as the pizza peel that is used to put pizzas in wood-fired ovens. It has a flat oval or rectangular piece attached to a long wooden handle. The peel has two advantages: you won't need to leave the oven door open as long, and you are able to stand farther away from the heat.

Go ahead and start baking with a pair of good potholders or oven mitts. Soon, one of your baking fans may give you a peel as a gift. A bit accident prone, I tended to pull the oven rack out past the tipping point when removing my bread, resulting in a wild grab to save the baking stone and breads from crashing to the floor (and usually burning myself in the process). A baker's peel has made my life calmer.

A great crust starts with the right amount of heat and steam.

STEP 13: BAKING

Three particular factors create bread with a terrific crust—scoring, high heat, and the right amount of steam. As discussed earlier, scoring helps the dough move in the right direction for that perfect-looking loaf. High heat kickstarts chemical processes that help the dough expand for the final time, while steam helps create an ideally thick and shiny crust on your bread.

PROVIDING THE RIGHT HEAT

In baking bread, high heat means having a super hot oven and an equally hot surface under the dough while it bakes. Your dough has been producing gases as part of the fermenting process, and a final expansion occurs when you put the bread in the oven. The heat of the oven speeds up the dough's chemical reactions, increasing gas production. In addition, carbon dioxide molecules dissolved in the dough turn into gas molecules at higher temperatures, and gas bubbles in the dough expand when heated. These effects all increase the size of the dough as it bakes into bread. This final expansion occurs in the first ten minutes the dough is in the oven. To maximize these effects, it is important to have a hot oven the moment the dough enters.

While commercial ovens are built to radiate heat even when the oven door is open, home ovens lose a significant amount of heat. After you close the door, the oven must regain the lost heat. By the time this happens, some damage has been done. The yeast cells are dying, gas-producing reactions are slowing down, and a crust is forming on the loaf, preventing expansion.

One way to avoid some of the loss of heat is to preheat your oven to 50 to 100 degrees higher than the desired final baking temperature. When you open the door and place the bread in, the loss of heat

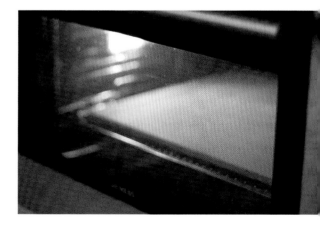

When using a baking stone, you must preheat the stone at the same time you preheate the oven to prevent the stone from cracking.

will lower the temperature, but by introducing a higher heat, you can compensate for some of that loss. Once you have put the breads into the oven and created steam using some of the techniques to follow, you can then turn the oven down to the final temperature.

Another way of adding and maintaining higher heat levels is to insulate your oven by putting regular bricks, firebricks, or flat slabs of stone (such as a piece of blue stone traditionally used for terraces and paths) in your oven. Don't use glazed tiles of any kind (the glaze may contain harmful lead); unglazed tiles are fine. These should be placed on the floor of the oven and on the top shelf to radiate heat downward. (A friend of mine on a Maine island adds some beach rocks to the floor of her oven.)

PRODUCING STEAM

The bursts of steam produced by a commercial oven are a real asset in baking bread. Steam does two things: first, it keeps the outside of the loaf from drying out until the dough has fully risen; second, it coagulates the starches on the outside of the loaf, which improves the color and texture of the crust. The steam condenses on the dough's surface and slows down the crust formation by keeping the surface damp and giving the loaf a longer time to develop and expand. The sugars in the dough dissolve in this water layer, increasing their concentration at the surface and eventually contributing to the browning of the loaf. The right amount of steam generally results in a thicker, browner, and shinier crust.

Being able to create a mini steam chamber within a heavy-duty baking container will be a life-altering experience for you. Using a fireproof Dutch oven baking container is, by far, the best way of producing bread that imitates what comes out of a commercial deck oven. The delicious crust and great open crumb, both aided by the steam, will woo you and you will never want to use any other baking method. These baking containers with lids are usually referred to as a Dutch ovens.

If you aren't baking with a Dutch oven, you can use a baking stone and still create steam. In fact, you'll find several ways to do so. Just keep reading to learn about a few of them.

Your grandmother's black cast-iron Dutch oven is last-a-lifetime durable, but the newer cast-iron cooking containers in rich colors will make your knees go weak.

Dutch ovens come in all shapes and sizes these days. You're sure to find one (or several) that can best accommodate the shape and size of the loaf you plan to bake.

USING A DUTCH OVEN

Ceramic glazed and cast-iron ovens are the most popular types for bread baking. Glass isn't heavy enough. Clay pots are too porous. Look for sales if you want to invest in one of the fancier brands with their gorgeous rich colors. Sometimes you can find black cast-iron Dutch ovens at yard sales—people seem to be tossing out their mother's or grandmother's cast iron. (If you do buy one second hand, be sure it has a lid.)

You can bake bread in any size Dutch oven, but you will get a better shape when the container is just big enough to allow the bread to expand. Just as a proofing container helps support the sides of dough as it proofs, a baking container helps the bread get better lift. When I bake for myself, I use a 4-quart Le Creuset-brand oven or a small glazed ceramic pot with round sides for making a perfect boule. (I seem to have collected a variety of sizes of Dutch oven containers to accommodate the breads I make.)

When I taught a baking course, many of my students decided to buy larger more-multipurpose Dutch ovens. In these, because the sides are not supporting the bread, the bread rises but the final shape is more of a half dome. I need to give credit to one of the bread testers, Judy Gradwohl, for her ingenuity: she places a smaller glass oven-safe bowl inside the Dutch oven. The dough rises to fit the smaller shape, but the Dutch oven still serves as a mini steam chamber for making a crispy crust on the loaf.

Dutch Ovens Today

Several companies such as Emile Henry, Staub, Lodge, and Le Creuset have been producing Dutch ovens for many generations. Now celebrity cooks are issuing their own lines of enameled cast-iron cooking items. These are sometimes a bit less expensive than the classic brands, though the ceramic color coatings don't "glow" as much. Whether you buy from a trusted manufacturer or a trusted chef, choose a Dutch oven that you'll want to hang onto and maybe even pass down. A good Dutch oven will last you more than a lifetime.

USING A BAKING STONE

Baking stones absorb the heat from the oven and distribute it across the bottom surface of the bread. The moisture that exits the bread creates a crackly crunchy surface where the dough and stone meet and helps you achieve a firm surface on the bottom of your breads. A baking stone imitates the stone or brick floors of commercial ovens, which retain their heat and radiate it onto the loaf of bread. **Note**: The baking stone must be *as hot as possible* when you put the bread on it, and you must preheat the baking stone *at the same time as you preheat the oven*, for up to half an hour before you bake. If you put a cold baking stone into a hot oven, the stone is likely to crack.

TOOLS & EQUIPMENT

Baking Stone

When buying a baking stone, I suggest you try a restaurant-supply store and buy the largest and thickest rectangular one available. The Internet is a good source for ordering baking stones,

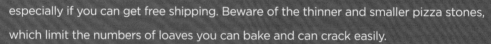

especially if you can get free shipping. Beware of the thinner and smaller pizza stones, which limit the numbers of loaves you can bake and can crack easily.

You can also make your own baking stone by putting a layer of firebricks (also called refractory bricks; used in making furnaces), terra-cotta tiles, or even regular red bricks (commonly used in building) on the metal rack in your oven. I leave the bricks in my oven because I find them helpful for all kinds of baking. **Note**: You will want to place your bread on the rack in the middle of the oven to prevent the top or bottom of it from getting too brown.

Remember that the baking stone needs to be hot by the time you are ready to put the loaves of bread on it. It's best to preheat the stone for thirty to forty-five minutes at 450 degrees Fahrenheit to be sure that the heat has completely penetrated the stone.

You provide your oven with steam while using a baking stone by several different methods. Here are three.

Water in a pan: My usual method for providing steam is to put a cast-iron pan on the rack above my bread and preheat it along with my baking stone. I put a cup of *boiling* water in the pan immediately after placing the shaped loaves in the oven. Be careful not to burn yourself (or

fog up your glasses) with the steam. In about ten minutes, open the oven door to see if any water remains in the pan. Take the pan out if there is any water in it. If no water remains, you can leave the pan in until the bread is baked. An empty pan won't make a difference, but extra water will. The steam is only valuable to the bread in the first phase of baking; after that, the oven should be hot and dry.

This baker is adding water to a container in the oven to create steam.

When I first started to introduce steam to my baking, I thought, "Ah, steam, the more the better." Wrong. I found that too much steam made for soggy-topped breads. Now I either put less water in the pan or remove the excess water about ten minutes after the bread has been in the oven.

Ice cubes and metal objects: One of the best suggestions for creating steam is in Ciril Hitz's book *Baking Artisan Bread*. Hitz suggests filling a loaf pan three-quarters full of metal objects, such as pie weights or metal hardware, or small stones and preheating them. After putting his shaped bread in the oven, Hitz drops ice cubes into his container of metal objects and quickly shuts the door.

Misting: An easy method for providing steam is to spritz your bread using a handheld mister. Because this may make the bread soggy, some home bakers prefer to spray the sides of the oven instead; they give the sides of the oven a couple of quick sprays before putting the bread in. Bakers usually use the bigger plant misters for this purpose; the larger size means you don't need to put your hand as far into the hot oven. Although other bakers have found misting effective, I have not and prefer to use different methods for generating steam.

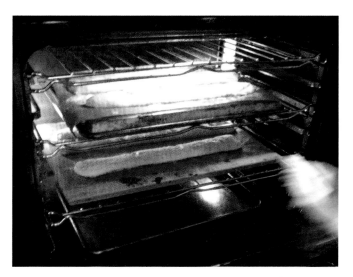

Misting the sides of the oven with a spray bottle is one way to add the necessary steam to your oven.

The easiest way to tell when your bread has finished baking is to test it with a thermometer. If it hits 205 degrees Fahrenheit, you're good to go.

KNOWING WHEN THE BREAD IS DONE

You've made sure your oven was hot enough and you've provided the right amount of steam at the beginning of the baking process. Now the question is, how will you know when the bread is done? Forget the old myth of knocking on the bottom of the loaf to see if it sounds hollow. Bread can make that sound even when it is slightly under- or overbaked.

A very simple way of knowing if bread is done is to test it with a thermometer. Most of the breads in this book will be fully baked when the loaf registers at 205 degrees Fahrenheit. Stick in the instant-read thermometer and you will know if your bread is ready or not.

Usually, you can also trust the time called for in the recipe of a cookbook. All the recipes in this book have been tested many times. I suggest you keep a record of each bread you bake, noting the proofing and baking times.

STEP 14: COOLING AND STORING

Hot bread out of the oven is almost irresistible, and I have cut many slices of warm bread for myself, my children, and friends. If you can summon the willpower, however, you should wait until the bread has completely cooled to cut it. Why? Because the bread needs to finish baking. Bread that hasn't cooled won't hold its structure; it will crumble as you cut it and as you add butter. You don't care about crumbling, you say? Then what about flavor? Flavors continue to develop until the bread cools. So have a little patience, put your bread on a rack, and let it finish baking. It will be worth the wait.

Wire racks differ in size and materials but they are essential for providing air around the surface of the bread to cool it down evenly. You'll notice that if you put bread on a flat surface to cool, the bottom won't be crispy. The best cooling rack is a heavy metal one with legs that allow for a decent amount of space between your counter and the rack. (Legs on racks can vary.) If you start with an inexpensive rack, you can always ask for a better model for a holiday or birthday!

While your bread is fresh, store it on the counter with a dishtowel draped over it to prevent it from drying out. (Freshly milled whole grains made with a sourdough starter ensure that your breads have a long shelf life.) When you finally do cut your loaf of bread, turn it onto the cutting board, open-side facing down to prevent the cut-side from drying out. You can leave bread out on the counter for a couple of days.

After that, store it in a breadbox with openings for air, or in a paper bag. After another day or two, wrap the bread in plastic to maintain some of the moisture and put it in the breadbox or refrigerator.

Your homemade bread will also freeze well. I often cut mine into two or three hunks so that I can take out a section when I need it. Or you can slice the whole loaf and then freeze it and only take out one slice at a time. Revive your stale bread by steaming it: put your slices or loaf in the top of a double boiler and boil a small amount of water in the bottom pan.

While you're going to be tempted to cut into that warm loaf straight out of the oven, allowing it to cool provides even greater benefits.

CHAPTER 4

Bread-Making Methods

In chapters 2 and 3, we covered fourteen steps of the bread-baking process to familiarize you with the typical steps in making artisan bread and what each different step usually entails, to acquaint you with the basic terminology used, and to give you a generalized picture of the process. In this chapter, I want to help you get started baking specific types of breads.

To do that, I will walk you through four methods for making bread, beginning with the easiest ones and then moving on to slightly more challenging ones. In the first lesson I will ask you to bake a loaf of mixed white and whole-wheat bread using commercial instant dry yeast. This bread recipe is so easy to complete that you will be on to the lesson-two bread almost immediately. For the second bread, which falls in the slow-fermented category, you will add more flavor and complexity to the bread by letting the dough ferment for a longer period of time.

The third method, and the next step up in your bread-baking experience, will use a *starter*, called a *preferment*. I will ease you into creating your own starter by making a preferment that will activate your bread and endow it with a depth of taste. From there, you can graduate to the fourth method, learning how to bake bread by creating your own wild-yeast starter.

By introducing you to these four basic methods of bread baking, I hope you will find your own comfort level. After experimenting with each of these four basic types of bread, you can then delve further into the method or methods that you prefer and that accommodate your particular lifestyle and taste. It's a good idea to read through this chapter at least once before beginning any recipes.

LESSON 1: BASIC BREAD-BAKING METHOD

I invite you to try our first baking lesson, a basic bread that combines white and whole-wheat flour and is perfect for everyday use. You just need enough time in your schedule (at least three hours) to allow the dough to proof and bake. Although I provide abbreviated versions of some instructions contained in chapters 2 and 3, please reread the full descriptions before trying any of the following lessons.

Before You Begin!

Each recipe provides you with a list of ingredients with both metric and US measurements, as well as a list of equipment you'll use. Most professional bakers and serious home bakers use a scale to measure ingredients because of the superior accuracy, and I hope you will convert to this method. The recipes also include approximate schedules, which you can look at to plan your baking. Finally, some recipes provide you with multiple options, such as two different baking methods. Be sure to follow the instructions set out for the option you have chosen.

All temperatures in these recipes are in degrees Fahrenheit. Yeast likes warm water. When mixing water, flour, and yeast, try to warm the water to between 85 and 95 degrees. Speaking of temperature, dough needs to proof in a space or room with a temperature of 72 to 80 degrees. Remember that, if you don't have a proofing basket, you could also use a greased bowl or colander, and you can cover whatever you use with either a damp dishtowel or plastic wrap. Make sure you perform the gluten windowpane or "finger poke" test (see chapter 2) to determine whether your dough has finished proofing.

Here's a little advice on Dutch ovens: If your recipe calls for using a Dutch oven and you happen to have two of them, feel free to bake two loaves simultaneously. If you only have one (as most people do), bake multiple loaves one after the other. Dust the bottom of the Dutch oven with a little coarse cornmeal to keep the bread from sticking and create a crispy bottom crust. If the Dutch oven you are using is very large, place your dough inside a smaller (1-quart) oven-safe bowl before putting it in the larger baking container. Once your dough is in the oven, you can choose to simply bake it in the lidded Dutch oven for the full amount of time called for, or you can take the lid off for the last 15 minutes of baking time to create a crisper top crust.

One last tip: Avoid using more flour than you need, which can dry out your finished bread and negatively affect its taste and consistency. A lot of the recipes in this book use very wet and sticky dough. The trick to handling it is to *wet* your hands—not flour them.

If you need help with a particular step, go back to the section in chapter 2 or 3 that discusses that step in more detail. Here's an index of helpful techniques and equipment to make it easier for you to refer back when you need to:

This bread may become one of your favorites. It is a flavorful balance of whole-wheat and white flours and, because you will be making it with instant dry yeast, the bread is guaranteed to rise. If you have a half hour to devote to making bread, you can revel in the pleasure of having a warm loaf that same day.

Yield: 1 medium loaf

SCALE AND MIX (5 minutes)

1. Place the yeast and warm water in a large mixing bowl.
2. Add the salt and mix thoroughly to integrate it into the yeast/ water mixture.
3. Add up to 4 cups of a mixture of wheat and white flour in even proportions (but only as much as is necessary to handle the bread) and mix with your hands, a large wooden spoon, or a Danish whisk.

FOLD (5 minutes)

1. Tilt the mixing bowl and, with a scraper or your hands (wetted to keep the dough from sticking to them), transfer the dough onto your lightly floured work surface.
2. Perform two sets of letter folds (eight folds in total) using the following technique:
   a. Gently shape the dough into a rectangle with the long side parallel with you (so it's running east to west).
   b. Pick up the right side and fold it over on itself so that one-third of the dough remains untouched.
   c. Pick up the left side and fold it over to cover the previous fold.
   d. Turn the dough perpendicular (north-south) to you and repeat the folds above.
   e. Repeat the steps above one more time to complete eight total folds.
3. Gather the dough into a ball and place it on your work surface.

Tip: A bench scraper is handy for folding dough if the dough is wet and difficult to work with. Slide the bench scraper under the dough and use the scraper to lift and fold the dough over onto itself. You can also leave wet dough in the bowl and perform the folds in the bowl.

KNEAD (10 minutes)

Using your preferred method, knead the dough for at least 10 minutes until it becomes soft, elastic, and begins to form gluten. You can use one of two methods (see chapter 2 for these and other methods):

Ingredients:
- White flour, 375 grams (3 cups)
- Whole-wheat flour, 120 grams (1 cup)
- Water, 474 grams (2 cups)
- Instant dry yeast, 7 grams (2 teaspoons)
- Salt, 5 grams (2 teaspoons)
- Coarse cornmeal (Option A)

Equipment:
- Scale or measuring cups and spoons
- Large mixing bowl
- Large wooden spoon or Danish whisk
- Proofing basket (such as a banneton, colander, or greased glass bowl)
- Dishtowel or plastic wrap
- Scoring device (such as a sharp razor or serrated knife)
- Dutch oven (Option A)
- Baking stone (Option B)
- Parchment paper (Option B)
- Rimless cookie sheet (Option B)
- Steam-generating container (metal pan filled with metal objects, Option B)

Using the Pinching Method:

1. Place a thumb on one side of the dough and your four fingers on the other side, pinching and closing your fingers until you divide the dough into two pieces.
2. Rotate your dough and pinch from the other direction.
3. Repeat over and over until the gluten develops.

Using the Bench-Kneading Method:

1. Place the palms of your hands against the center portion of the dough ball, press down, and push the dough away from you, stretching it out.
2. Fold the far end of the dough over onto the portion closest to you.
3. Turn the ball around in the opposite direction, and push and fold again.
4. Repeat these steps until the dough is soft and smooth.
5. Perform the windowpane gluten test to check whether the dough is ready.

FIRST PROOF (45 minutes)

Put the dough in a proofing basket, cover it with a damp dishtowel or plastic wrap, and place it in a warm location until the dough has doubled in size, about 45 minutes.

FOLD (5 minutes)

Fold the dough using two complete sets of envelope folds (eight folds).

SECOND PROOF (30 minutes)

Place the dough back in the basket or bowl and let it rest for 30 minutes.

SHAPE (10 minutes)

1. Shape the dough into a round (boule) form by first cupping your hands around the ball of dough with your thumbs resting on the top and your other fingers touching the back toward the bottom.
2. Rotate the dough in a circular fashion—using the edges of your hands to tuck the bottom underneath as you go—until you create the desired surface tension. You should now have a nice taut ball of dough.

Tip: You'll find plenty of other ways to shape dough. Look on the Internet for illustrated tutorials and videos on the subject, then try them all and find what works for you.

THIRD PROOF AND PREHEAT (30 minutes)
OPTION A: DUTCH OVEN

1. Place your dough in a proofing basket (or other round form) to rise.
2. Let the dough proof in a warm location, covered with a damp dishtowel or plastic wrap, for approximately 30 minutes.
3. Preheat the Dutch oven and lid at 450 degrees during the 30 minutes of proofing time.

OPTION B: BAKING STONE

1. Transfer your dough to parchment paper placed on top of a rimless cookie sheet.
2. Let the dough proof in a warm location, covered with a damp dishtowel or plastic wrap, for approximately 30 minutes.
3. Preheat the baking stone and steam-generating container (metal container filled with metal objects) at 450 degrees during the 30 minutes of proofing time.

BAKE (30–45 minutes)
OPTION A: DUTCH OVEN

1. Score the bread with a large X.
2. Take the Dutch oven out of the hot oven.
3. Sprinkle coarse cornmeal into the bottom of the container to keep the dough from sticking.
4. Slide the dough from the proofing bowl into the hot baking container.
5. Put the lid on the Dutch oven and quickly transfer the baking container to the oven.
   Note: The Dutch oven will act as a miniature steam chamber, which is why you do not need to introduce steam.
6. Bake for 45 minutes at 450 degrees or bake for 30 minutes, remove the lid, and then bake for 15 more minutes until the bread achieves the desired golden color.

OPTION B: BAKING STONE

1. Score the dough with a large X.
2. Slide the dough, still on the parchment paper (it doesn't burn), onto your baking stone.
3. Introduce steam into the oven by pouring approximately one cup of water into your steam-generating container (the hot metal objects that have been preheating in a metal pan). Be very careful not to burn yourself when introducing steam.
4. Bake for 30 to 35 minutes at 450 degrees.

COOL (30 minutes)

Let the bread cool completely on a wire rack before slicing it.

SCHEDULE

Active Time: 35 minutes
Total Time: 3 hours and 35 minutes

+ Scale and mix: 5 minutes
+ Fold: 5 minutes
+ Knead: 10 minutes
+ First proof: 45 minutes
+ Fold: 5 minutes
+ Second proof: 30 minutes
+ Shape: 10 minutes
+ Third proof and preheat: 30 minutes
+ Bake: 30–45 minutes
+ Cool: 30 minutes

To Remove the Lid or Not

The lid on a Dutch oven retains the moisture in the container that helps the bread rise and brown. Deciding whether to keep the lid on for the entire baking time or to remove it after a period of time will depend on your oven heat and your personal preferences for crust and color. Dough will have a crunchier crust if the lid is on the whole time, but the advantage of taking the lid off toward the end is that you can watch over the color of the crust as it bakes.

LESSON 2: OVERNIGHT FERMENTATION

To use this method, mix the ingredients and let the dough proof overnight. During the proofing, the dough has time to ferment—a process that adds flavor to the bread. Then simply pop the bread in the oven the next day and you have two exceptional breads.

The key to success in this method is high hydration. In chapter 1, I wrote about how manufacturers during the Industrial Revolution reduced the amount of water in dough to prevent it from sticking to their equipment. But the right balance of water to flour is crucial to making the best bread. By including more water in your dough, you will get the best flavor and most nutrients out of your bread.

When Jim Lahey's overnight no-knead high-moisture bread became all the rage, I realized that his recipe model was identical to the recipe for my mother's oatmeal bread, which was always available in our house. My mother proofed the dough overnight to develop a more complex taste; and its high-moisture content created healthier bread. Plus, her recipe included fiber from rolled oats and iron from molasses.

Wet Dough

The greatest difference between the recipes in this book and others you may have used in the past is that these recipes mostly use very wet dough. (Refer to the first chapter of the book for the historical transformation to dry dough and the scientific and health rationale for going back to wet dough.) It takes practice to get used to the wet dough. All of the test bakers were cautious as they worked with their dough, questioning if it would rise sufficiently. Fortunately, they refrained from adding too much flour at my request and the breads turned out wonderfully. You will have to find the right balance as you practice with these recipes. Err on the wet side, but add flour if the dough is unmanageable.

Ann Van Stelten's Oatmeal Bread

Living every moment fully even though she was terminally ill with cancer, my mother taught me and the homecare worker helping our family how to make her oatmeal bread. By doing so, not only did my mother find a way to continue providing fresh homemade bread for our family but she also provided the aide, an older woman on a limited income, with the means of saving money on food. My mother was pleased when the aide brought a loaf of bread she had baked at home to show her. Today, my brother and I make this bread—especially at holiday get-togethers—as a way of continuing my mother's legacy and thanking her for providing us with healthy, easy-to-make bread in the pre–Jim Lahey days. The bread makes great sandwiches, but I actually prefer it as toast.

Yield: 2 loaves (7x3-inch) or 2 boules

Ingredients:
- White flour (unbleached), 750 grams (6 cups)
- Water, 237 grams (1 cup)
- Oat flakes, 60 grams (¾ cup)
- Butter, 5 grams (1 teaspoon)
- Salt, 6 grams (1 teaspoon)
- Light molasses, 15 grams (¼ cup)
- Dry instant yeast, 4 grams (2 teaspoons)

Equipment:
- Scale or measuring cups and spoons
- Large mixing bowl (8 cups or larger)
- Wooden spoon or Danish whisk (optional)
- Proofing basket or similar
- Dishtowel or plastic wrap
- 1 or 2 Dutch ovens (Option A)
- 2 loaf pans to accommodate 6 cups of dough (Option B)
- Steam-generating container (metal pan filled with metal objects) (Option B)
- Wire cooling rack

Day One
SCALE AND MIX (10 minutes)
1. Scale the salt, butter, and rolled oats and place them in the mixing bowl.
2. Scale and add warm water.
3. Scale and add the yeast, molasses, and flour. Mix well by hand or using a large wooden spoon or Danish whisk.

PROOF (12–16 hours)
Cover the dough in the mixing bowl with a damp towel or plastic wrap and leave it at room temperature for 12 to 16 hours (usually overnight).

Day Two
DIVIDE AND SHAPE (10 minutes)
Place your dough on a work surface. The shape you give it at this point depends on which option you go with.

OPTION A: DUTCH OVEN
1. Divide the dough into two pieces.
2. Gently roll the pieces into round balls.

OPTION B: LOAF PAN
1. Divide the dough into two pieces.
2. Shape each piece into two rectangular shapes and place them perpendicular to you.
3. Roll each rectangle into a loaf: Lift the bottom third of dough and place the edge in the center of the rectangle. Lift the top portion and fold it down and over the bottom portion (like a letter). Roll the dough into a log shape, and tuck both short ends under the log.
4. Place the dough in loaf pans.

SECOND PROOF AND PREHEAT (2–3 hours)

Let the dough proof until it has doubled in size, which will take 2 to 3 hours, depending on the temperature of your kitchen.

OPTION A: DUTCH OVEN

1. Place your dough in a proofing basket (or other round form) to rise.
2. Let the dough proof in a warm location, covered with a damp dishtowel or plastic wrap.
3. Preheat the oven, Dutch ovens, and lids to 450 degrees for the last 30 minutes of proofing time.

OPTION B: LOAF PAN

1. Cover your dough (already in the loaf pan) with a dishtowel or plastic wrap and allow it to proof in a warm location.
2. Preheat the oven to 350 degrees for the last 30 minutes of proofing time.

BAKE

OPTION A: DUTCH OVEN (45–60 minutes)

1. Take the Dutch ovens and lids out of the oven, place the dough in the containers, replace the lids, and return them to the oven.
2. Bake with the lid on for 45 minutes, or bake for 30 minutes, remove the lid, and continue baking for 15 more minutes until your bread achieves the desired crust and caramel color.

Note: If you have two Dutch ovens, you can bake the loaves simultaneously. Otherwise, bake one loaf and then the other.

OPTION B: LOAF PAN (75 minutes)

Bake at 350 degrees for 75 minutes until the tops of the loaves are a golden caramel color.

COOL (30 Minutes)

Let the bread cool completely on a wire rack before slicing it. Pan loaves especially will not hold their shape if they are too warm when sliced.

> ## SCHEDULE
>
> **Active Time:** 20 minutes
> **Total Time:** 16–21 hours
>
> **Day One**
> ❖ Scale and mix: 10 minutes
> ❖ Proof: 12–16 hours
>
> **Day Two**
> ❖ Divide and shape: 10 minutes
> ❖ Proof and preheat: 2–3 hours
> ❖ Bake: 45–75 minutes
> ❖ Cool: 30 minutes

LESSON 3: PREFERMENT METHOD

Preferments are mixtures (mainly flour and water) that you make and allow to ferment before you mix the bread dough. With this wondrous ingredient, you can achieve most of sourdough bread's complexity of flavor without the work of maintaining and feeding a starter.

The French call the preferment a *poolish* (because the preferment is thought to have originated in Poland before coming to France), and Italians refer to the preferment as a *biga*. The English name is *sponge*, a reflection of the appearance of a preferment after twelve hours, when the surface is covered with small holes and indentations like a natural sea sponge. Some recipes call for a preferment called a *soaker*, presumably because it is made of grains or seeds that are soaked overnight. *Poolish*, *biga*, sponge, or soaker—a preferment is made for one-time use.

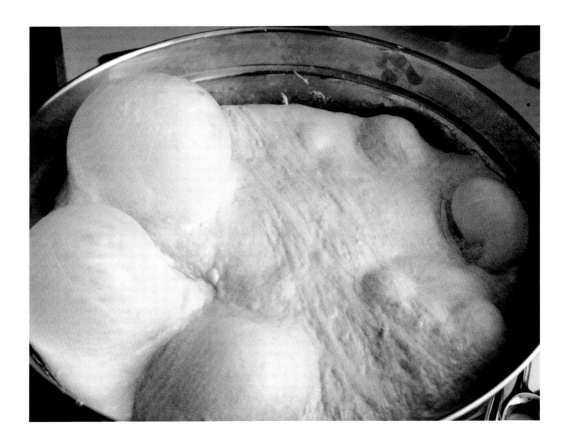

Anadama Bread

Ingredients:

Preferment:
- Water, 118 grams (½ cup)
- Coarse cornmeal, 83 grams (½ cup)

Dough:
- Bread flour, 318 grams (2½ cups)
- Water, 118 grams (½ cup)
- Molasses, 136 grams (½ cup)
- Instant yeast, 11 grams (1 tablespoon)
- Butter, 16 grams (1 tablespoon)
- Salt, 10 grams (1¼ teaspoons)

Equipment:
- Scale or measuring cups and spoons
- Lidded container
- Large mixing bowl
- Small mixing bowl
- Wooden spoon or Danish whisk (optional)
- Dishtowel or plastic wrap
- Bench scraper (optional)
- Wire cooling rack
- Dutch oven with lid (Option A)
- Medium loaf pan (Option B)

According to an old New England legend, the genesis of this bread occurred when a fisherman's wife walked out on her demanding husband with dinner half prepared. The fisherman was furious and swore: "Ana, damn her." Then, being a quick-thinking man, the fisherman tossed the abandoned ingredients—cornmeal and molasses—together with some flour and yeast and put the concoction in the oven to bake. The result was delicious Anadama bread, which is a favorite in the Boston area. You will find that the preferment adds richness to the taste.

Yield: 1 medium loaf

Day One
MAKE PREFERMENT (5 minutes)

Mix the water and cornmeal in a small bowl.

PROOF (12 hours)

Place the mixture in a container with a tight lid (preferably three times the size of the dough to allow for expansion) and set it aside in a warm location overnight.

Day Two
MIX (5 minutes)

1. Place the molasses, butter, and preferment mixture in a large bowl.
2. In a small bowl, mix the yeast and water together, then add this mixture to the large bowl.
3. Mix all ingredients by hand or using a wooden spoon or Danish whisk.
4. Add 159 grams (1¼ cups) flour and all of the salt to the mixture in the large bowl and mix thoroughly.
5. Add the remaining 159 grams (1¼ cups of flour) a bit at a time until the dough gathers together into a ball.

Note: Do not add all of the flour unless the dough requires it. At the same time remember that all flour varies and you might need to add even *more* than the total 318 grams (2½ cups) called for in the recipe.

KNEAD (10 minutes)

Knead the dough using the pinching method or the bench-kneading method until it's smooth and elastic.

FIRST PROOF (60–90 minutes)

Place the dough in a lightly greased bowl, cover it with a damp towel or plastic wrap, and put it in a warm location to rise until the dough has doubled in volume.

FOLD, DIVIDE, AND SHAPE (10 minutes)

1. Transfer the dough onto a work surface.
2. Perform one set of letter folds (four folds).
3. Divide the dough into two pieces using a knife or bench scraper.
   Tip: Try to cut dough in one motion and not multiple times. Each cut damages the webs of gluten you have carefully created during the folding and kneading processes.
4. If using a Dutch oven, shape the dough into a large boule. If using a loaf pan, shape the dough into a loaf.

SECOND PROOF AND PREHEAT (40 minutes)

Let the dough proof until it has doubled in size (approximately 40 minutes), and allow the oven to preheat for the last 30 minutes.

OPTION A: DUTCH OVEN

1. Place the boule in a large bowl or proofing basket, cover the bowl with a damp towel or plastic wrap, and allow the dough to proof in a warm location.
2. Preheat the oven, with Dutch oven and lid inside, to 475 degrees for 30 minutes.

OPTION B: LOAF PAN

1. Place the dough into greased loaf pan, cover with a damp towel or plastic wrap, and allow the dough to proof in a warm location.
2. Preheat the oven to 375 degrees for 30 minutes.

BAKE (35–45 minutes)

OPTION A: DUTCH OVEN (45 minutes)

1. Remove the Dutch oven and lid from the oven.
2. Sprinkle the bottom of the Dutch oven with coarse cornmeal.
3. Transfer the dough into the Dutch oven, and put the container (with lid) back in the oven.
4. Bake 45 minutes with lid on, or bake for 30 minutes with the lid on, and then remove the lid and continue baking for another 15 minutes until the bread is golden.

OPTION B: LOAF PAN (35 minutes)

Place the loaf pans in the oven and bake at 375 degrees for 35 minutes.

COOL (30 minutes)

Allow the bread to cool completely on a wire rack before cutting it.

LESSON 4: SOURDOUGH (WILD YEAST) BREAD-BAKING METHOD

Now you're ready for the big time. It's not that any of the other bread-baking methods are less worthy, but highly hydrated sourdough breads produce the pinnacle of flavor, crumb, and crust. You will have a tremendous sense of accomplishment when you produce your sourdough breads and delight in their taste.

Don't be intimidated. Feeding a sourdough starter is easy, and once you know how to do it, you can easily transform a white-flour starter to a whole-wheat or rye sourdough starter. Suddenly you have numerous flavor options to experiment with, bake, and enjoy. Sourdough baking is both fun and rewarding.

Making a Wild-Yeast Sourdough Starter

Starter causes the bread to rise and, most importantly, adds a subtle complexity of taste, sometimes a slightly sour flavor. To make a wild-yeast starter for your bread, you must first activate the dormant yeast and bacteria that already exist in flour. As the flour and water start their own chemical reaction of fermenting, the wild yeast and bacteria "wake up." The fermenting process attracts and captures wild yeast from the air. In combination with yeast, bacteria cause the sugars in the flour to ferment. This progression creates carbon dioxide gas and acid. (It is this acid, not the wild yeast, that gives the breads their tanginess.) Once the yeast has built up its strength, the baker interrupts the process and adds this natural live leavening agent—the starter—to the dough.

To make the wild-yeast sourdough starter, first you must find five days in a row when you will be able to take ten minutes each morning and night to *grow* (make) your starter. It's not much time to devote to creating this amazing symbiotic culture, which will deliver excellent bread, but you must be consistent throughout the process. After the first five days, you can continue to feed a starter on a regular basis, or you can store it in the refrigerator until you plan to bake bread again. (If you do store it, refer to the directions for reviving your culture on page 90).

Wild yeast starters fall into two major categories that bakers refer to as *liquid starter* and *stiff starter*. Because a liquid starter is easier to use and maintain, most of the formulas in this book are based on it.

The following schedule is based on feeding your starter for five days and baking on the sixth day. But, if your schedule permits you to bake on Day Five rather than Day Six, go ahead and bake.

Yield: Approximately 700 grams of mother starter

Day One
GENERATE YOUR MOTHER STARTER

The first step in generating a mother starter is to create the *seed* from flour and water. The wild yeast in the flour and air, mixed with bacteria, will begin to ferment. You will know that the starter is fermenting when it begins to grow in volume, bubble up, and then collapse and you notice an acidic odor. Look for bubbles that are about ¼ to ½ inch in diameter and look active. The bubbles that form as wild yeast ferments are irregular and will sometimes burst.

1. Scale 450 grams (3½ cups) of white flour, 50 grams (⅓ cup) of rye flour, and 500 grams (2¼ cups) of water, placing each in your container.
2. Cover the container, and let the starter ferment in a warm location for 24 hours.

Day Two
BEGIN THE TWELVE-HOUR FEEDING SCHEDULE

Now it's time to feed your hungry starter—every 12 hours for several days.

MORNING

1. Remove all but 250 grams (½ cup) of starter from the container (throw away the excess).
2. Scale and add 250 grams (2 cups) of white flour (at this point, you can continue with the combination of rye and white flour or just use white flour) and 250 grams (1⅛ cups) of water.
3. Mix the ingredients together and let the container stand in a warm place for 12 hours.

EVENING

Repeat the morning process.

Day Three
REDUCE THE AMOUNT OF STARTER

The yeast and bacteria are stronger now. You'll need to reduce the amount of starter to maintain a reasonably sized mixture. Today or tomorrow, the starter should have a batterlike consistency and be full of bubbles.

Ingredients:
- Water
- White bread flour
- Rye flour

Equipment:
- Digital scale or measuring cups and spoons
- Large container with lid (mason jar or plastic food-storage tub, for example)

MORNING

1. Remove all but 200 grams (1 cup) of starter from the container.
2. Scale and add 250 grams (2 cups) of white flour and 250 grams (1⅛ cups) of water.
3. Mix the ingredients together and let the container stand in a warm place for 12 hours.

EVENING

Repeat the morning process.

Day Four
CONTINUE TO FEED THE STARTER

Your starter is almost ready to use at this point—just a bit more feeding to go.

MORNING

Repeat the procedure from yesterday using the same reduced quantities.

EVENING

Repeat the morning process.

Day Five
REPEAT OR BAKE

As mentioned, you can use your starter today (see Day Six for instructions), feed it for one more day and then use it, or feed it for one more day and then store it until you're ready to use it. The choice is entirely yours.

MORNING

Repeat the procedure from yesterday using the same quantities.

EVENING

Repeat the morning process.

Day Six
BAKE

Go ahead—bake your bread. Just use whatever quantity of starter is called for in your recipe. Or, if you don't plan to bake for a few days, you can slow down the pace of the starter activity by putting it in the refrigerator.

STORE

If you retard your starter (put it in the fridge), you will need to wake it up to make it vigorous and healthy again.

The rule is that you should refresh the starter the night before *and* the morning of the day you plan to bake.

EVENING

1. Remove all but 200 grams (1 cup) of starter from the container.
2. Scale and add 250 grams (2 cups) of flour (all white or half and half) and 250 grams (1⅛ cups) of water.
3. Mix the ingredients and let the container stand in a warm place for 12 hours.

MORNING

1. Remove all but 200 grams of starter from the container.
2. Scale and add 250 grams of flour (all white or half and half) and 250 grams of water.
3. Mix the ingredients together and use immediately in bread baking.

Beyond Day Six
Mother Starter

Because you will want to keep some starter for future baking, you will need to maintain the starter. Save the remainder to keep as your "mother starter" supply for all future bread baking. Simply continue to feed the starter on a regular schedule using the same amounts of ingredients last used. You can begin to drop the amount of starter to 125 grams (¾ cup) at any point when the starter looks "lively," which means it is expanding and contracting—a process you can note by traces left on the side of your container—and has developed bubbles. As the population of yeast grows, it goes through the food quicker. After a few weeks, if you are continuing to feed the starter daily, you can even drop the starter to 100 grams (½ cup).

Mac McConnell's Multigrain Bread

Ingredients:

Starter Feed:

- Premade sourdough starter, 50 grams (¼ cup)
- White flour, 200 grams (1½ cups)
- Water, 200 grams (1 cup)

Dough:

- White flour, 240 grams (1¾ cups)
- Whole-wheat flour, 92 grams (¾ cup)
- Rye flour, 37 grams (⅓ cup)
- Flax seeds, 16 grams (¼ cup)
- Millet seeds, 16 grams (¼ cup)
- Sesame seeds, 16 grams (¼ cup)
- Pumpkin seeds, roasted and unsalted, 16 grams (¼ cup)
- Sunflower seeds, roasted and unsalted, 16 grams (¼ cup)
- Water, 304 grams (1⅓ cups)
- Salt, 10 grams (2 teaspoons)
- Sourdough starter, 148 grams (¾ cup)

Tom "Mac" McConnell, the creator of this recipe, is a genius with bread. Although Mac takes the same analytical and precise approach to bread baking that he did to mechanical engineering (he holds a master's degree in the field), he also connects emotionally with bread through taste, smell, and touch.

The grains in this bread provide a strong complexity and slight crunch, yet the bread is moist and delicious, not dry like some multigrain breads. This is my favorite bread recipe in this book. I hope you will incorporate sourdough bread into your life—it's truly extraordinary.

Yield: 2 boules

Day One
PREPARE SEEDS (5 minutes)

Prepare the seeds by mixing them with 50 grams (¼ cup) of water and allowing them to soak for at least 4 hours or overnight.

FEED STARTER (5 minutes)

The night before you begin your recipe, scale and mix the ingredients for the sourdough starter feed. Put a lid on the container, and place the mixture in the refrigerator overnight.

Day Two
FEED STARTER (5 minutes)

The next morning, repeat the steps to feed the starter, but use the mixture immediately in your recipe in the amount called for.

SCALE AND MIX (10 Minutes)

1. Combine the three flours in a large mixing bowl.
2. In a small bowl, combine the salt with 25 grams (1¾ tablespoons) of water, and set it aside.
3. Mix 229 grams (1 cup) of warm water with the sourdough starter until the starter breaks up into pea-size particles.
4. Pour the mixture of water and sourdough starter into the bowl containing the flours.
5. Add the salt/water mixture that you set aside and blend all ingredients together.

KNEAD (10 minutes)

Knead the dough using the pinching method or the traditional bench-kneading method. **Note:** This dough, like others in this book, will be moister than you may be accustomed to, but try to refrain from using additional flour.

FIRST PROOF (45 minutes)

Place the dough in a greased bowl or proofing basket, cover it with a damp towel or plastic wrap, and let it proof in a warm location until it doubles in size.

FOLD (5 minutes)

Place the dough on a lightly floured work surface and fold it using two complete sets of letter folds (eight folds in total).

SECOND PROOF (45 minutes)

Place the dough back into its bowl or basket, re-cover it with a damp towel or plastic wrap, and let it proof in a warm location for another 45 minutes.

DIVIDE AND PRESHAPE (10 minutes)

Place the dough on a lightly floured work surface, cut it into two pieces, and gently preshape them each into boule form.

THIRD PROOF (20 minutes)

Again, place the dough into two bowls or baskets, cover each with a damp towel or plastic wrap, and let them proof in a warm location for another 20 minutes.

FINAL SHAPING (5 minutes)

Transfer the dough onto a work surface and shape each piece into a boule, making sure that the final forms have the proper smoothness and elasticity and holds their shape.

Equipment:

- Scale or measuring cups and spoons
- Large mixing bowl
- 3 small-to-medium mixing bowls
- Wooden spoon or Danish whisk (optional)
- Proofing basket or similar
- Dishtowel or plastic wrap
- Bench scraper (optional)
- Scoring tool
- 1 or 2 Dutch ovens with lids (Option A)
- Baking stone (Option B)
- Parchment paper (Option B)
- Rimless cookie sheet (Option B)
- Steam-generating container (metal container filled with small metal objects, Option B)

PROOF AND PREHEAT OVEN (2 hours)
OPTION A: DUTCH OVEN

1. Place the dough seam-side up (the bottom of the shaped loaf should face up, toward you) in a lightly floured banneton or some similar container with a round bottom.
2. Cover the dough with a damp towel or plastic wrap and let it proof in a warm location.
3. During the last 30 minutes of proofing time, preheat the oven and your baking equipment to 450 degrees.

OPTION B: BAKING STONE

1. Cover a rimless cookie sheet with parchment paper and place the two boules on it.
2. Cover the dough with a damp towel and let it proof for 2 hours in a warm location.
3. During the last half hour of proofing time, pre-heat the oven, your baking stone, and your steam-generating container to 375 degrees.

BAKE (45 minutes)
OPTION A: DUTCH OVEN

1. Score each boule with your favorite design.
2. Remove the baking container from the oven and take off the lid.
3. Sprinkle the bottom of the container with coarse cornmeal to prevent the dough from sticking.
4. Transfer the dough (seam-side down) into the Dutch oven, put the lid back on, and return it to the oven for 30 minutes.
5. Take off the lid and continue baking for another 15 to 20 minutes until the bread is the desired golden caramel color.

OPTION B: BAKING STONE

1. Score each boule with your favorite design.
2. Slide the parchment paper and dough onto the hot baking stone.
3. Pour approximately 1 cup of water into the steam-generating container and close the oven door quickly to capture the steam. Be very careful so you don't get burned.
4. Bake at 375 degrees for 45 minutes until brown and crusty.

COOL (30 minutes)

Allow the bread to cool completely on a wire rack before cutting it.

PART II:

The Recipes

CHAPTER 5

Yeasted Breads

You'll find two types of dry yeast on the market: active dry yeast and instant active dry yeast. Instant active dry yeast is superior because it gives bread better lift and texture, plus it doesn't have to be proofed (mixed with water first). You can use active dry and instant yeast interchangeably in recipes.

Instant yeast is a bit more powerful than active dry yeast. Some bakers make adjustments in quantity, but I recommend using whatever amount the recipe calls for.

The instant-yeasted breads in this chapter are the simplest for beginners to bake. Our featured master baker in this chapter and owner of several Maryland bakeries, Ned Atwater, advises the home baker to pick one style of bread that he or she likes and just keep repeating that bread formula over and over, practicing to make perfect. Ned's advice is to "stay simple and be patient—soon you will be baking great bread," and I encourage you to take it. This is essentially the philosophic approach of the book: select one type of bread baking that fits your taste preference and your schedule, conquer that bread, and then move on to the next challenge.

Bran Bread

Ingredients:

+ White flour, 437–563 grams (3½–4½ cups)
+ Wheat bran or oat bran, 111 grams (1½ cup)
+ Water, 474 grams (2 cups)
+ White sugar, 25 grams (3 tablespoons)
+ Instant dry yeast, 3 grams (1½ teaspoons)
+ Salt, 6 grams (1½ teaspoons)
+ Coarse cornmeal (Option A)

Equipment:

+ Scale or measuring cups and spoons
+ Large mixing bowl
+ Wooden spoon or Danish whisk (optional)
+ Proofing basket
+ Dishtowel or plastic wrap
+ Scoring tool
+ Dutch oven with lid (Option A)
+ 9x5-inch loaf pan (Option B)
+ Wire cooling rack

Bran, the hard coating on grains, is particularly important to our diets because of its high fiber content. It also enhances the flavor of the bread. Unfortunately, many popular food products are refined, which means that they have removed the bran. This is why it's all the more important to use whole grains. Try this recipe and be healthier!

Yield: 1 loaf or boule or two smaller ones

SCALE AND MIX (5 minutes)

1. Scale the water and sugar and mix them together.
2. Stir in the yeast until it dissolves.
3. Add the bran.

REST (10 minutes)

Let the dough rest. (Bran takes a while to absorb water.)

SCALE AND MIX (5 minutes)

1. Add 125 grams (1 cup) of flour and stir.
2. Add the salt.
3. Add more flour and stir until the dough is stiff. **Note**: You do not have to use all of the remaining flour.

KNEAD (10 minutes)

Either using the pinching method in a bowl or kneading on a work surface, work the dough until it is shiny and smooth and the gluten has developed.

FIRST PROOF (2–3 hours)

Place the dough in a proofing basket or greased bowl, cover it with a damp towel or plastic wrap, and put it in a warm place until the dough has doubled in size.

FOLD AND REST (10 minutes)

1. Remove the bread from the bowl and place it on a work surface.
2. Perform one set of letter folds (four folds).
3. Allow the dough to rest for 5 minutes on the work surface.

SHAPE (5 minutes)

OPTION A: DUTCH OVEN

Shape your dough into a boule.

OPTION B: LOAF PAN

1. Roll the dough into a cylinder and tuck in the ends.
2. Place the dough, seam-side down, into the greased loaf pan.

SECOND PROOF AND PREHEAT (1 hour)
OPTION A: DUTCH OVEN

1. Place the dough back into the proofing basket, cover it with a damp towel or plastic wrap, and put it in a warm place to proof.
2. Preheat the oven, Dutch oven, and lid to 350 degrees for the last 30 minutes of proofing time.

OPTION B: LOAF PAN

1. Cover the pan with a damp towel or plastic wrap and place it in a warm location to proof until the dough has doubled in size.
2. Preheat the oven to 350 degrees during the last 30 minutes of proofing time.

SCORE AND BAKE
OPTION A: DUTCH OVEN (50 minutes)

1. Score the dough with a simple X or crosshatch pattern (#).
2. Carefully remove the hot baking container from the oven and take off the lid.
3. Sprinkle coarse cornmeal into the bottom of the container.
4. Transfer the dough into the container.
5. Put the lid on the Dutch oven and bake for 30 minutes, then take off the lid and bake for another 15 minutes or until the bread is the desired golden caramel color.

OPTION B: LOAF PAN (55–65 minutes)

1. Score the dough with a single straight line down its length.
2. Place the dough-filled pan in the oven and bake for 50 to 60 minutes.

COOL (30 minutes)

Let the bread cool completely on a wire rack.

SCHEDULE

Active Time: 35 minutes
Total Time: 6 hours and 20 minutes

- Scale and mix: 5 minutes
- Rest: 10 minutes
- Scale and mix: 5 minutes
- Knead: 10 minutes
- First proof: 2–3 hours
- Fold and rest: 10 minutes
- Shape: 5 minutes
- Second proof and preheat: 1 hour
- Score and bake: 50–65 minutes
- Cool: 30 minutes

Focaccia

Ingredients:
- White flour, 437–500 grams (3½–4 cups)
- Water, 237 grams (1 cup)
- Olive oil, 93 grams (½ cup)
- Instant dry yeast, 4 grams (2 teaspoons)
- Salt, 18 grams (1 tablespoon)
- Sugar, 26 grams (2 tablespoons)
- Coarse cornmeal, enough for dusting

Toppings:
- Olive oil, 24 grams (2 tablespoons)
- 1 medium onion, diced
- Garlic cloves, 2 minced
- Parmesan cheese, grated, 14 grams (¼ cup)
- Salt, coarse, 18 grams (1 tablespoon)
- Freshly ground black pepper, to taste
- Rosemary, chopped, 4 grams (2 tablespoons)

Equipment:
- Scale or measuring cups and spoons
- Large mixing bowl
- Small mixing bowl
- Wooden spoon or Danish whisk (optional)
- Proofing basket or bowl
- Dishtowel or plastic wrap
- Large baking sheet
- Parchment paper (optional)
- Pastry brush
- Small frying pan
- Wire cooling rack

Focaccia is—like a thick, doughy pizza crust—a quick and easy bread to make and crown with various toppings. The origins of this bread go back to ancient Roman times, when flatbreads were baked in the center of the oven and called by the Latin name *focus* (meaning "hearth" or "fireplace"). Today, focaccia can range from a thin flatbread to a puffier, more cakelike version. Some focaccias are relatively plain, with just garlic, sea salt, and grated cheese covering them, while others can be rich and filling, topped with onion, various meats, vegetables, and different spices and types of olives. My favorite toppings include potato, tomato, and rosemary (of which I have an exuberant bush in my kitchen garden). Experiment with your favorite toppings. Think of focaccia as a palette for your culinary expression. Be fearless!

Yield: 1 rectangle (8x11-inch)

SCALE AND MIX (10 minutes)
1. Scale and mix the yeast, salt, and water.
2. Add the sugar.
3. Scale the flour into a large bowl.
4. Add the yeast/salt/water mixture to the flour.
5. Add the olive oil.
6. Mix well.

KNEAD (10 minutes)
Using the pinching or bench-kneading technique, knead the dough until it is smooth and elastic.

FOLD (5 minutes)
1. Turn the dough out onto a work surface and complete one set of letter folds (a total of four folds).
2. Roll the dough into a ball.

FIRST PROOF (45 minutes)
Place the dough in a proofing basket or greased bowl, brush the top of it with olive oil, cover it with a damp towel or plastic wrap, and allow it to proof in a warm location until it has doubled in size.

SHAPE (15 minutes)
1. Coat a baking pan, cookie sheet, or sheet pan (a pan with edges, sometimes called a jelly roll pan) with a little olive oil. If you use parchment paper, you won't have to worry about the focaccia sticking to the bottom of the pan.
2. Sprinkle the bottom of pan or parchment paper with coarse cornmeal.

3. Transfer the dough to the pan.

4. Gently lift and stretch the dough by placing your hands under one end of it and with quick, smooth gestures, raising it up into the air. Keeping your hands underneath the dough, apply enough pressure to stretch it out to the edges of the baking sheet. **Tip:** Use little flipping actions, not pulls. You want to stretch the dough out so that it will become a rectangular shape about ½ inch in thickness.

SECOND PROOF (15 minutes)

Cover the dough on the baking sheet with a damp dishtowel and allow it to proof in a warm place for 15 minutes.

PREHEAT (30 minutes)

Preheat the oven to between 400 and 425 degrees Fahrenheit.

PREPARE TOPPINGS AND DOUGH (20 minutes)

1. Sauté the sliced onion in a small frying pan with olive oil over low heat for 15 minutes until the slices caramelize.

2. As soon as the dough is fully proofed, take off the dishtowel. With your fingertips, make indentations (think *dimples*) about ½ inch deep across the surface of the dough (with a few inches between them).

3. Brush the dough's surface with olive oil.

4. Scatter the caramelized onions, garlic, cheese, salt, pepper, and rosemary over the surface of the dough.

BAKE (20 minutes)

Bake on the bottom rack of the oven for 15 to 20 minutes or until the top is golden but still soft and the bottom is a bit crunchy.

COOL (30 minutes)

Let the bread cool completely on a wire rack before cutting.

SCHEDULE

Active Time: 1 hour
Total Time: 3 hours and 20 minutes

- Scale and mix: 10 minutes
- Knead: 10 minutes
- Fold: 5 minutes
- First proof: 45 minutes
- Shape: 15 minutes
- Second proof: 15 minutes
- Preheat: 30 minutes
- Prepare toppings and dough: 20 minutes
- Bake: 20 minutes
- Cool: 30 minutes

Irish Brown Wheaten Bread

Ingredients:
+ White flour, 125 grams
  (1 cup)
+ Whole-wheat flour,
  240 grams (2 cups)
+ Buttermilk and/or low-fat milk,
  575 grams (2½ cups)
+ Rolled oats, 40 grams
  (½ cup)
+ Salt, 6 grams (1 teaspoon)
+ Baking soda, 8 grams
  (1 heaping teaspoon)
+ Unsalted butter, 16 grams
  (1 tablespoon)

Equipment:
+ Scale or measuring cups
  and spoons
+ Large mixing bowl
+ Wooden spoon
+ 9x5 loaf pan or 10-inch
  cast-iron frying pan
+ Wire cooling rack

With the introduction and easy availability of baking soda in the mid nineteenth century, the Irish began to make bread by combining baking soda with buttermilk. Together, they are a great leavening agent; the lactic acid in buttermilk interacts with baking soda to produce carbon dioxide bubbles, causing the bread to rise. Buttermilk also helps preserve the dough. The Irish baked the dough in cast-iron skillets or in three-legged pots (called Bastibles) that they placed directly over a turf fire.

Traditional Irish soda bread contains only flour, baking soda, buttermilk, and salt. The soda bread made with whole wheat is also called wheaten bread or cake bread and is said to be more closely associated with northern Ireland; the soda bread made with white flour, also referred to as farl, is said to be more closely associated with the south. Sometimes the breads include caraway seeds for variety. When raisins are part of the mix, the bread is known as Spotted Dog.

Irish soda bread, whether made of whole-wheat or white flour, typically has an X cut into the center. Some people associate this with the Christian iconography of the cross, others with the Irish fascination with fairy myths, which suggests that cutting the dough "lets the fairies out" so they don't jinx your bread. However, the X probably evolved from practical considerations: the cuts help the dough rise, allow the heat to reach the deepest part of the bread, and make it easier to divide the bread at the table.

The quick preparation and baking time plus the use of whole-wheat grains make this an easy and healthy bread for daily consumption. I owe this recipe to a great friend and chef I met in the Berkshires (Massachusetts), Bob Luhmann. Bob may have a German surname, but he owns a house in Ireland and is more Irish than the Blarney stone.

Yield: 1 loaf

PREHEAT (30 minutes)

Preheat the oven to 425 degrees for about 30 minutes before baking your bread.

MIX (5 minutes)

1. Scale and blend the dry ingredients in a mixing bowl.
2. Cut the butter into small pieces and use your fingers to work it into the dry mix until the butter is the size of small peas.
3. Add the buttermilk and mix until it begins to hold together.
   Tip: Stop when the mixture begins to form a ball. If you overwork the dough, the gluten will overdevelop and the bread will be heavy.

SCORE AND BAKE (50 minutes)

1. Grease your cast-iron frying pan or loaf pan and place your dough in it.
2. Dust the top of the dough with flour.
3. If using the frying pan, score a large X across the dough. If using the loaf pan, score the dough once lengthwise.
4. Place your pan on the middle rack of the oven and bake for 45 minutes.

COOL (30 minutes)

Let your bread cool completely on a wire rack before cutting it.

SCHEDULE

Active Time: 10 minutes

Total Time: 2 hours

❖ Preheat: 30 minutes

❖ Mix: 5 minutes

❖ Score and bake: 50 minutes

❖ Cool: 30 minutes

Rustic Wheat Bread

Ingredients:
+ White flour, 375 grams (3 cups)
+ Whole-wheat flour, 120 grams (1 cup)
+ Water, 474 grams (2 cups)
+ Instant dry yeast, 4 grams (2 teaspoons)
+ Salt, 5 grams (1 teaspoon)
+ Coarse cornmeal (Option A)

Equipment:
+ Scale or measuring cups and spoons
+ Large mixing bowl
+ Large wooden spoon or Danish whisk (optional)
+ Proofing basket
+ Dishtowel or plastic wrap
+ Scoring tool
+ Dutch oven (Option A)
+ Baking stone (Option B)
+ Parchment paper (Option B)
+ Rimless cookie sheet (Option B)
+ Steam-generating container (Option B)
+ Wire cooling rack

You may remember this recipe from chapter 4. This is a very simple recipe that allows you to enjoy wholesome homemade bread on a regular basis. The recipe in chapter 4 contains more detail, so if you're still a little unsure of the steps involved, you may want to refer back to it or to the detailed descriptions of the steps in previous chapters.

Yield: 1 medium loaf

SCALE AND MIX (5 minutes)
1. Place the yeast and warm water in a large mixing bowl.
2. Add the salt and mix thoroughly to integrate.
3. Add up to 4 cups of a mixture of wheat and white flour in even proportions (but only as much as is necessary to handle the bread) and mix.

FOLD (5 minutes)
1. Transfer the dough onto a lightly floured work surface.
2. Perform two sets of letter folds (eight folds in total).
3. Gather the dough into a ball and place it on your work surface.

KNEAD (10 minutes)
Using your preferred kneading method, knead the dough for at least 10 minutes until it becomes soft and elastic and begins to form gluten.

FIRST PROOF (45 minutes)
Put the dough in a proofing basket, cover it with a damp dishtowel or plastic wrap, and place it in a warm location until the dough has doubled in size, about 45 minutes.

FOLD (5 minutes)
Fold the dough using two complete sets of envelope folds (eight folds).

SECOND PROOF (30 minutes)
Place the dough back in the basket or bowl and let it rest for 30 minutes.

SHAPE (10 minutes)
Shape the dough into a boule.

THIRD PROOF AND PREHEAT (30 minutes)

OPTION A: DUTCH OVEN

1. Place the dough in a proofing basket, cover it with a damp towel or plastic wrap, and allow it to proof in a warm location.
2. Preheat the Dutch oven and lid at 450 degrees during the same 30 minutes of proofing time.

OPTION B: BAKING STONE

1. Transfer your dough to parchment paper placed on top of a rimless cookie sheet.
2. Let the dough proof in a warm location, covered with a damp dishtowel or plastic wrap, for approximately 30 minutes.
3. Preheat the baking stone and steam-generating container (metal container filled with metal objects) at 450 degrees during the 30 minutes of proofing time.

SCORE AND BAKE

OPTION A: DUTCH OVEN (50 minutes)

1. Score the bread with a large X.
2. Take the Dutch oven out of the hot oven.
3. Sprinkle coarse cornmeal into the bottom of the container,
4. Transfer the dough from the proofing bowl into the hot baking container.
5. Put the lid on the Dutch oven and bake for 30 minutes, then take off the lid and bake for another 15 minutes or until the bread is the desired golden caramel color.

OPTION B: BAKING STONE (40 minutes)

1. Score the dough with a large X.
2. Slide the dough, still on the parchment paper (it doesn't burn), onto your baking stone.
3. Introduce steam into the oven by pouring approximately 1 cup of water into your steam-generating container and quickly close the oven door. (Be very careful not to burn yourself when introducing steam.)
4. Bake for 30 to 35 minutes at 450 degrees.

COOL (30 minutes)

Let the bread cool completely on a wire rack before slicing it.

SCHEDULE

Active Time: 40 minutes

Total Time: 3 hours and 40 minutes

❖ Scale and mix: 5 minutes

❖ Fold: 5 minutes

❖ Knead: 10 minutes

❖ First proof: 45 minutes

❖ Fold: 5 minutes

❖ Second proof: 30 minutes

❖ Shape: 10 minutes

❖ Third proof and preheat: 30 minutes

❖ Score and bake: 40–50 minutes

❖ Cool: 30 minutes

Swedish Limpa Bread

Ingredients:

+ White flour, 284 grams (2½ cups)
+ Rye flour, 255 grams (2½ cups)
+ Light molasses, 120 grams (1/3 cup)
+ Bitter ale, 284 grams (1½ cups)
+ Unsalted butter, 42 grams (3 tablespoons)
+ Salt, 15 grams (1 tablespoon)
+ Active dry yeast, 11 grams (1 tablespoon and ½ teaspoon)
+ Malt powder, 19 grams (3 tablespoons), or brown sugar, 25 grams (¼ cup)
+ Zest of an orange Aniseed seeds, 2 grams (1 teaspoon)
+ Fennel seeds, 3 grams (1 tablespoon)
+ Coarse cornmeal (Option A)

Equipment:

+ Small saucepan
+ Large mixing bowl
+ Wooden spoon or Danish whisk (optional)
+ Proofing basket or bowl
+ Dishtowel or plastic wrap
+ Scoring tool
+ Dutch oven with lid (Option A)
+ Baking stone (Option B)
+ Rimless cookie sheet (Option B)
+ Parchment paper (Option B)
+ Steam-generating container (Option B)
+ Wire cooling rack

According to legend, this Swedish bread was made from the *wort*, or brewer's yeast, found at the bottom of the barrel after the beer-making process was finished. To contrast with the acidity of the yeast, the bakers added the sweet and strong flavoring of orange. The combination of orange and fennel is terrific, and the taste becomes even more complex with the addition of anise (or sometimes caraway) seeds.

I lived in Stockholm for several years, and the large underground farmers' market with sparkling fresh fish and bakers' stalls was paradise. Because you could buy a half or even a quarter of a loaf of bread, I took advantage of the opportunity to try the multitude of Scandinavian breads. Among them I discovered my favorite: the limpa. This bread will surprise you and your family. Don't mask the flavor of the bread—serve it with soups or salads, or with simple sandwich fillings. The Swedes like it for breakfast with slices of hard-boiled eggs on top.

Yield: 1 large bâtard

SCALE AND MIX (10 minutes)

1. Place the molasses, ale, and butter in a small saucepan and stir over low heat until the butter is dissolved. Allow to cool.
2. Scale and add to the large mixing bowl the flours (reserve 30 grams [heaping ¼ cup] of the white to add if the dough is too wet to handle), malt powder or brown sugar, yeast, orange zest, aniseed, and fennel seeds.
3. Add the cooled wet mixture from first step to the flour mixture and blend until the flour is completely moistened.

KNEAD (10 minutes)

Using the pinching or bench-kneading method, knead the dough in the bowl or on the counter. Work with dough until it becomes smooth and shiny and gluten develops.

Tip: If the dough remains too sticky while kneading, add some of the 30 grams of flour you reserved earlier. But remember, less flour is always better.

FIRST PROOF (20 minutes)

Place the dough in a proofing basket or greased bowl, cover it with a damp towel or plastic wrap, and put it in a warm location to proof.

FOLD (5 minutes)

Perform one complete letter fold.

SECOND PROOF (1–2 hours)

Put the dough back in the proofing basket, cover it with a damp dishtowel or plastic wrap, and place it in a warm location until the dough has doubled in size.

FOLD (5 minutes)

Perform one complete letter fold.

THIRD PROOF (30 minutes)

Cover the dough and allow it to rest on your work surface.

SHAPE (5 Minutes)

Shape the dough into or bâtard.

FOURTH PROOF AND PREHEAT (60 minutes)

OPTION A: DUTCH OVEN

1. Place the dough back into the proofing basket, cover it with a damp dishtowel or plastic wrap, and let it proof in a warm location until it doubles in size.
2. Preheat your oven, Dutch oven, and lid at 450 degrees for the last 30 minutes.

OPTION B: BAKING STONE

1. Cover a cookie sheet with parchment paper.
2. Place the dough on the parchment paper, cover it with damp towel or plastic wrap, and allow it to proof in a warm location until it doubles in size.
3. Preheat the oven, baking stone, and steam-generating container at 375 degrees for the last 30 minutes of the proof.

SCORE (5 minutes)

Using your scoring tool, cut four diagonal slashes or one long slash lengthwise on the bâtard loaf.

BAKE

OPTION A: DUTCH OVEN (45 minutes)

1. Remove the hot Dutch oven from the oven and sprinkle the bottom with coarse cornmeal.
2. Transfer the dough to the Dutch oven, replace the lid, and return the container to the oven.
3. Bake for 30 minutes, then take off the lid and bake for another 15 minutes or until the bread is the desired golden caramel color.

OPTION B: BAKING STONE (50–60 minutes)

1. Slide the dough (still on the parchment paper) directly onto the baking stone.
2. Pour approximately 1 cup of water into the metal pan to create steam, and quickly close the oven door (be careful not to burn yourself!).
3. Turn the oven temperature down to 350 degrees and bake for 50 to 60 minutes.

COOL (30 minutes)

Let the bread cool completely on a wire rack before cutting it.

SCHEDULE

Active Time: 40 minutes

Total Time: 6 hours

+ Scale and mix: 10 minutes
+ Knead: 10 minutes
+ First proof: 20 minutes
+ Fold: 5 minutes
+ Second proof: 1–2 hours
+ Fold: 5 minutes
+ Third proof: 30 minutes
+ Shape: 5 minutes
+ Fourth proof and preheat: 60 minutes
+ Score: 5 minutes
+ Bake: 45–60 minutes
+ Cool: 30 minutes

Whole-Wheat Bread with Hazelnuts and Currants

You'll find lots of bread recipes calling for walnuts and raisins, but few that combine hazelnuts (a delicious nut) and currants (which I like better than raisins). This is great breakfast bread, with its rich flavor and filling energy boost. You will be your own champion if you bake and start the day with this bread.

Yield: 1 large boule or bâtard or 2 small loaves

MAKE PREFERMENT (5 minutes)

1. Mix the whole-wheat flour with the water.
2. Add the yeast and stir.

PROOF (2 hours)

Put the mix in a container, put the lid on, and place it in a warm location for 2 hours.

MIX (5 minutes)

1. Mix the rye flour and salt.
2. Add the butter and break it up in the flour using your hands or two knives until the bits are the size of small peas.
3. Combine the butter-flour mixture with the preferment.
4. Add the white flour until the dough will form a ball. (Use only as much flour as necessary. A wet dough is preferable.)
5. Add the hazelnuts and currants.

KNEAD (10 minutes)

Using the pinching or bench-kneading method, knead the dough until it is silky and smooth and has developed the proper amount of gluten.

FIRST PROOF (2 hours)

Place the dough in a proofing basket or greased bowl, cover it with a dishtowel or plastic wrap, and place it in a warm location until the dough has doubled in volume.

DIVIDE AND SHAPE (5 minutes)

1. Turn the dough out onto your work surface and divide it into two equal parts, or leave it as one large ball, about 8 inches in diameter.
2. Shape into one or two boules or bâtards.

Ingredients:

+ Whole-wheat flour, 240 grams (2 cups)
+ Light or medium rye flour, 51 grams (½ cup)
+ White flour, 375 grams (3 cups)
+ Instant dry yeast, 2 grams (1 teaspoon)
+ Water, 474 grams (2 cups)
+ Unsalted butter, 38 grams (3 tablespoons)
+ Salt, 12 grams (2 teaspoons)
+ Toasted or roasted hazelnuts, finely chopped, 56 grams (½ cup)
+ Dried currants, 58 grams (½ cup)
+ Coarse cornmeal (Option A)
+ Equipment:
+ Scale or measuring cups and spoons
+ 4-cup plastic container with lid
+ Large mixing bowl
+ Wooden spoon or Danish whisk (optional)
+ Proofing basket or bowl
+ Dishtowel or plastic wrap
+ Scoring tool
+ Dutch oven with lid (Option A)
+ Baking stone (Option B)
+ Steam-generating container (Option B)
+ Wire cooling rack

SECOND PROOF AND PREHEAT (1 hour)

Place the dough back into the proofing basket or greased bowl, cover it with a damp towel or plastic wrap, and allow it to proof in a warm location.

OPTION A: DUTCH OVEN

During the last 30 minutes of proofing, preheat your oven, Dutch oven, and lid to 475 degrees.

OPTION B: BAKING STONE

During the last 30 minutes of proofing, preheat your oven, baking stone, and steam-generating container to 375 degrees.

SCORE AND BAKE

OPTION A: DUTCH OVEN (50 minutes)

1. Score your dough with your desired design, such as a large X or crosshatch (#) pattern.
2. Take the Dutch oven and lid out of the oven and sprinkle the bottom of the container with coarse cornmeal.
3. Place your dough in the bottom of the Dutch oven.
4. Put the lid on the Dutch oven and bake for 45 minutes, or bake for 30 minutes and then take off the lid and bake for another 15 minutes or until the bread is the desired golden caramel color.

OPTION B: BAKING STONE (50–65 minutes)

1. Using a scoring instrument, make a large X or crosshatch (#) pattern on the top of the dough.
2. Transfer the dough from the basket to the hot baking stone.
3. Pour approximately 1 cup of water into the steam-generating container and quickly shut the oven door (be careful not to burn yourself!).
4. Bake for 45 to 60 minutes.

COOL (30 minutes)

Let the bread cool completely on a wire rack before cutting it.

SCHEDULE

Active Time: 30 minutes
Total Time: 7 hours

- Make preferment: 5 minutes
- Proof: 2 hours
- Mix: 5 minutes
- Knead: 10 minutes
- First proof: 2 hours
- Divide and shape: 5 minutes
- Second proof and preheat: 1 hour
- Score and bake: 50–65 minutes
- Cool: 30 minutes

Spelt is an ancient grain with a high nutritional value and a slightly nutty flavor. This recipe comes from Ned Atwater, owner and baker of Naturally Leavened Bread (see profile on page 203). Although almost all the breads Ned bakes for his customers are naturally leavened with a sourdough starter, he is choosing to share this easy recipe that uses instant dry yeast instead as a way to encourage you to try spelt flour. You have no excuse—anyone can make a bread with instant yeast. But you'll still deserve bragging rights when you produce a crackling-crusted loaf of bread from a grain that dates back to the fifth millennium BC. Serve a slice of spelt with a hearty sharp cheese to complement the bread's flavor.

Yield: 2 boules or bâtards

SCALE AND MIX (5 minutes)

In a medium bowl, scale and mix the spelt flour, yeast, and 300 grams (1½ cups) of the water (room temperature).

FIRST PROOF (20 minutes)

Place the dough in a proofing basket, cover it with a damp towel or plastic wrap, and allow it to proof for 20 minutes in a warm location.

MIX AND KNEAD (15 minutes)

1. Mix the salt into the remaining 100 grams (½ cup) of water and add this to the dough.
2. Use the pinching method or bench-kneading method to work the dough until the proper gluten develops. **Tip:** Kneading must be done *gently* because the gluten in spelt flour is fragile.
3. Add the walnuts.

SECOND PROOF AND FOLD (65 minutes)

1. Return the dough to a proofing basket or greased bowl, cover it with a damp towel or plastic wrap, and allow it to proof in a warm location for 30 minutes.
2. Complete one set of letter folds (four folds total) in the basket.
3. Allow the dough to proof for another 30 minutes.

DIVIDE AND PRESHAPE (5 minutes)

1. Divide the dough into two equal parts.
2. Preshape the dough into two boules or bâtards.

THIRD PROOF (30 minutes)

Place the dough back into the proofing basket or greased bowl, cover it with a damp towel or plastic wrap, and allow it to proof in a warm location.

Ingredients:
- Whole spelt flour, 500 grams (4½ cups)
- Water, 400 grams (1½ cups)
- Instant dry yeast, 5 grams (1 teaspoon)
- Salt, 9 grams (1½ teaspoons)
- Walnuts, chopped, 125 grams (1⅓ cups)
- Coarse cornmeal (Option A)

Equipment:
- Scale or measuring cups and spoons
- Medium mixing bowl
- Small mixing bowl
- Wooden spoon or Danish whisk (optional)
- Proofing basket or bowl
- Bench scraper (optional)
- Scoring tool
- Dutch oven with lid (Option A)
- Baking stone (Option B)
- Rimless cookie sheet (Option B)
- Parchment paper (Option B)
- Steam-generating container (Option B)
- Wire cooling rack

FOLD (5 minutes)

Complete two letter folds (for a total of eight folds).

FOURTH PROOF (2 hours)

Place the dough back into the proofing basket or greased bowl, cover it with a damp towel or plastic wrap, and allow it to proof in a warm location for 2 hours.

FINAL SHAPING (5 minutes)

Shape your dough into its final boule or bâtard forms.

FIFTH PROOF AND PREHEAT (2 hours)

1. Place your shaped dough seam-side up in your proofing basket, cover it with a damp dishtowel, and allow it to proof in a warm location for 2 hours.
2. During the last 30 minutes of proofing, preheat your oven and Dutch oven (with lid) or baking stone to 450 degrees.

SCORE AND BAKE (50 minutes)
OPTION A: DUTCH OVEN

1. Score the dough with your favorite pattern.
2. Take your Dutch oven and lid out of the oven.
3. Dust the bottom of the Dutch oven with coarse cornmeal.
4. Transfer your dough from its proofing location into the Dutch oven seam-side down.
5. Put the lid on the Dutch oven and bake for 30 minutes, then take off the lid and bake for another 15 minutes or until the bread is the desired golden caramel color.

OPTION B: BAKING STONE

1. Score your dough using whatever pattern you like.
2. Transfer your loaves to the preheated baking stone.
3. Pour 1 cup of water into your steam-generating container and quickly close the oven door (be careful not to let the steam burn you!).
4. Bake at 450 degrees for 45 minutes until your bread is brown and crusty.

COOL (30 minutes)

Let the bread cool completely on a wire rack before cutting it.

Fougasse comes from the Latin word focus, meaning "fireplace" or "hearth." The origin of this type of bread dates back to ancient Rome, when it was baked in the wood ashes of the baker's oven as the fire reached its peak temperature. By baking this thin (1½-inch-high) bread in the ashes, bakers could assess the heat of their ovens and determine whether the ovens were ready for regular-size loaves of bread. This unusual bread, with its multiple openings, has many variations in different parts of Europe, but the recipe below is from southern France. This version may be baked plain or with the addition of herbs such as rosemary and thyme. Pieces of anchovies or olives are also common additions.

Note: This dough calls for a sourdough starter. See chapter 4 for more specific instructions on making and feeding starters. If you don't have any on hand, you'll have to make some about a week before you can begin this recipe. If you already have some in the refrigerator, you'll just need to feed it the night before and morning of making this bread.

Yield: 4 small loaves

Day One
FEED STARTER (5 minutes)

The night before you begin your recipe, scale and mix the ingredients for the sourdough starter feed. Put a lid on the container, and place the mixture in the refrigerator overnight.

Day Two
FEED STARTER (5 minutes)

The next morning, repeat the steps to feed the starter, but use the mixture immediately in your recipe in the amount called for.

SCALE AND MIX (5 minutes)

1. Scale and combine in a large bowl the flour, salt, and yeast.
2. In another bowl, scale the water and sourdough starter, and break up the starter in the water until they're blended.
3. Add the water/starter mixture to the flour mixture and blend.

KNEAD (10 minutes)

1. Using either the pinching technique or the bench-kneading method, work the dough until it becomes smooth and elastic and forms a strong gluten. **Note:** The dough will be drier than many of the recipes in this book.

Ingredients:
Starter Feed:
- Premade sourdough starter, 50 grams (¼ cup)
- White flour, 200 grams (1½ cups)
- Water, 200 grams (1 cup)

Dough:
- White flour, 513 grams (1 heaping cup)
- Whole-wheat flour, 27 grams (⅛ cup)
- Water, 373 grams (1⅔ cup)
- Salt, 12 grams (2 teaspoons)
- Instant dry yeast, 3 grams (2 scant teaspoons)
- Sourdough starter, 54 grams (scant ⅓ cup)
- Olive oil, 16 grams (1 tablespoon and 1 teaspoon)
- Rosemary, 3 stems (each 6 inches long), chopped

Equipment:
- Large mixing bowl
- Small mixing bowl
- Wooden spoon or Danish whisk (optional)
- Proofing basket or bowl
- Dishtowel or plastic wrap
- Bench scraper (optional)
- Parchment paper
- 2 large baking sheets
- Pastry brush
- Rolling pin (optional)
- Scoring tool
- Baking stone
- Steam-generating container
- Wire cooling rack

2. Add the olive oil and integrate it into the dough.

3. Add the chopped rosemary and knead the dough again to combine all ingredients.

FIRST PROOF (1 hour)

Place the dough in a proofing basket or greased bowl, cover it with a damp dishtowel or plastic wrap, and let it proof in a warm location for 1 hour.

DIVIDE AND PRESHAPE (5 minutes)

1. Divide the dough into four pieces.

2. Roll each piece into a ball.

3. Fold each piece using the circle method (for a refresher, see chapter 2).

SECOND PROOF (20–30 minutes)

Place the dough back into the proofing basket, cover it with a damp dishtowel, and allow it to proof in a warm location for up to 30 minutes.

FINAL SHAPING (5 minutes)

Starting with one ball of dough and using a rolling pin or your hands, spread the dough into a slightly oval shape that's about 12 inches long, 9 inches wide, and 1 to 1¼ inches thick. Leave the other balls of dough covered to keep them from dying out. **Note:** If the dough is too thin, the fougasse will be brittle; if it is too thick, the bread won't have the nice crunch you want to achieve. Experiment until you find the right thickness.

SCORE (5 minutes)

The most traditional shape of fougasse uses voids in the bread to imitate the shaft of wheat. (The center cut symbolizes the shaft of the wheat and the cuts to the sides represent kernels of grain.)

1. Cut one long slash (the stem) in the center of the oval using your scoring tool.
2. Make four to five cuts (the kernels) on either side of this center line at 45 degree angles, each a couple of inches apart. Be sure to leave some dough between the center cut and the kernels as well as between the kernels and the outer edges of the dough.

TRANSFER DOUGH (5 minutes)

Cover your baking sheets with parchment paper and transfer the dough to them following these steps.

Note: This movement requires delicacy and speed.

1. Fold the dough in half along the center cut of the dough.
2. Fold the top of the bread over the bottom half. The dough will now be folded in quarters.
3. Gently pick up the bread and quickly move it onto the parchment paper.
4. Open up each fold in reverse order.

   Tip: At this point, you may want to enlarge the diagonal slashes a bit with your fingers to be sure they are open wide enough so that when the bread swells and bakes the openings won't close and hide the wheat pattern. If you break the dough, just wet the two pieces and reconnect them. (Dab a little rosemary in that place and no one will notice.)
5. Brush the dough with olive oil (mixed with some chopped rosemary, if more is desired).

THIRD PROOF AND PREHEAT (1 hour)

1. Allow the dough to proof on the baking sheets covered with a damp dishtowel or plastic wrap for 1 hour in a warm location.
2. Preheat the oven, baking stone, and steam-generating container to 450 degrees 30 minutes before baking.

BAKE (30 minutes)

1. Transfer the dough, still on the parchment paper, onto the baking stone.
2. Pour approximately 1 cup of water into the pan filled with metal objects to create steam and quickly close the oven door (be careful not to burn yourself!).
3. Bake at 450 degrees for 15 minutes.
4. If your oven heats unevenly (most ovens do!), turn your baking sheets.
5. Bake for another 15 minutes until the bread is slightly crispy and the tops are evenly browned.
6. Brush the bread again with olive oil to give it a sheen.

COOL (30 minutes)

Let the bread cool completely on a wire rack before cutting it.

SCHEDULE

Active Time: 45 minutes

Total Time: 4 hours and 15 minutes

Day One
- Feed starter: 5 minutes

Day Two
- Feed starter: 5 minutes
- Scale and mix: 5 minutes
- Knead: 10 minutes
- First proof: 1 hour
- Divide and preshape: 5 minutes
- Second proof: 20–30 minutes
- Final shaping: 5 minutes
- Score: 5 minutes
- Transfer dough: 5 minutes
- Third proof and preheat: 1 hour
- Bake: 30 minutes
- Cool: 30 minutes

CHAPTER 6

Slow-Fermenting Breads

The marvelous convenience of the slow-fermenting method is that all of the proofing can be completed overnight rather than in various stages over a day. These breads fit more easily into most home bakers' schedule.

Another reason I'm a big advocate of this method is that slow-fermented dough contains greater hydration than most other types of dough. Using less flour and more water allows the grains to gel properly and release more nutrients, so the goal in baking healthier breads is always to retain as much water as possible. The long fermenting times allow you to skip several of the proofing stages, when many bakers can't help but add more flour because they are manipulating the dough.

A couple of the recipes in this chapter use sourdough starter. (Head back to chapter 4 for a refresher on the subject.) If you don't have any, you'll need to make some about a week before you make your bread, but doing so will save you time in the future because you can store it for long periods. If you already have some in the fridge, you just need to feed it with water and flour the night before and the morning of using it.

Beer Bread

Ingredients:

+ White flour, 375 grams (3 cups)
+ Salt, 9 grams (1½ teaspoon)
+ Instant dry yeast, 4 grams (2 teaspoons)
+ Water, 178–237 grams (¾ to 1 cup)
+ Mild lager, 79 grams (⅓ cup)
+ White vinegar, 13 grams (1 tablespoon)
+ Coarse cornmeal (Option A)

Equipment:

+ Scale or measuring cups and spoons
+ Large mixing bowl
+ Wooden spoon or Danish whisk (optional)
+ Proofing basket or bowl
+ Dishtowel or plastic wrap
+ Scoring tool
+ Dutch oven with lid (Option A)
+ Baking stone (Option B)
+ Rimless cookie sheet (Option B)
+ Parchment paper (Option B)
+ Steam-generating container (Option B)
+ Wire cooling rack

Whole-Wheat Beer Bread

For a whole-wheat version of the Beer Bread recipe, substitute 1 cup of whole-wheat flour for 1 cup of white flour and add 2 tablespoons honey or sugar. This bread has a slightly acidic taste, and the dense crumb makes it a great sandwich bread with a healthy, robust flavor.

Beer breads are undergoing a certain renewal. Some attribute their growing popularity to the increase in available craft beer or the focus on local food, by extension local breweries. Other points of view suggest that making bread with American beer is a way for bakers to break from French bread-making traditions and make breads with an American "stamp." No matter what your reason is for making beer bread (an excuse for sampling different beers perchance?), you will quickly learn that your bread will mirror the flavor of the beer's ingredients (though to a lesser and lighter degree than that of the beer itself). I find it interesting to see what color and taste stout or dark beers add to the bread.

I'll repeat my favorite mantra: select the method of bread making that is ideal for your schedule and taste, and then explore deeper while staying in the confines of that method. Many Americans like to slither and slide all over the map as we look for instant gratification. We can learn from some of the other cultures that stress the opposite—concentrating on one thing and using patience and repetition to achieve perfection. Taking this in-depth approach is a good philosophy with beer-bread making. Experiment within the recipe; try different beers, different flours. You will enjoy the experimenting—and be able to immediately drink to your success when you find the ultimate beer bread.

Yield: 1 medium loaf

Day One
MEASURE AND MIX (5 minutes)

1. Scale and mix the flour, salt, and yeast.
2. Measure and add the water, beer, and vinegar, and mix well.

   Tip: As you mix, bring the bottom of the dough up onto the top to be sure the dough is well integrated.

PROOF (12 hours)

Place the dough in a proofing basket or greased bowl, cover it with a damp towel or plastic wrap, and leave it at room temperature for approximately 12 hours.

Day Two
KNEAD (10 minutes)

Transfer the dough onto a lightly floured work surface and perform three to four full letter folds (twelve to sixteen total folds) to create gluten and encourage the dough to form a ball.

PROOF AND PREHEAT (2 hours)

OPTION A: DUTCH OVEN

1. Place the dough in a proofing basket or greased bowl (or let it sit on your work surface), cover it with a damp towel or plastic wrap, and allow it to proof in a warm location for 2 hours.

2. Preheat your oven, Dutch oven, and lid to 450 degrees during the last 30 minutes of proofing time.

OPTION B: BAKING STONE

1. Cover a rimless cookie sheet with parchment paper and transfer the dough to it.

2. Preheat your oven, baking stone, and steam-generating container to 450 degrees during the last 30 minutes of proofing time.

SCORE AND TRANSFER DOUGH (5 minutes)

OPTION A: DUTCH OVEN

1. Score the dough with whatever pattern you like, such as a large X or square.
2. Remove the hot Dutch oven and lid from the oven.
3. Sprinkle a small amount of coarse cornmeal into the bottom of the container.
4. Transfer the proofed dough into the Dutch oven.
5. Put the lid on the Dutch oven and return it to the oven.

OPTION B: BAKING STONE

1. Score the dough with whatever pattern you like, such as a large X or square.
2. Slide both the dough and the parchment paper into the oven directly onto the baking stone.
3. Pour approximately 1 cup of hot water into the container of hot metal objects and quickly close the oven door. (Be careful not to burn yourself!)

BAKE (45–60 minutes)

OPTION A: DUTCH OVEN

Bake for 30 minutes, then remove the lid and bake for the last 15 minutes until the bread is a golden caramel color and appears to have a crispy crust.

OPTION B: BAKING STONE

Bake for 45 to 60 minutes. **Tip:** An instant-read thermometer should register 210 degrees.

COOL (30 minutes)

Allow the bread to cool completely on a wire rack before cutting it.

SCHEDULE

Active Time: 20 minutes

Total Time: 16 hours

Day One

❖ Measure and mix: 5 minutes

❖ Proof: 12 hours

Day Two

❖ Knead: 10 minutes

❖ Proof and preheat: 2 hours

❖ Score and transfer dough: 5 minutes

❖ Bake: 45–60 minutes

❖ Cool: 30 minutes

Ann Van Stelten's Oatmeal Bread

Ingredients:
+ White flour, 750 grams (6 cups)
+ Water, 237 grams (1 cup)
+ Oat flakes, 60 grams (¾ cup)
+ Butter, 5 grams (1 teaspoon)
+ Salt, 6 grams (1 teaspoon)
+ Light molasses, 15 grams (¼ cup)
+ Instant dry yeast, 4 grams (2 teaspoons)
+ Coarse cornmeal (Option A)

Equipment:
+ Scale or measuring cups and spoons
+ Large mixing bowl
+ Wooden spoon or Danish whisk (optional)
+ Proofing basket
+ Dishtowel or plastic wrap
+ Bench scraper (optional)
+ Dutch oven (Option A)
+ 2 small loaf pans (Option B)
+ Steam-generating container (Option B)
+ Wire cooling rack

You may remember this recipe from chapter 4—I remember it from a childhood filled with the smell of baking bread. This was my mother's recipe for oatmeal bread, a staple in our home growing up. The recipe in chapter 4 contains more detail, so if you're still a little unsure of the steps involved, you may want to refer back to it or to the detailed descriptions of the steps in previous chapters.

Yield: 2 small loaves or 2 boules

Day One
SCALE AND MIX (10 minutes)

1. Scale the salt, butter, and rolled oats and place them in the mixing bowl.
2. Scale and add the warm water.
3. Scale and add the yeast, molasses, and flour. Mix well.

PROOF (12–16 hours)

Cover the dough in the mixing bowl with a damp towel or plastic wrap and either place it in the refrigerator or leave it at room temperature for 12 to 16 hours (usually overnight).

Day Two
DIVIDE AND SHAPE (10 minutes)
OPTION A: DUTCH OVEN

1. Divide the dough into two pieces.
2. Gently roll the pieces into round balls.

OPTION B: LOAF PAN

1. Divide the dough into two pieces.
2. Shape each piece into two rectangular shapes and place them perpendicular to you.
3. Roll each rectangle into a loaf and place them in the pans (see chapter 2 for more detailed instructions).

PROOF AND PREHEAT (2–3 hours)
OPTION A: DUTCH OVEN

1. Place your dough into proofing baskets.
2. Let the dough proof in a warm location, covered with damp dishtowels or plastic wrap, for 2–3 hours until the dough has doubled in size.
3. Preheat the oven, Dutch oven and lid to 450 degrees for the last 30 minutes of proofing.

OPTION B: LOAF PAN

1. Cover your dough (already in the loaf pan) with a dishtowel or plastic wrap and allow it to proof in a warm location until the dough has risen above the edge of the loaf pan.

2. Preheat the oven to 350 degrees for the last 30 minutes of proofing.

BAKE

OPTION A: DUTCH OVEN (45–60 minutes)

1. Take the Dutch oven and lid out of the oven, and sprinkle the bottom of the container with cornmeal.

2. Place the dough in the container, replace the lid, and return it to the oven.

3. Bake for 30 minutes, remove the lid, and continue baking for 15 more minutes until your bread achieves the desired crust and caramel color.

OPTION B: LOAF PAN (75 minutes)

Bake at 350 degrees for 75 minutes until the tops of the loaves are a golden caramel color.

COOL (30 minutes)

Let the bread cool completely on a wire rack before slicing it.

SCHEDULE

Active Time: 20 minutes

Total Time: 21 hours

Day One
* Scale and mix: 10 minutes
* Proof: 12–16 hours

Day Two
* Divide and shape: 10 minutes
* Proof and preheat: 2–3 hours
* Bake: 45–75 minutes
* Cool: 30 minutes

Louis Hutchins's Overnight Bread

Ingredients:

Starter Feed:
- ✦ Premade sourdough starter, 50 grams (¼ cup)
- ✦ White flour, 200 grams (1½ heaping cups)
- ✦ Water, 200 grams (1 cup)

Dough:
- ✦ White flour, 425 grams (3 heaping cups)
- ✦ Salt, 12 grams (2 teaspoons)
- ✦ Water, 300 grams (1¼ cup)
- ✦ Sourdough starter, 120 grams (½ cup)
- ✦ Coarse cornmeal (Option A)

Equipment:
- ✦ Scale or measuring cups and spoons
- ✦ Large mixing bowl
- ✦ Small mixing bowl
- ✦ Wooden spoon or Danish whisk (optional)
- ✦ Dishtowel or plastic wrap
- ✦ Bowl scraper
- ✦ Dutch oven with lid (Option A)
- ✦ Baking stone (Option B)
- ✦ Rimless cookie sheet (Option B)
- ✦ Parchment paper (Option B)
- ✦ Steam-generating container (Option B)
- ✦ Wire cooling rack

Louis Hutchins lives outside Boston, Massachusetts with his wife and two children. A busy man and a committed home baker, Louis found time to create two versions of no-knead overnight-fermenting bread that use a sourdough starter. The first recipe is for a boule and the second recipe produces three extraordinary baguettes. (For more information on Louis, see his profile on page 189.) These breads are easier to make than most sourdough recipes because they are based on one long fermenting (proofing) phase. The recipes are written for the bread to be prepared in the evening, fermented overnight, and baked the next day, but you can adjust the timing to bake it in one day (starting in the morning and finishing 12 hours later).

Yield: 1 boule

Day One
FEED STARTER (10 minutes)

1. In the morning, scale 50 grams (¼ cup) of your existing sourdough starter (toss out the rest) and add 100 grams (1 cup) white flour and 100 grams (½ cup) water to it. Blend everything together, put a lid on the container, and place it back in the refrigerator.
2. In the evening, repeat what you did in the morning—50 grams of existing starter with an added 100 grams each of flour and water. Use the mixture immediately.

SCALE AND MIX (5 minutes)

1. Scale the flour and salt and combine them.
2. Scale the water and sourdough starter and combine them in a separate bowl.
3. Break up the starter by hand or with a spoon until it is well blended with water.
4. Combine the water and flour mixtures and mix them thoroughly using a large wooden spoon or a Danish whisk.

PROOF (8–12 hours)

Cover the bowl with a damp dishtowel or plastic wrap and allow it to proof in a warm location. **Note:** The dough in this recipe will not rise that much. Watch for a uniform pattern of bubbles on its surface. As the yeast activates, it *begins* to make bubbles, but the dough isn't fully proofed until the bubbles appear across the surface—not just in one area.

Day Two
TRANSFER DOUGH AND FOLD (10 minutes)

1. Cover a rimless cookie sheet with parchment paper.

2. Using a bowl scraper, carefully scoop the dough from the bowl and onto the cookie sheet.

3. Allow the dough to rest, covered with a damp towel or plastic wrap, in a warm location for 5 minutes.

4. Perform one set of letter fold (four folds) and place the dough seam-side down on the cookie sheet.

FIRST PROOF (5 minutes)

Cover the dough with a damp towel or plastic wrap and allow it to proof in a warm location for 5 minutes

KNEAD (5 minutes)

Carefully pick up the dough by scooping it with your palms underneath it, and then slowly rotate the dough in your hands, at the same time tucking it up into itself until you create the proper elasticity. (This action is similar to preshaping.)

SCHEDULE

Active Time: 30 minutes
Total Time: 15 hours

Day One
❖ Feed starter: 10 minutes
❖ Scale and mix: 5 minutes
❖ Proof: 8–12 hours

Day Two
❖ Transfer and fold: 10 minutes
❖ First proof: 5 minutes
❖ Knead: 5 minutes
❖ Second proof and preheat: 1 hour
❖ Bake: 50 minutes
❖ Cool: 30 minutes

SECOND PROOF AND PREHEAT (30–60 minutes)

1. Place the dough back on the cookie sheet.

2. Sprinkle the top of the dough with flour, and then cover it with a damp towel or plastic wrap.

3. Allow the dough to proof in a warm location for 30 minutes to 1 hour.

4. Preheat the oven, Dutch oven, and lid (Option A) or the oven, baking stone, and steam-generating container (Option B) at 450 degrees during the last 30 minutes of proofing.

BAKE (50 minutes)
OPTION A: DUTCH OVEN

1. Remove the Dutch oven from the oven and take off the lid.

2. Sprinkle the bottom of the container with coarse cornmeal.

3. Place the dough into the Dutch oven seam-side down, replace the lid, and return it to the oven.

4. Bake for 30 minutes, remove the lid, and continue baking for 20 minutes until the bread reaches the desired golden color.

OPTION B: BAKING STONE

1. Transfer the dough and parchment paper from the cookie sheet onto the preheated baking stone.

2. Carefully add 1 cup of water to the steam-generating container and quickly close the oven door (being careful not to burn yourself). Remove the container after 10 minutes.

3. Continue to bake the bread for approximately 40 more minutes until you achieve the desired crust and color.

COOL (30 minutes)

Let the bread cool completely on a wire rack before cutting it.

Louis's Easy Baguettes

Ingredients:

Starter Feed:
* Premade sourdough starter, 50 grams (¼ cup)
* White flour, 200 grams (1½ cups)
* Water, 200 grams (1 cup)

Dough:
* White flour, 425 grams 3 heaping cups)
* Sea salt, 7 grams (scant 1 teaspoon)
* Water, 300 grams (1⅜ cups)
* Sourdough starter, 120 grams (¾ cup)

Equipment:
* Scale or measuring cups and spoons
* 2 large mixing bowls
* Wooden spoon or Danish whisk (optional)
* Couche (optional)
* 2 proofing baskets
* Dishtowel or plastic wrap
* Bench scraper (optional)
* Scoring tool
* Baking stone
* Rimless cookie sheet
* Parchment paper
* Steam-generating container
* Transfer tool
* Wire cooling rack

These baguettes are easier to make than many other recipes while having the authentic taste of real French baguettes.

Yield: 3 baguettes

Day One
FEED STARTER (10 minutes)

1. In the morning, scale 50 grams (¼ cup) of your existing sourdough starter (toss out the rest) and add 100 grams (1 cup) white flour and 100 grams (½ cup) water to it. Blend everything together, put a lid on the container, and place it back in the refrigerator.
2. In the evening, repeat what you did in the morning—50 grams of existing starter with an added 100 grams each of flour and water. Place the mixture back in the refrigerator.

SCALE AND MIX (5 minutes)

1. Scale and mix the water and sourdough starter, breaking the starter up to the size of small peas.
2. Measure and add the salt and flour. **Tip**: As you mix, bring the bottom of the dough up onto the top so the ingredients are well integrated.

FIRST PROOF (12 hours)

Place the dough in a proofing basket or greased bowl, cover it with a damp towel or plastic wrap, and leave it at room temperature for approximately 12 hours.

Day Two
SECOND PROOF (45 minutes)

Transfer the dough into a new proofing basket, cover it with a damp towel or plastic wrap, and allow it to proof for 45 minutes.

FOLD (5 minutes)

Perform one complete set of letter folds (four folds) in the basket.

THIRD PROOF (45 minutes)

Cover the dough with a damp towel or plastic wrap and allow it to proof for 45 more minutes in a warm location.

DIVIDE AND PRESHAPE (5 minutes)

Divide the dough into three pieces and roll each into a log shape.

FOURTH PROOF (20–30 minutes)

Re-cover the pieces of dough with a damp or floured towel and let them proof for 20 to 30 minutes until they puff up a bit.

FINAL SHAPING, FIFTH PROOF, AND PREHEAT (50 minutes)

1. Shape the dough into baguette forms (see chapter 2 for instructions).
2. Place the forms on a floured couche. If you don't have one, place the baguettes on a parchment-paper-lined cookie sheet.
3. Allow the dough to proof for 45 minutes.
4. During the last 30 minutes of the proofing time, preheat the oven, baking stone, and steam-generating container to 450 degrees.

SCORE AND TRANSFER (5 minutes)

1. Score the dough in a pattern you like.
2. Transfer the dough from the couche using a transfer tool or slide the dough and paper off the cookie sheet and onto the preheated baking stone.

STEAM AND BAKE (25 minutes)

1. Carefully pour 1 cup of water into the preheated steam-generating container and quickly close the oven door (be careful not to burn yourself!).
2. Let the steam fill the oven for 10 minutes and then (again, very carefully) remove the steam-generating container. Bake for 10 to 15 more minutes until the bread is the desired golden color.

COOL (30 minutes)

Allow the bread to cool completely on a wire rack before cutting it.

SCHEDULE

Active Time: 40 minutes

Total Time: 17 hours

Day One
+ Feed starter: 10 minutes
+ Scale and mix: 5 minutes
+ Proof: 12 hours

Day Two
+ Second proof: 45 minutes
+ Fold: 5 minutes
+ Third proof: 45 minutes
+ Divide and preshape: 5 minutes
+ Fourth proof: 20–30 minutes
+ Final shaping, fifth proof, and preheat: 50 minutes
+ Score and transfer: 5 minutes
+ Steam and bake: 25 minutes
+ Cool: 30 minutes

CHAPTER 7

Prefermented Breads

Preferments are a simple solution, time- and energy-wise, to adding a depth of flavor to your bread. They're made just once and added to the dough, not fed regularly like a starter.

Our featured baker for this chapter, Solveig Tofte of Sun Street Breads in Minneapolis, Minnesota, loves working with preferments. She notes, "I gain great pleasure from the complex taste achieved with one or multiple preferments. For Sun Street's farmers' markets, I used two or three preferments. I don't think it is entirely necessary, but it's what I love about breads. If you preferment equal parts semolina and water and add a little yeast, you get this kind of cool buttery flavor and amazing strength. A rye sponge has a very clean spicy flavor. So you can marry those two in one loaf and have this bread with a kind of haunting rye and buttery semolina flavor . . . it's esoteric and fun for me."

Note: Some of the recipes in this chapter use sourdough starter. See chapter 4 for specific instructions on making and feeding starters.

Anadama Bread

Ingredients:

Preferment:
- Water, 118 grams (½ cup)
- Coarse cornmeal, 83 grams (½ cup)

Dough:
- White flour, 318 grams (2½ cups)
- Water, 118 grams (½ cup)
- Instant dry yeast, 11 grams (1 tablespoon)
- Molasses, 136 grams (½ cup)
- Butter, 16 grams (1 tablespoon)
- Salt, 10 grams (1¼ teaspoons)
- Coarse cornmeal (Option A)

Equipment:
- Scale or measuring cups and spoons
- Lidded container
- Large mixing bowl
- Small mixing bowl
- Wooden spoon or Danish whisk (optional)
- Proofing basket or bowl
- Dishtowel or plastic wrap
- Bench scraper (optional)
- Dutch oven with lid (Option A)
- Medium loaf pan (Option B)
- Wire cooling rack

You'll remember the recipe for this rich New England-style bread and its colorful origins from chapter 4. This is a great recipe to begin your journey with preferments.

Yield: 1 medium loaf or boule

Day One
MAKE PREFERMENT (5 minutes)

Mix the water and cornmeal in a small bowl.

PROOF (12 hours)

Place the mixture in a container with a tight lid (preferably three times the size of the dough to allow for expansion) and leave it in a warm location overnight.

Day Two
SCALE AND MIX (5 minutes)

1. Place the molasses, butter, and preferment mixture in a large bowl.
2. In a small bowl, mix the yeast and water together, then add this mixture to the large bowl and stir.
3. Add half of the flour and all of the salt to the mixture in the large bowl and mix thoroughly.
4. Add the remaining flour a bit at a time until the dough gathers together into a ball.

KNEAD (10 minutes)

Knead the dough using the pinching method or the bench-kneading method until it's smooth and elastic.

FIRST PROOF (60–90 minutes)

Place the dough in a proofing basket or greased bowl, cover it with a damp towel or plastic wrap, and put it in a warm location to rise until the dough has doubled in volume.

FOLD, DIVIDE, AND SHAPE (10 minutes)

1. Transfer the dough onto a work surface.
2. Perform one set of letter folds (four folds).
3. Divide the dough into two pieces.
4. If using a Dutch oven, shape the dough into a large boule. If using a loaf pan, shape the dough into a loaf form.

SECOND PROOF AND PREHEAT (40 minutes)
OPTION A: DUTCH OVEN

1. Place the boule in a proofing basket or bowl, cover it with a damp towel or plastic wrap, and allow the dough to proof in a warm location until it has doubled in size.
2. Preheat the oven, Dutch oven, and lid to 475 degrees for the last 30 minutes.

OPTION B: LOAF PAN

1. Place the dough into a greased loaf pan, cover it with a damp towel or plastic wrap, and allow it to proof in a warm location until it has doubled in size.
2. Preheat the oven to 375 degrees for the last 30 minutes of proofing.

BAKE
OPTION A: DUTCH OVEN (45 minutes)

1. Remove the Dutch oven and lid from the oven.
2. Sprinkle the bottom of the Dutch oven with coarse cornmeal.
3. Transfer the dough into the Dutch oven, replace the lid, and immediately return the Dutch oven to the oven.
4. Bake for 45 minutes.

OPTION B: LOAF PAN (35 minutes)

Place the loaf pan in the oven and bake at 375 degrees for 35 minutes.

COOL (30 minutes)

Allow the bread to cool completely on a wire rack before cutting it.

SCHEDULE

Active Time: 30 minutes
Total Time: 16 hours

Day One
+ Make preferment: 5 minutes
+ Proof: 12 hours

Day Two
+ Scale and mix: 5 minutes
+ Knead: 10 minutes
+ First proof: 60–90 minutes
+ Fold, shape, and divide: 10 minutes
+ Second proof and preheat: 40 minutes
+ Bake: 35–45 minutes
+ Cool: 30 minutes

Baguette with Bran Flakes

Ingredients:

Starter Feed:

+ Premade sourdough starter, 50 grams (¼ cup)

+ White flour, 200 grams (1½ cups)

+ Water, 200 grams (1 cup)

Preferment:

+ White flour, 250 grams (2 cups)

+ Water, 250 grams (1 cup)

+ Instant dry yeast, 1 pinch

+ Salt, 1 gram (¼ teaspoon)

Bran Mixture:

+ Water, 60 grams (¼ cup)

+ Bran flakes, 60 grams (1 cup)

+ Sourdough starter, 1 pinch

Dough:

+ White flour, 820 grams (6½ cups)

+ Water, 465 grams (2 cups)

+ Sourdough starter, 80 grams (¼ cup)

+ Instant dry yeast, 2 grams (1 teaspoon)

+ Malt, 4 grams (1 tablespoon)

+ Salt, 21 grams (1 tablespoon)

If made correctly, a baguette can evoke thoughts of a flavor-filled picnic on the banks of the Seine or in a mountain meadow. Add a sweet Normandy butter, a wedge of pâté, a bottle of wine, and a pleasant companion—who could want more? Unfortunately, many baguettes made on this side of the Atlantic are missing the light texture and crumb of traditional baguettes and suffer from a sad blandness.

One of the tricks to making a great baguette is learning how to correctly shape and score the dough (see chapters 2 and 3 for the how-tos). It's not too difficult. Take a bit of time to practice, and don't expect to get that trademark lightness and crunch if you merely roll the dough into a log form and make a few quick cuts. **Tip:** Don't try speaking French to your baguette unless your accent is good; the results could be disastrous.

Thomas "Mac" McConnell created the following baguette recipe while working at Berkshire Mountain Bakery and helping me develop recipes for this book. The bran adds a nice flavor to the baguettes, and if you follow the scoring technique described in detail in chapter 3, your baguette should have "lips" that bake into crispy crusts, giving you superb baguette crunchiness. *Bonne chance!*

Yield: 8 baguettes

Day One
FEED STARTER (10 minutes)

1. In the morning, scale 50 grams (¼ cup) of your existing sourdough starter (toss out the rest) and add 100 grams (1 cup) white flour and 100 grams (½ cup) water to it. Blend everything together, put a lid on the container, and place it back in the refrigerator.

2. In the evening, repeat what you did in the morning—50 grams of existing starter with an added 100 grams each of flour and water. Place the mixture back in the refrigerator.

MAKE PREFERMENT (5 minutes)

1. Scale and mix together the preferment ingredients.

2. Put the mixture in a large lidded container that will allow the preferment to double or triple in size.

MAKE BRAN MIXTURE (5 minutes)

1. Scale and mix together the ingredients for the bran mixture.

2. Place the mixture in a small container with a lid. **Note:** The bran mixture will not expand like the preferment.

PROOF (12–16 hours)

Allow the preferment and bran mixture to rest in a warm location and the sourdough starter to rest in the refrigerator for 12 to 16 hours or overnight.

Day Two
SCALE AND MIX (5 minutes)

1. Scale and put in a bowl the white flour, yeast, and malt.
2. In this order, add and mix in the water, preferment, bran mixture, 80 grams (⅓ cup) of the sourdough starter, and the salt.

KNEAD (5–10 minutes)

Using the pinching or bench-kneading method, knead the dough until it has developed the proper amount of gluten.

FIRST PROOF (45–60 minutes)

Place the dough in a proofing basket or greased bowl, cover it with a damp towel or plastic wrap, and allow it to proof in a warm location.

FOLD (5 minutes)

1. Pat the dough into a rectangle on your work surface.
2. Perform one to two letter folds (four to eight folds).

SECOND PROOF (30–45 minutes)

Place the dough back into the proofing basket or on a work surface, cover it with a damp towel or plastic wrap, and allow it to proof in a warm location.

DIVIDE AND PRESHAPE (10 minutes)

1. Place the dough on your work surface with the sticky side up.
2. Divide the dough into eight equal pieces.
3. Gently shape the eight pieces as follows: Form a rectangle from each piece and place it perpendicular (north-south) on the work surface. Fold over the top third and press the dough with your thumbs and the bottom of your palms. Gently roll the top over and keep rolling to the end—as if you were rolling up a miniature carpet—to create cylinders.

THIRD PROOF (20 minutes)

Allow the baguettes to proof, lightly covered with a damp towel or plastic wrap, in a warm location.

FINAL SHAPING (10 minutes)

Give the baguettes their final shape according to the instructions in chapter 2.

Equipment:
- Scale or measuring cups
- 2 medium mixing bowls
- Wooden spoon or Danish whisk (optional)
- Large lidded container
- Small lidded container
- Proofing basket or bowl
- Dishtowel or plastic wrap
- Bench scraper (optional)
- Parchment paper (Option A)
- 2 rimless cookie sheets (Option A)
- Couche (Option B)
- Transfer tool (peel, smooth board, or cardboard, Option B)
- 2 baking stones
- Steam-generating container
- Scoring tool
- Wire cooling rack

FOURTH PROOF AND PREHEAT (60 minutes)

OPTION A: PARCHMENT PAPER

1. Line two rimless cookie sheets with parchment paper and put four baguettes on each. Cover them with a damp towel and put them in a warm location to proof.
2. During the last 30 minutes of this proofing phase, preheat your oven, baking stones, and steam-generating container to 475 degrees.

OPTION B: COUCHE

1. Put the first baguette on a lightly floured couche (a piece of heavy linen).
2. Pull the fabric up into a fold or wave shape next to the baguette, and place the second baguette on the bottom of the fold. Continue until all eight baguettes are lined up on the couche with folds of linen separating each.
3. During last half hour of this proofing phase, preheat your oven, baking stones, and steam-generating container to 475 degrees.

SCORE (5 minutes)

Using a scoring tool, make five cuts at a 45 degree angle along an imaginary line that runs the length of each baguette. Follow the directions described in chapter 3.

TRANSFER (5 minutes)

OPTION A: PARCHMENT PAPER

Slide the baguettes—still on the parchment paper—onto the baking stones.

OPTION B: COUCHE

1. Position a length of smooth wood or a piece of heavy cardboard (one as long as the baguette and 4 to 6 inches wide) at a 45 degree angle to the first baguette resting on the couche.
2. Roll the baguette onto the transfer tool.
3. Position your transfer tool with the baguette on it next to a baking stone.
4. Pull away your transfer tool with a quick action so that the baguette "jumps" onto the baking stone.
5. Repeat with the other baguettes.

BAKE (20 minutes)

1. Create steam by pouring about 1 cup of hot water into the metal objects in the steam-generating container and quickly shut the oven door. (Be careful not to burn yourself!)
2. Bake the baguettes at 475 degrees for 20 minutes until they become golden in color. If water remains in the pan after 10 minutes, remove it. Otherwise, you can leave it in the oven.

COOL (30 minutes)

Allow the baguettes to cool completely on a wire rack before slicing them.

SCHEDULE

Active Time: 70 minutes
Total Time: 21 hours

Day One
+ Make preferment: 5 minutes
+ Make bran mixture: 5 minutes
+ Feed starter: 10 minutes
+ Proof: 12–16 hours
+ Day Two
+ Scale and mix: 5 minutes
+ Knead: 5–10 minutes
+ First proof: 45–60 minutes
+ Fold: 5 minutes
+ Second proof: 30–45 minutes
+ Divide and preshape: 10 minutes
+ Third proof: 20 minutes
+ Final shaping: 10 minutes
+ Fourth proof and preheat: 60 minutes
+ Score: 5 minutes
+ Transfer: 5 minutes
+ Bake: 20 minutes
+ Cool: 30 minutes

Eating something loosely translated as "old shoe" may not sound particularly appealing, but don't be afraid: this bread from Italy was dubbed ciabatta not for its flavor or texture but for its irregular shape, which resembles that of a carpet slipper or a flattened worn-in shoe. Ciabatta usually has a crispy crust with a soft interior and a rather large crumb, meaning it has many holes or air pockets. If you're looking to spice things up, add jalapeño and cheese, chocolate, or herbs.

Yield: 1 medium ciabatta

Day One
MAKE PREFERMENT (5 minutes)

1. Scale and combine the flour and water for the preferment.
2. Add the salt and yeast and mix until well blended.
3. Place the mixture in a container that will allow the preferment to double or triple in volume, and secure the lid tightly on the container.

PROOF (12 hours)

Let the preferment stand in a warm place for 12 hours or overnight.

Day Two
SCALE AND MIX (5 minutes)

1. Scale and place in a large bowl the water, olive oil, and 450 grams of the preferment you made.
2. Add to the wet ingredients the flour, salt, and yeast.

Ingredients:

Preferment:
- White flour, 227 grams (1¾ cups)
- Water, 227 grams (1 cup)
- Instant dry yeast, 1 pinch
- Salt, 1 pinch

Dough:
- White flour, 523 grams (1¾ cups)
- Water, 338 grams (1½ cups)
- Olive oil, 15 grams (1 tablespoon)
- Instant dry yeast, 2 grams (1 teaspoon)
- Preferment, 450 grams (2 cups)

Equipment:
- Scale or measuring cups and spoons
- Small mixing bowl
- Large mixing bowl
- Wooden spoon or Danish whisk (optional)
- Large lidded container
- Proofing basket
- Bench scraper (optional)
- Parchment paper
- Rimless cookie sheet
- Baking stone
- Steam-generating container
- Wire cooling rack

KNEAD (10 minutes)

3. Using the pinching or bench-kneading technique, knead the dough by hand until it has developed enough gluten.

FIRST PROOF AND FOLD (2–3 hours)

1. Place your dough in a proofing basket, cover it with a damp towel or plastic wrap, and let it proof in a warm location. You may also leave your dough, covered, on your work surface to proof.

2. Perform one set of letter folds (four folds) every 45 minutes during the proof. **Tip:** If you are proofing the dough in a bowl, you can perform the letter folds right in the bowl. If you are proofing the dough on your work surface, you can perform the letter folds there; you may want to use a wet bench scraper to help lift the edges of the dough because it will be wet and may stick to the counter.

SHAPE (5 minutes)

Shaping ciabatta dough is challenging because the dough is very wet and a special delicate hand-action is necessary. Your goal is to retain as much air in the dough as possible.

1. Dust your work surface and the top of the ciabatta dough with flour.

SCHEDULE

Active Time: 30 minutes

Total Time: 18 hours and 30 minutes

Day One
- Make preferment: 5 minutes
- Proof: 12 hours

Day Two
- Scale and mix: 5 minutes
- Knead: 10 minutes
- First proof and fold: 2–3 hours
- Shape: 5 minutes
- Divide: 5 minutes
- Second proof and preheat: 1–2 hours
- Bake: 20–30 minutes
- Cool: 30 minutes

2. Place the dough in center of your work surface.

3. Gently shape the dough into a rectangle about 1 to 2 inches tall, 14 inches wide, and 14 inches long.

4. Cover a rimless cookie sheet with parchment paper.

5. Place your hands under one end of the dough and, with quick and smooth gestures, raise the dough up into the air.

6. Keeping your hands underneath the dough, apply enough pressure to stretch out the dough to the edges of the baking sheet. (Use little flipping actions—not pulls—to create a rectangular shape.)

DIVIDE (5 minutes)

1. Place the rectangular dough back on your work surface.

2. Cut the dough into four strips between 10 and 12 inches long and about 4 inches wide. **Tip:** If you want, you could cut the ciabatta into small rectangles, which are great for sandwiches. (Just remember that they will bake faster.)

3. Lift and place the shaped loaves back onto the parchment-paper-lined baking sheet. Place the loaves far enough apart (3 to 4 inches) to allow the dough to expand without touching its neighbor.

SECOND PROOF AND PREHEAT (1–2 hours)

1. Cover the dough with a damp towel or plastic wrap (brush the plastic with olive oil to prevent sticking) and allow it to proof in a warm location.

2. Preheat the oven, baking stone (on the middle rack), and steam-generating container to 450 degrees during the last 30 minutes of proofing time.

BAKE (20–30 minutes)

1. Gently transfer the ciabatta dough and the parchment paper onto the baking stone.

2. Carefully pour approximately 1 cup of hot water into the metal objects to create steam and quickly close the oven door (be careful not to burn yourself!).

3. Bake for 20 to 30 minutes.

COOL (30 minutes)

Allow the loaves to cool completely on a wire rack before cutting them.

Solveig Tofte's Farm Girl Beer Bread

Ingredients:

Whole-Wheat Sourdough Starter Feed:

+ Premade sourdough starter, 50 grams (¼ cup)
+ Whole-wheat flour, 200 grams (1½ cups)
+ Water, 200 grams (1 cup)

Whole-Wheat Preferment (Levain):

+ Whole-wheat flour, 102 grams (¾ cup)
+ Water, 71 grams (⅓ cup)
+ Whole-wheat sourdough starter, 10 grams (⅛ cup)

Rye Soaker:

+ Rye or oat flakes (not instant), 191 grams (2¼ cups)
+ Water, 64 grams (¼ cup)

Dough:

+ White flour, 408 grams (3¼ cups)
+ Whole-wheat flour, 102 grams (¾ cup)
+ Instant dry yeast, 2 grams (1 teaspoon)
+ Scotch ale or Saison beer, 224 grams (1 cup)
+ Salt, 11 grams (2 teaspoons)
+ Water, 35 grams (2¼ tablespoons)
+ Coarse cornmeal, enough for dusting

Solveig's baking philosophy contains two major themes: the importance of temperature to dough and a love of preferments. "Truly, it was an ah-ha moment (during practice for the [Bread Baker Guild of America's] Coupe du Monde) when I discovered how critical temperature is to the outcome of a bread. If a certain dough was within the range of 75 or 76 degrees, it would be perfect; otherwise, less than exceptional."

Solveig recommends two types of beer for her bread: Scotch ale and Saison beer. Your local wine and beer store will carry both of these items. If you are interested in trying something new, you can check the Internet for different brands, but Samuel Adams carries both Saison and Scotch ale.

Note: This recipe requires a whole-wheat sourdough starter. To convert a regular sourdough starter (see page 89 for the recipe), feed the starter twice with whole-wheat flour 12 hours apart—once in the evening before and once in the morning of the day you make this bread).

Yield: 2 medium loaves

Day One

FEED STARTER (10 minutes)

1. In the morning, scale 50 grams (¼ cup) of your existing sourdough starter (toss out the rest) and add 100 grams (1 cup) whole-wheat flour and 100 grams (1½ cups) water to it. Blend everything together, put a lid on the container, and place it back in the refrigerator.

2. In the evening, repeat what you did in the morning—50 grams of existing starter with an added 100 grams each of flour and water. Place the mixture back in the fridge.

MAKE PREFERMENT (5 minutes)

3. Scale and mix the whole-wheat flour, water (heated to 78 degrees), and starter.

4. Place the mixture in a lidded container with enough space for the preferment to at least double in size.

MAKE RYE SOAKER (5 minutes)

Scale and mix the rye or oat flakes and the water (heated to 78 degrees) and place the mixture in a lidded container.

PROOF (12 hours)

Let all mixtures stand for 12 hours or overnight, the preferment and soaker in a warm location and the starter in the refrigerator.

Day Two

SCALE AND MIX (5 minutes)

1. Scale and mix the flours and the yeast.
2. Combine the salt and 35 grams (2½ teaspoons) of water in a small bowl.
3. Add the beer and preferment to the flour mixture.
4. Add the water and salt mixture to the beer and flour mixture and blend well.
5. Add and mix in the rye soaker.

KNEAD (10 minutes)

1. Knead the dough using the pinching or bench-kneading technique for approximately 5 minutes until the dough becomes somewhat elastic and shiny.
2. Let the dough rest for a few minutes, then continue to knead for 5 more minutes until the proper gluten has developed.

Equipment:
- Scale or measuring cups and spoons
- Large mixing bowl
- Small mixing bowl
- Wooden spoon or Danish whisk (optional)
- Large lidded container
- Medium lidded container
- 2 proofing baskets
- Dishtowel or plastic wrap
- Bench scraper (optional)
- Scoring tool
- Dutch oven
- Wire cooling rack

FIRST PROOF AND FOLD (2 hours)

1. Place the dough in a proofing basket, cover it with a damp towel, and put it in a warm location to proof.
2. At the end of the first hour, fold the dough using one to two complete letter folds (four to eight total folds).

DIVIDE AND PRESHAPE (5 minutes)

Using a bench scraper or knife, divide the dough into two even (roughly 550-gram) pieces and gently preshape them into round forms (boules).

SECOND PROOF (20 minutes)

Place the dough in proofing baskets, cover them with damp towels or plastic wrap, and allow the dough to rest for 20 minutes to give the gluten enough time to relax and be ready to form the links necessary to help bread rise.

FINAL SHAPING (5 minutes)

Give the preshaped boules their final shape.

THIRD PROOF AND PREHEAT (1 hour)

1. Dust the proofing containers with an equal mixture of rye flakes and white flour.
2. Place the shaped dough into the baskets seam-side up.
3. Allow the dough to proof, covered with a damp towel or plastic wrap, in a warm location for 1 hour.
4. During last half hour of proofing time, preheat the oven, Dutch oven, and lid to 475 degrees.

SCORE AND BAKE (45 minutes)

1. Dust the tops of the boules with flour and score them with a crosshatch pattern (#).
2. Carefully remove the Dutch oven from the oven and take off the lid.
3. Sprinkle the bottom of the container with coarse cornmeal.
4. Transfer a boule to the baking container, seam-side down.
5. Put the lid back on and place the Dutch oven back into the oven.
6. Bake at 450 degrees for 30 to 35 minutes. Remove the lid and bake a bit longer until the bread is the desired golden color.
7. Repeat these steps to bake the second boule when the first is done.

COOL (30 minutes)

Allow each loaf to cool completely on a wire rack for 30 minutes before slicing it.

From the boot-heel region of Italy, Puglia (Apulia) and the surrounding area comes another artisanal bread, pugliese. Pugliese is an Italian white bread with a fairly airy crumb made with a preferment—called a *biga* in Italian—which acts as a leavening agent. Pugliese makes a good slicing bread for sandwiches.

Yield: 1 bâtard

Day One
MAKE PREFERMENT (5 minutes)

Scale and blend the flour, water, and yeast until they start to form a ball.

KNEAD (5 Minutes)

Knead the dough using the pinching or bench-kneading method until it forms a smooth ball.

PROOF (12 hours)

Put the preferment in a container (big enough to allow it to double in volume), close the lid, and

allow it to proof in a warm place for 12 hours. (You can also store this preferment in the refrigerator for up to four days. Just bring it back to room temperature before using it.)

Day Two
MIX (5 minutes)

1. Scale and combine in a large bowl the yeast and water (between 80 and 95 degrees).
2. Add the preferment and break it up until it dissolves into the water.
3. Blend in the flours and the salt.

KNEAD (10 minutes)

Knead the dough using the pinching method while adding up to 300 grams (2½ cups) more flour, 50 grams (½ cup) at a time, until it develops the right amount of gluten. **Note:** Be careful not to add too much flour because this dough should be very wet.

FIRST PROOF (3 hours)

Place the dough in a proofing basket or greased bowl, cover it with a damp towel or plastic wrap, and put it in a warm location for up to 3 hours.
Note: The dough will rise but may not double in volume.

Ingredients:
Preferment:
- White flour, 63 grams (½ cup)
- Water, 40 grams (¼ cup)
- Instant dry yeast, 2 grams (1 teaspoon)

Dough:
- White flour, 375 grams (3 cups)
- Whole-wheat flour, 50 grams (½ cup)
- Water, 355 grams (1½ cups)
- Instant dry yeast, 2 grams (1 teaspoon)
- Salt, 7 grams (1 teaspoon)

Equipment:
- Scale or measuring cups and spoons
- Large lidded container
- Large mixing bowl
- Wooden spoon or Danish whisk (optional)
- Proofing basket or bowl
- Dishtowel or plastic wrap
- Scoring tool
- Dutch oven with lid (Option A)
- Baking stone (Option B)
- Parchment paper (Option B)
- Rimless cookie sheet (Option B)
- Steam-generating container (Option B)
- Wire cooling rack

SHAPE (5 minutes)

Transfer the dough to a lightly floured work surface and shape it into a bâtard.

SECOND PROOF AND PREHEAT (1 hour)
OPTION A: DUTCH OVEN

1. Place the dough in a proofing basket, cover it with a damp towel or plastic wrap, and let it proof in a warm location for 1 hour.
2. During the last 30 minutes of proofing, preheat the oven, Dutch oven, and lid to 450 degrees.

OPTION B: BAKING STONE

1. Cover a rimless cookie sheet with parchment paper.
2. Place the dough on the baking sheet, cover it with a damp towel or plastic wrap, and allow it to proof in a warm location for 1 hour.

During the last 30 minutes of proofing, preheat the oven, baking stone, and steam-generating container to 450 degrees.

SCORE AND BAKE
OPTION A: DUTCH OVEN (35–40 minutes)

1. Score the dough with one cut along the length of it.
2. Take the hot Dutch oven from the oven and remove the lid.

SCHEDULE

Active Time: 35 minutes

Total Time: 18 hours

Day One
- Make preferment: 5 minutes
- Knead: 5 minutes
- Proof: 12 hours

Day Two
- Mix: 5 minutes
- Knead: 10 minutes
- First proof: 3 hours
- Shape: 5 minutes
- Second proof and preheat: 1 hour
- Score and bake: 35–45 minutes
- Cool: 30 minutes

3. Sprinkle coarse cornmeal into the bottom of the baking container.

4. Transfer the dough to the Dutch oven, seam-side down.

5. Replace the lid on the Dutch oven and return both to the oven.

6. Bake at 450 degrees for 30 minutes. After
   30 minutes, lift the lid and check on the bread. If you don't have the desired golden caramel color, bake for another 5 minutes until you do.

OPTION B: BAKING STONE (50 minutes)

1. Score the dough with one cut along the length of it.

2. Slide the dough and parchment paper onto the baking stone.

3. Pour approximately 1 cup of water into the metal pan to create steam and quickly close the oven door (be careful not to burn yourself).

4. Bake for 45 minutes or until the bread is golden brown in color.

COOL (30 minutes)

Allow the bread to cool completely on a wire rack before slicing it.

Saison Beer and Scotch Ale

History documents Saison beer as originating from the Wallonia area of Belgium (the French-speaking region). The beer was commonly made in local farmhouses for the workers during the harvesting season. It had a relatively low alcohol content, which was fortunate because records indicate that workers were allotted a significant number of liters to keep them "refreshed" during the hot haying season. This artisanal beer began to disappear, but a revival of interest has sparked an increase in its production, especially in the United States.

Saison is a somewhat difficult beer to characterize because of variation due to its homemade qualities. Saison beers can range from light to dark in color and usually include herbs and spices to produce the distinctive bitter taste. Many of the beers are very fruity in aroma and tend to be semi-dry. Jeremy White, an employee at Samuel Adams, channeled his love of Belgian beers into creating a Lemon Pepper Saison, which Samuel Adams now distributes nationally. The beer's peppery flavor contrasts a sweetness of vanilla and a complex spice called Grains of Paradise with its pepper and ginger tangs.

Scotch ale originally comes from Edinburgh, Scotland, and usually contained a higher alcohol content, which caused the ale to be called a "wee heavy" beer. Samuel Adams produces its own Scotch ale, which it advertises as using a "rare peat-smoked malt commonly used by distillers of Scotch malt whiskey. This unique malt gives Samuel Adams Scotch Ale its distinct subtle smoky character and deep amber hue." No wonder these beers add a characteristic tang to your bread!

CHAPTER 8

Sourdough Breads

Sourdough breads all use a starter made from flour and water that has undergone a chemical reaction, producing bacteria (the good kind, like those in yogurt) and yeast, which work together in a harmonious relationship. The yeast produced in a starter is referred to as *wild yeast* because it forms naturally and is not commercially produced. The wild yeast is responsible for causing a bread to rise and obtain *good lift*, and the bacteria in the starter is essential for providing the nice tang or slightly sour, complex taste. When you use sourdough starter, the bread is lighter and has a better crumb, is easier to digest and provides more nutrients, and is stronger and more complex in flavor. You can make sourdough breads from most flours. In fact, rye flour responds better to sourdough than to commercial yeast. See page 89 for instructions on how to make your own sourdough starter.

Master baker, Richard Bourdon, bakes only sourdough breads at his Berkshire Mountain Bakery in Housatonic, Massachusetts. Richard is fully committed to ensuring that his breads benefit from a long fermentation process. "Fermentation," he explains, "unlocks the nutrients present in the grains. The process allows your body to better absorb minerals during digestion. I want the people who eat my bread to gain maximum minerals and vitamins … therefore, these grains must be fermented."

Cherry Pecan Bread

Ingredients:

Starter Feed:

+ Premade sourdough starter, 50 grams (¼ cup)
+ White flour, 200 grams (2 cups)
+ Water, 200 grams (1 cup)

Dough:

+ Whole-wheat flour, 200 grams (1½ cups)
+ White flour, 190 grams (1½ cups)
+ Water, 347 grams (1¾ cups)
+ Sourdough starter, 125 grams (¾ cup)
+ Salt, 9 grams (1½ teaspoons)
+ Cherries, dried, 120 grams (¾ cup)
+ Pecans, chopped, 92 grams (¾–1 cup)
+ Coarse cornmeal, enough for dusting

Equipment:

+ Scale or measuring cups and spoons
+ Large mixing bowl
+ Medium mixing bowl
+ Small mixing bowl
+ Wooden spoon or Danish whisk (optional)
+ Lidded container
+ Proofing basket or bowl
+ Dishtowel or plastic wrap
+ Bench scraper (optional)
+ Dutch oven with lid
+ Scoring device
+ Wire cooling rack

Combining fruits and nuts adds moisture, crunch, and sweetness to any bread. Cherries and pecans are a great combination, though you can substitute cranberries and walnuts or other preferences. This recipe calls for several proofing times and a proofing basket or bowl to allow for maximum gluten development to give the bread as open a crumb as possible. Enjoy this healthy bread that is great for all occasions.

Yield: 2 medium loaves

Day One
FEED STARTER (10 minutes)

1. In the morning, scale 50 grams (¼ cup) of your existing sourdough starter (toss out the rest) and add 100 grams (1 cup) of white flour and 100 grams (½ cup) of water to it. Blend everything together, put a lid on the container, and place it back in the refrigerator.

2. In the evening, repeat what you did in the morning—50 grams of existing starter with an added 100 grams each of flour and water. Put the lid on the container and place it back in the refrigerator to sit overnight. This amount of starter will give you enough for the recipe and some extra to store in the refrigerator for another baking.

Day Two
SCALE AND MIX (15 minutes)

1. Scale and mix 300 grams (1½ cups) water and 125 grams (scant ¾ cups) sourdough starter, breaking up the starter until it is integrated into the water. Set the mixture aside.

2. Scale the flours and place them in the large bowl.

3. Scale 47 grams (¼ cup) water with the salt and set aside.

4. Pour the water/starter mixture into the large bowl containing the flour and mix until it forms a ball.

5. Allow the mixture to rest for 10 minutes.

6. Add the salt/water mixture and work it into the dough until it is integrated.

KNEAD AND REST (25 minutes)

1. Knead for 1 minute and then rest the dough for 4 minutes.

2. Repeat over a period of 25 minutes (for a total of five kneads and five rests) or until the dough is smooth and elastic and has formed a proper amount of gluten.

MIX (5 minutes)

1. Add the cherries and pecans to the dough.

2. Knead until the cherries and pecans are integrated into the dough.

FIRST PROOF (1 hour)

Place the dough in a proofing basket or greased bowl, cover it with a damp towel or plastic wrap, and allow it to proof in a warm location.

FOLD (5 minutes)

Perform two to four sets of letter folds (for a total of eight to sixteen folds).

SECOND PROOF (1 hour)

Place the dough in a proofing basket or greased bowl, cover it with a damp towel or plastic wrap, and allow it to proof in a warm location.

DIVIDE AND PRESHAPE (10 minutes)

1. Divide the dough into two equal pieces.
2. Transfer the dough onto a lightly floured work surface.
3. Gently shape the dough into two boules or bâtards.

THIRD PROOF (20 minutes)

Place the dough in proofing baskets or greased bowls, cover them with damp towels or plastic wrap, and allow them to proof in a warm location.

FINAL SHAPE (5 minutes)

Give your dough its final boule or bâtard shape.

FOURTH PROOF (2 hours)

4. Place the dough in lightly floured proofing baskets, cover them with damp towels or plastic wrap, and allow them to proof.
5. During the last 30 minutes of proofing time, preheat the oven, Dutch oven, and lid to 450 degrees.

SCORE AND BAKE (50 minutes)

1. Score the dough of the first loaf: for a boule, use a simple pattern; for a bâtard, make a single cut down the length of the loaf.
2. Remove the Dutch oven and lid from the oven.
3. Sprinkle coarse cornmeal into the bottom of the Dutch oven.
4. Transfer the dough into the Dutch oven, replace the lid, and return it to the oven.
5. Bake for 45 minutes or bake for 30 minutes, remove the lid, and bake for another 15 minutes until the bread reaches the desired golden color. Repeat process with second loaf.

COOL (30 minutes)

Let the bread cool completely on a wire rack before cutting it.

SCHEDULE

Active Time: 1 hour
Total Time: 19 hours

Day One
✦ Feed starter: 10 minutes

Day Two
✦ Scale and mix: 15 minutes
✦ Knead and rest: 25 minutes
✦ Mix: 5 minutes
✦ First proof: 1 hour
✦ Fold: 5 minutes
✦ Second proof: 1 hour
✦ Divide and preshape: 10 minutes
✦ Third proof: 20 minutes
✦ Final shape: 5 minutes
✦ Fourth proof: 2 hours
✦ Score and bake: 50 minutes
✦ Cool: 30 minutes

Paris Night

Ingredients:

Starter Feed:

- Premade sourdough starter, 50 grams (¼ cup)
- Rye flour, 200 grams (1½ cups)
- Water, 200 grams (1 cup)

Preferment:

- Whole-rye flour, 81 grams (¾ cup)
- Water, 80 grams (⅓ cup)
- Rye sourdough starter, 40 grams (⅛–¼ cup)

Dough:

- White flour, 121 grams (1 cup)
- Whole-wheat flour, 202 grams (1¾ cups)
- Rye flour, 81 grams (¾ cup)
- Water, 300 grams (1½ cups)
- Salt, 5 grams (1 teaspoon)
- Instant dry yeast, 3 grams (1 teaspoon)
- Milk powder, 6 grams (1 tablespoon)
- Raisins, 150 grams (1 cup)
- Canola oil, 12 grams (1 tablespoon)
- Mild honey, 12 grams (1 tablespoon)
- Walnut pieces, 57 grams (½ cup)
- Coarse cornmeal (Option A)

Clear Flour Bakery owners, Christy Timon and Abe Faber (see their profile on page 196), have generously shared a favorite recipe with us. They sent me the large-batch formula, which I converted to a smaller portion for home baking (with a few emails to Abe). I then asked Louis Hutchins to test this recipe. First, Louis bought a loaf of Paris Night bread from Clear Flour Bakery and sampled it at home. Then, he began testing. The first batch wasn't entirely successful, so he called the bakery, and Abe made some suggestions. After Louis baked a few more batches, he was pleased with the results and dropped by Clear Flour to show Christy and Abe his final product and—nervously—solicit their reaction. They declared Louis's bread a success, a fine replica of their Paris Night. Now it's your turn to try. And if you live in the Boston area, be sure to drop in to Clear Flour and share a slice of your version of Paris Night!

You'll shape this bread into a bâtard, which is an ideal shape for fruit-and-nut-filled bread. Dough has to work harder to rise with fruit and nuts in it, and the oval bâtard shape doesn't require as much lift as a boule does. **Note:** This recipe requires a rye sourdough starter. You can convert a regular sourdough starter using two feedings, 12 hours apart, of rye flour.

Yield: 2 medium bâtards

Day One

FEED STARTER (10 minutes)

1. In the morning, scale 50 grams (¼ cup) of your existing sourdough starter (toss out the rest) and add 100 grams (¾ cup) of rye flour and 100 grams (½ cup) of water to it. Blend everything together, put a lid on the container, and place it back in the refrigerator.

2. In the evening, repeat what you did in the morning—50 grams of existing starter with an added 100 grams each of flour and water. Put the lid on the container and place it back in the refrigerator to sit overnight. This amount of starter will give you enough for the recipe and some extra to store in the refrigerator for another baking.

MAKE PREFERMENT (5 minutes)

1. Scale the rye flour, water, and rye sourdough starter for the preferment and place these ingredients in a large bowl.

2. Break up the starter until it is the size of small peas and continue to mix until the starter is nearly incorporated. Place the mixture in a container that will allow it to double or triple in volume and affix the lid.

PROOF (8 hours)

Let the mixture stand in a warm location until a dome has formed on the top, approximately 8 hours.

SOAK RAISINS (5 minutes)

1. Scale the raisins and cover them with hot water (80 degrees).
2. Immediately drain and shake the raisins in a colander to remove any excess water.
3. Place the raisins in a small bowl and cover. Let stand overnight at room temperature.

Day Two

SCALE (5 minutes)

1. Scale and place in a large bowl the white flour, whole-wheat flour, whole-rye flour, and milk powder.
2. Scale and add to the bowl the honey, canola oil, and water for the dough.

MIX (15 minutes)

1. Knead using the pinching or bench-kneading method for approximately 5 minutes or until the dough begins to become elastic and shiny.
2. Add the rye preferment and knead for approximately 5 more minutes, and then add the yeast and salt.
3. Knead for another few minutes.
4. Add and mix in the walnuts and presoaked raisins.

PROOF (1 hour)

Place the dough in a proofing basket or greased bowl, cover it with a damp towel or plastic wrap, and allow it to proof in a warm location.

DIVIDE AND REST (20 minutes)

Divide the dough into two pieces using a bench scraper or wet knife and allow it to rest for 20 minutes.

Equipment:

- Scale or measuring cups and spoons
- 2 large mixing bowls
- 2 small mixing bowls
- Wooden spoon or Danish whisk (optional)
- Colander
- Proofing baskets or bowls
- Dishtowel or plastic wrap
- Bench scraper
- Scoring tool
- Dutch oven with lid (Option A)
- Transfer tool (Option A)
- Baking stone (Option B)
- Rimless cookie sheet (Option B)
- Parchment paper (Option B)
- Steam-generating container (Option B)
- Wire cooling rack

SCHEDULE

Active Time: 45 minutes

Total Time: 17 hours

Day One

+ Feed starter: 10 minutes
+ Make preferment: 5 minutes
+ Proof: 8 hours
+ Soak raisins: 5 minutes

Day Two

+ Scale: 5 minutes
+ Mix: 15 minutes
+ Proof: 1 hour
+ Divide and rest: 20 minutes
+ Shape: 5 minutes
+ Final proof and preheat: 1½–2 hours
+ Score: 5 minutes
+ Bake: 35 minutes
+ Cool: 30 minutes

SHAPE (5 minutes)

Shape the dough into two bâtards.

FINAL PROOF AND PREHEAT (1½–2 hours)

OPTION A: DUTCH OVEN

1. Place the shaped dough seam-side up in lightly floured proofing baskets or bowls.
2. Cover the dough with a damp dishtowel or plastic wrap and allow it to rise in a warm place for 1½–2 hours.
3. During the last 30 minutes, place the Dutch oven and lid in the oven and preheat it to 475 degrees.

OPTION B: BAKING STONE

1. Place the shaped dough seam-side down on a parchment-covered rimless baking sheet.
2. Cover the dough with a damp dishtowel or plastic wrap and allow it to rise in a warm place for 1½ to 2 hours.
3. Place the baking stone and steam-generating container in the oven and preheat it to 450 degrees.

SCORE (5 minutes)

Score each loaf with a chevron pattern (this pattern suits the bâtard shape) by making several 45 degree cuts angling toward—but not touching—an imaginary center line that runs the length of the loaf (you should end up with several broken V-shaped cuts). Four cuts down each side should be sufficient.

BAKE (35 minutes)

OPTION A: DUTCH OVEN

1. Remove the Dutch oven and lid from the oven.
2. Roll one of the loaves onto a transfer tool (a wooden board or stiff piece of cardboard) and gently deposit the loaf into the hot Dutch oven. (**Alternative:** Let the dough proof on parchment paper, which you can then pick up like a stretcher to transfer your loaf into the Dutch oven.)
3. Place the lid on the Dutch oven, reduce the oven temperature to 450 degrees, and bake for 25 minutes.
4. Remove the lid from the Dutch oven and bake for another 5 to 10 minutes or until the loaf is a medium brown and has a good crust. Repeat process with the second loaf.

OPTION B: BAKING STONE

1. Slide the parchment paper with the shaped loaves directly onto the hot baking stone.
2. Pour approximately 1 cup of water over the hot metal objects in the steam-generating container (be careful of the steam) and quickly close the oven door.
3. Bake for 33 to 36 minutes.

COOL (30 minutes)

Let the bread cool completely on a wire rack before cutting it.

Khorasan, or KAMUT (its trademarked name), is an ancient grain that bakes into delicious bread with a nutty taste and a golden interior color. When a US airman brought khorasan grains from Egypt to his family farm in Montana, the family called the grain "King Tut's wheat." Despite its noble name, the grain never achieved much commercial success and eventually disappeared from public awareness.

In the late 1970s, a man named Bob Quinn revived interest in the grain, trademarked the name KAMUT, and sold KAMUT flour to the emerging health-food constituency interested in organic, genetically unaltered grains. Today, KAMUT, like spelt, is attracting a following of wheat-sensitive individuals who find that KAMUT is suitable for them as a wheat substitute. Ask your family or guests if they've ever been served bread made from a grain that has its own Egyptian hieroglyphic symbols!

Yield: 1 boule or bâtard

Day One
FEED STARTER (10 minutes)

1. In the morning, scale 50 grams (¼ cup) of your existing sourdough starter (toss out the rest) and add 100 grams (1 cup) white flour and 100 grams (½ cup) water to it. Blend everything together, put a lid on the container, and place it back in the refrigerator.

2. In the evening, repeat what you did in the morning—50 grams of existing starter with an added 100 grams each of flour and water. Put the lid on the container and place it back in the refrigerator to sit overnight. This amount of starter will give you enough for the recipe and some extra to store in the refrigerator for another baking.

MAKE PREFERMENT (5 minutes)

Scale the flour, water, and sourdough starter for the preferment and mix them together.

PROOF (12–16 hours)

Place the preferment mixture in a container that will allow it to double or triple in volume, affix the lid, and set it in a warm location for 12 to 16 hours or overnight.

Day Two
SCALE AND MIX (5 minutes)

1. Scale and mix the flours, water, and yeast for the dough.
2. Add and mix in 135 grams (1¼ cup) preferment and the salt.

Ingredients:

Starter Feed:
- Premade sourdough starter, 50 grams (¼ cup)
- White flour, 200 grams (2 cups)
- Water, 200 grams (1 cup)

Preferment:
- KAMUT flour, 129 grams (1⅛ cups)
- Water, 129 grams (⅝ cups)
- Sourdough starter, 69 grams (⅓ cup)

Dough:
- KAMUT flour, 370 grams (3¼ cups)
- White flour, 100 grams (¾ cup)
- Water, 383 grams (scant 2 cups)
- Instant dry yeast, 5 grams (2 teaspoons)
- Salt, 11 grams (2 teaspoons)
- Preferment, 135 grams (1¼ cups)
- Coarse cornmeal, enough for dusting

Equipment:
- Scale or measuring cups and spoons
- 1 small mixing bowl
- 1 large mixing bowl
- Wooden spoon or Danish whisk (optional)
- Lidded container
- Proofing basket or bowl
- Dishtowel or plastic wrap
- Scoring tool
- Dutch oven with lid
- Wire cooling rack

KNEAD (15 minutes)

1. Knead with the pinching technique or the bench-kneading method on your work surface until gluten develops.
2. Continue to mix until the dough is smooth and has strength. **Note:** KAMUT flour will take longer than most flours to develop strength.

FIRST PROOF AND FOLD (2–3 hours)

1. Place the dough in a proofing basket or greased bowl, cover it with a damp towel or plastic wrap, and allow it to proof in a warm location for 1 hour.
2. Perform one set of letter folds (total of four folds) at the end of the first hour and then let the dough proof for another hour.
3. Perform another set of letter folds (total of four folds) at the end of the second hour.
4. Continue proofing for another hour if necessary.

PRESHAPE (5 minutes)

Preshape the dough into a boule.

SECOND PROOF (30 minutes)

Place the dough back in the proofing basket or greased bowl, cover it with a damp towel or plastic wrap, and allow it to proof in a warm location.

SHAPE (5 minutes)

Give the dough its final boule or bâtard shape.

THIRD PROOF AND PREHEAT (2 hours)

1. Place the dough in the proofing basket again, cover it with a damp towel or plastic wrap, and allow it to proof in a warm location.
2. During the last 30 minutes of proofing time, put the Dutch oven and lid into the oven and preheat it to 475 degrees.

SCORE AND BAKE (50 minutes)

1. Score the loaf in a favorite pattern using a scoring tool.
2. Remove the Dutch oven and lid from the oven and sprinkle bottom of the container with coarse cornmeal to keep the dough from sticking.
3. Transfer the dough into the hot container, replace the lid, and return the set to the oven.
4. Bake at 475 degrees for 45 minutes or take the lid off for the last 10 to 15 minutes or until the bread is crusty and a golden color.

COOL (30 minutes)

Let the bread cool completely on a wire rack before cutting it.

SCHEDULE

Active Time: 50 minutes
Total Time: 23 hours

Day One
- Feed starter: 10 minutes
- Make preferment: 5 minutes
- Proof: 12–16 hours

Day Two
- Scale and mix: 5 minutes
- Knead: 15 minutes
- First proof and fold: 2–3 hours
- Preshape: 5 minutes
- Second proof: 30 minutes
- Shape: 5 minutes
- Third proof and preheat: 2 hours
- Score and bake: 50 minutes
- Cool: 30 minutes

This recipe comes from Jim Amaral, master baker of Borealis Breads in Portland, Maine. Jim highlights his home state at his bakery, which he named after the aurora borealis, the surreal northern lights that can be seen in Maine. Jim features Maine wheat in his signature bread, Katahdin, which is the name of the highest mountain in Maine and is famous as the end (or beginning) of the Appalachian Trail. The mountain is also part of my family lore because my parents, on one of the first weekends after they were married, climbed Katahdin in a heavy rainstorm, managing the famous Knife Edge Trail that has claimed the lives of nineteen people. I think you'll enjoy this bread given the same Native American name as the great mountain. **Note:** A whole-wheat sourdough starter is required for this recipe. You can convert a regular sourdough starter using two feedings, 12 hours apart, of whole-wheat flour. Though the flavor of the bread won't be quite the same, you can use a regular sourdough starter if you forget to make a whole-wheat starter.

Yield: 2 medium boules

Day One
FEED STARTER (10 minutes)

1. In the morning, scale 50 grams (¼ cup) of your existing sourdough starter (toss out the rest) and add 100 grams (¾ cup) whole-wheat flour and 100 grams (½ cup) water to it. Blend everything together, put a lid on the container, and place it back in the refrigerator.

2. In the evening, repeat what you did in the morning—50 grams of existing starter with an added 100 grams each of flour and water. Put the lid on the container and place it back in the refrigerator to sit overnight. This amount of starter will give you enough for the recipe and some extra to store in the refrigerator for another baking.

Day Two
SCALE AND MIX (5 minutes)

1. Scale and place the water and sourdough starter for the dough in a medium bowl.
2. Blend the mixture until the starter is broken into pea-size pieces.
3. Add the whole-wheat flour for the dough to the water/sourdough mixture and mix thoroughly.

KNEAD (15 minutes)

1. Knead using the pinching technique or bench-kneading method until the dough begins to become elastic and shiny, approximately 10 minutes.
2. Add the salt.
3. Knead for approximately 5 more minutes or until the dough has achieved the proper gluten strength.

Ingredients:
Starter Feed:
- Premade sourdough starter, 50 grams (¼ cup)
- Whole-wheat flour, 200 grams (1½ cups)
- Water, 200 grams (1 cup)

Dough:
- Whole-wheat flour, 530 grams (4½ cups)
- Water, 318 grams (1⅝ cups)
- Sourdough starter, 135 grams (¾ cup)
- Salt, 15 grams (1 tablespoon)
- Coarse cornmeal (Option A)

Equipment:
- Scale or measuring cups and spoons
- Large bowl
- Small bowl
- Wooden spoon or Danish whisk (optional)
- Lidded container
- Proofing baskets or bowls
- Dishtowel or plastic wrap
- Bench scraper
- Scoring tool
- Dutch oven with lid (Option A)
- Baking stone (Option B)
- Rimless cookie sheet (Option B)
- Parchment paper (Option B)
- Steam-generating container (Option B)
- Wire cooling rack

FIRST PROOF (1–2 hours)

Place the dough in a proofing basket or greased bowl, cover it with a damp towel or plastic wrap, and allow it to proof in a warm location.

FOLD, DIVIDE, AND SHAPE
(10 minutes)

1. Place the dough on your work surface and perform two sets of letter folds (total of eight folds).
2. Let the dough rest for a few minutes and then divide it into two pieces.
3. Gently shape the dough into boules.

SECOND PROOF AND PREHEAT (1–2 hours)
OPTION A: DUTCH OVEN

1. Place the loaves seam-side up in proofing baskets, cover them with a damp towel or plastic wrap, and let the dough rise in a warm location until it has doubled in size.
2. During the last 30 minutes of proofing time, place your Dutch oven and lid in the oven and preheat it to 475 degrees.

OPTION B: BAKING STONE

1. Place the loaves seam-side up on a parchment-paper-covered rimless cookie sheet.
2. Cover the loaves with a damp dishtowel or plastic wrap and let the dough rise in a warm location until it has doubled in size.
3. During the last 30 minutes of proofing time, place your baking stone and steam-generating container in the oven and preheat it to 475 degrees.

SCORE AND BAKE (85–115 minutes)
OPTION A: DUTCH OVEN

1. Score the dough with your favorite pattern.
2. Remove the Dutch oven from the oven.
3. Sprinkle the bottom of the Dutch oven with coarse cornmeal.
4. Place one loaf, seam-side down, in the bottom of the Dutch oven.
5. Bake with the lid on for 40 minutes, then remove the lid and bake for approximately 40 more minutes or until the dough is a golden color.
6. Repeat with second loaf.

OPTION B: BAKING STONE

1. Score the dough with your favorite pattern.
2. Slide the loaves and parchment paper directly onto the hot baking stone.
3. Pour approximately 1 cup of water over the hot metal objects in the steam-generating container (be careful of the steam) and quickly close the oven door.
4. Bake at 450 degrees for 20 minutes.
5. Turn the oven down to 350 degrees and bake 1½ hours longer or until the dough is golden colored.

COOL (30 minutes)

Let the bread cool completely on a wire rack before cutting it.

SCHEDULE
Active Time: 45 minutes
Total Time: 19 hours
Day One
❖ Feed sourdough starter: 10 minutes
Day Two
❖ Scale and mix: 5 minutes
❖ Knead: 15 minutes
❖ First proof: 1–2 hours
❖ Fold, divide, and shape: 10 minutes
❖ Second proof and preheat: 1–2 hours
❖ Score and bake: 85–115 minutes
❖ Cool: 30 minutes

Mac McConnell's Multigrain Bread

Remember this recipe from chapter 4? If store-bought multigrain bread has left you disappointed, Tom "Mac" McConnell's multigrain bread is sure to renew your faith in this healthy alternative to white bread. You may want to refer back to it or to the detailed descriptions of the steps in chapters 2 and 3 if you're still a little unsure of the steps involved.

Yield: 2 boules

Day One
PREPARE SEEDS (5 MINUTES)

Prepare the seeds by mixing them with 50 grams (¼ cup) of water and allowing them to soak for at least 4 hours or overnight.

FEED STARTER (5 minutes)

The night before you begin your recipe, scale and mix the ingredients for the sourdough starter feed. Put a lid on the container, and place the mixture in the refrigerator overnight.

Day Two
FEED STARTER (5 minutes)

The next morning, repeat the steps to feed the starter, but use the mixture immediately in your recipe in the amount called for.

SCALE AND MIX (10 Minutes)

1. Scale and combine the flours in a large bowl.
2. In a small bowl, combine the salt with 25 grams (1¾ tablespoons) of water, and set it aside.
3. Mix 229 grams (1 cup) of warm water with the sourdough starter until the starter breaks up into pea-size particles.
4. Pour the mixture of water and sourdough starter into the bowl containing the flours.
5. Add the salt/water mixture that you set aside and blend all ingredients together.

KNEAD (10 minutes)

Knead the dough using the pinching method or the traditional bench-kneading method.

FIRST PROOF (45 minutes)

Place the dough in a greased bowl or proofing basket, cover it with a damp towel or plastic wrap, and let it proof in a warm location.

Ingredients:
Starter Feed:
- Premade sourdough starter, 50 grams (¼ cup)
- White flour, 200 grams (1½ cups)
- Water, 200 grams (1 cup)

Dough:
- White flour, 240 grams (1¾ cups)
- Whole-wheat flour, 92 grams (¾ cup)
- Rye flour, 37 grams (⅓ cup)
- Flax seeds, 16 grams (¼ cup)
- Millet seeds, 16 grams (¼ cup)
- Pumpkin seeds, roasted and unsalted, 16 grams (¼ cup)
- Sesame seeds, 16 grams (¼ cup)
- Sunflower seeds, roasted and unsalted, 16 grams (¼ cup)
- Water, 304 grams (1⅓ cups)
- Salt, 10 grams (2 teaspoons)
- Sourdough starter, 148 grams (¾ cup)

Equipment:
- Scale or measuring cups and spoons
- Large mixing bowl
- 3 small-to-medium mixing bowls
- Wooden spoon or Danish whisk (optional)
- Proofing basket or similar
- Dishtowel or plastic wrap
- Bench scraper (optional)
- Scoring tool
- 1 to 2 Dutch ovens with lids (Option A)
- Baking stone (Option B)
- Parchment paper (Option B)
- Rimless cookie sheet (Option B)
- Steam-generating container (metal container filled with small metal objects) (Option B)

FOLD (5 minutes)

Place the dough on lightly floured work surface and fold it using two complete letter-fold sets (eight folds).

SECOND PROOF (45 minutes)

Place the dough back into its bowl or basket, recover it with a damp towel or plastic wrap, and let it proof in a warm location for another 45 minutes.

DIVIDE AND PRESHAPE (10 minutes)

Divide the dough into two pieces, and gently preshape them each into boule form.

THIRD PROOF (20 minutes)

Place the dough into two bowls or baskets, cover each with a damp towel or plastic wrap, and let them proof in a warm location.

FINAL SHAPING (5 minutes)

Transfer the dough onto a work surface and shape each piece into a boule, making sure that the final forms have the proper smoothness and elasticity and hold their shape.

PROOF AND PREHEAT (2 hours)
OPTION A: DUTCH OVEN

1. Place the dough seam-side up (the bottom of the shaped loaf should face up, toward you) in a lightly floured banneton or some similar container with a round bottom.
2. Cover the dough with a damp towel or plastic wrap and let it proof for 2 hours in a warm location.
3. During the last 30 minutes of proofing time, preheat the oven and your baking equipment to 450 degrees.

OPTION B: BAKING STONE

1. Cover a rimless cookie sheet with parchment paper and place the two boules on it.
2. Cover the dough with a damp towel and let it proof for 2 hours in a warm location.
3. During the last half hour of proofing time, pre-heat the oven, your baking stone, and your steam-generating container to 375 degrees.

BAKE (50 minutes)
OPTION A: DUTCH OVEN

1. Score each boule with your favorite design.
2. Remove the baking container from the oven and take off the lid.
3. Sprinkle the bottom of the container with coarse cornmeal to prevent the dough from sticking.
4. Transfer the dough (seam-side down) into the Dutch oven, put the lid back on, and return it to the oven for 30 minutes.
5. Take off the lid and continue baking for another 15 to 20 minutes until the bread is the desired golden caramel color.

OPTION B: BAKING STONE

1. Score each boule with your favorite design.
2. Slide the parchment paper and dough onto the hot baking stone.
3. Pour approximately 1 cup of water into the steam-generating container and close the oven door quickly to capture the steam (be very careful so you don't get burned!).
4. Bake at 375 degrees for 45 minutes until brown and crusty.

COOL (30 minutes)

Allow the bread to cool completely on a wire rack before cutting it.

SCHEDULE

Active Time: 1 hour
Total Time: 18 hours

Day One
+ Prepare seeds: 5 minutes
+ Feed starter: 5 minutes

Day Two
+ Feed starter: 5 minutes
+ Scale and mix: 10 minutes
+ Knead: 10 minutes
+ First proof: 45 minutes
+ Fold: 5 minutes
+ Second proof: 45 minutes
+ Divide and preshape: 10 minutes
+ Third proof: 20 minutes
+ Final shaping: 5 minutes
+ Proof and preheat: 2 hours
+ Bake: 50 minutes
+ Cool: 30 minutes

Olive Bread

Ingredients:

Starter Feed:
- Premade sourdough starter, 50 grams (¼ cup)
- White flour, 200 grams (2 cups)
- Water, 200 grams (1 cup)

Dough:
- White flour, 389 grams (scant 4 cups)
- Whole-wheat flour, 243 grams (2¼ cups)
- Water, 460 grams (2¼ cups)
- Sourdough starter, 220 grams (1⅛ cup)
- Salt, 15 grams (1 tablespoon)
- Olives, 95 grams (¾ cup)
- Coarse cornmeal, enough for dusting

Equipment:
- Scale or measuring cups and spoons
- Large mixing bowl
- Small mixing bowl
- Wooden spoon or Danish whisk (optional)
- Lidded container
- Proofing basket or bowl
- Dishtowel or plastic wrap
- Scoring tool
- Dutch oven with lid
- Wire cooling rack

If you are passionate about olives, you have a whole world to explore because there are as many olives as there are stars in the sky, and each can have its own flavor depending on the brine. This recipe was based on Kalamata olives—those dark, meaty olives from Greece—but I urge you to experiment with the wide range of olives available from many countries. You can use them whole (pitted), but I like to coarsely chop the olives.

Yield: 1 large loaf

Day One
FEED STARTER (10 minutes)

1. In the morning, scale 50 grams (¼ cup) of your existing sourdough starter (toss out the rest) and add 100 grams (1 cup) white flour and 100 grams (½ cup) water to it. Blend everything together, put a lid on the container, and place it back in the refrigerator.

2. In the evening, repeat what you did in the morning—50 grams of existing starter with an added 100 grams each of flour and water. Put the lid on the container and place it back in the refrigerator to sit overnight. This amount of starter will give you enough for the recipe and some extra to store in the refrigerator for another baking.

Day Two
SCALE AND MIX (5 minutes)

1. Scale 400 grams (2 cups) of water and 200 grams (1⅛ cup) of the sourdough starter.
2. Break up the starter until the water and starter are blended.
3. Scale 60 grams (¼ cup) of water and the salt. Mix and set aside.
4. Scale and add the flours needed for the dough to the water/starter mixture and mix thoroughly.
5. Add the salt/water mixture and combine all ingredients.

KNEAD (10 minutes)

Knead the dough using the pinching technique on a slightly floured work surface until the dough reaches the proper stage of gluten development.

FIRST PROOF (3 hours)

Place the dough in a proofing basket or greased bowl, cover it with a damp towel or plastic wrap, and allow it to proof in a warm location.

FOLD (5–10 minutes)

Perform two to three letter folds (total of eight to twelve folds).

SECOND PROOF (3 hours)

Place the dough back in its proofing basket, cover it with a damp dishtowel or plastic wrap, and let it proof again in a warm location for another 3 hours.

SHAPE (10 minutes)

Shape the dough into a boule.

THIRD PROOF AND PREHEAT (1 hour)

1. Cover the dough with a damp dishtowel or plastic wrap and allow it to proof in warm location until it nearly doubles in size.
2. During the last 30 minutes of proofing time, place your Dutch oven and lid in the oven and preheat to 450 degrees.

SCORE AND BAKE (50 minutes)

1. Score the dough with a simple pattern.
2. Remove your Dutch oven and lid from the oven.
3. Sprinkle the bottom of the Dutch oven with cornmeal.
4. Transfer the loaf to the Dutch oven, cover it, and bake at 450 degrees for 30 minutes.
5. Remove the lid and bake for another 15 minutes.

COOL (30 minutes)

Allow the bread to cool completely on a wire rack before cutting it.

SCHEDULE

Active Time: 50 minutes

Total Time: 21 hours

Day One
- Feed starter: 10 minutes

Day Two
- Scale and mix: 5 minutes
- Knead: 10 minutes
- First proof: 3 hours
- Fold: 5–10 minutes
- Second proof: 3 hours
- Shape: 10 minutes
- Third proof and preheat: 1 hour
- Score and bake: 50 minutes
- Cool: 30 minutes

Perfect Bread

Ingredients:

Starter Feed:
- Premade sourdough starter, 50 grams (¼ cup)
- White flour, 200 grams (2 cups)
- Water, 200 grams (1 cup)

Dough:
- White flour, 200 grams (2 cup)
- Whole-wheat flour, 200 grams (1¾ cups)
- Water, 280 grams (1⅓ cups)
- Salt, 10 grams (1½ teaspoon)
- Sourdough starter, 160 grams (¾ cup)
- Coarse cornmeal, enough for dusting

Equipment:
- Scale or measuring cups and spoons
- Large mixing bowl
- Small mixing bowl
- Wooden spoon or Danish whisk (optional)
- Lidded container
- Proofing basket or bowl
- Dishtowel or plastic wrap
- Scoring tool
- Dutch oven with lid
- Wire cooling rack

Richard Bourdon, the master baker and owner of Berkshire Mountain Bakery, developed a half-and-half mixture of whole-wheat- and white-flour bread, which he calls "the perfect bread." "If you like white bread, then you will enjoy this bread because it is half white. If you like whole wheat, then you'll be happy, too, because the bread is half whole wheat," he says. Richard's breads all use sourdough starter, and the doughs have high hydration and long fermenting times.

Yield: 1 large loaf or two medium loaves

Day One
FEED STARTER (10 minutes)

1. In the morning, scale 50 grams (¼ cup) of your existing sourdough starter (toss out the rest) and add 100 grams (1 cup) white flour and 100 grams (1/2 cup) water to it. Blend everything together, put a lid on the container, and place it back in the refrigerator.

2. In the evening, repeat what you did in the morning—50 grams of existing starter with an added 100 grams each of flour and water. Put the lid on the container and place it back in the refrigerator to sit overnight. This amount of starter will give you enough for the recipe and some extra to store in the refrigerator for another baking.

Day Two
SCALE AND MIX (5 minutes)

1. Scale the flours for the dough.
2. Scale 80 grams (scant ⅓ cup) water and add the salt. Set aside.
3. Mix 200 grams (1 cup) water with the starter for the dough, breaking up the sourdough starter until it is thoroughly blended with the water.
4. Add the salt/water mixture to the starter/water mixture and mix well.

KNEAD (10 minutes)

Knead the dough with the pinching or bench-kneading method until it feels smooth and silky and has developed the proper amount of gluten.

FIRST PROOF AND FOLD (1½ hours)

1. Cover the dough and allow it to proof in a warm location.
2. Every 30 minutes, perform one set of letter folds (four folds per set).

DIVIDE AND PRESHAPE (5 minutes)

1. Divide the dough into two small pieces or leave it as one large loaf.
2. Gently preshape the dough into boules or bâtards.

SECOND PROOF (30 minutes)

Cover the dough with a damp dishtowel or plastic wrap and allow it to set in a warm place.

FINAL SHAPE (5 minutes)

1. Shape the dough by cupping your hands around the ball of dough, with your little fingers on the bottom and your other fingers resting on the top, and drawing the dough toward you.
2. Lift, turn, and place the dough on its original place on the work surface. Draw the dough across the work surface several times until a netting forms on the dough's surface and the dough holds its form.

THIRD PROOF AND PREHEAT (2–3 hours)

1. Cover the dough with a damp dishtowel or plastic wrap and allow it to set in a warm place. **Tip:** If you have shaped a boule and want more support for the dough while it proofs, place it in a banneton or floured colander/strainer.
2. During the last 30 minutes of proofing, put your Dutch oven and lid in the oven and preheat to 475 degrees.

SCORE AND BAKE (50 minutes)

1. Score the dough in your favorite pattern.
2. Remove your Dutch oven and lid from the oven.
3. Sprinkle the bottom of the Dutch oven with coarse cornmeal.
4. Gently transfer the dough into Dutch oven, replace the lid, and return it to the oven.
5. Bake for 30 minutes, remove the lid, and bake for another 15 minutes.

COOL (30 minutes)

Allow the bread to cool completely on a wire rack before cutting.

SCHEDULE

Active Time: 45 minutes

Total Time: 19 hours

Day One
+ Feed starter: 10 minutes

Day Two
+ Scale and mix: 5 minutes
+ Knead: 10 minutes
+ First proof and fold: 1½ hours
+ Divide and preshape: 5 minutes
+ Second proof: 30 minutes
+ Final shape: 5 minutes
+ Third proof and preheat: 2–3 hours
+ Score and bake: 50 minutes
+ Cool: 30 minutes

Rye Bread

Ingredients:

Starter Feed:
- Premade sourdough starter, 50 grams (¼ cup)
- Rye flour, 200 grams (generous 1½ cups)
- Water, 200 grams (1 cup)

Dough:
- White flour, 350 grams (3½ cups)
- Rye flour, 100 grams (generous ¾ cup)
- Whole-wheat flour, 50 grams (½ cup and 2 tablespoons)
- Water, 370 grams (1¾ cups)
- Sourdough starter, 100 grams (½ cup)
- Salt, 11 grams (2 teaspoons)
- Coarse cornmeal, enough for dusting

Equipment:
- Scale or measuring cups and spoons
- Large mixing bowl
- Small mixing bowl
- Lidded container
- Proofing basket or bowl
- Dishtowel or plastic wrap
- Scoring tool
- Dutch oven with lid
- Wire cooling rack

Rye has been a much undervalued and underappreciated grain in this country, but now that Americans have become familiar with French and Italian breads, there is a growing interest in rye breads from elsewhere in Europe—the Netherlands, Belgium, Germany, Scandinavia, and the Eastern European countries.

Because rye has less gluten than wheat does, rye bread can be dense. A bread composed solely of rye flour and baked in a loaf pan truly feels and looks like a brick. I prefer using just enough rye flour combined with the right mixture of white flour to provide a great rye taste. Getting the right combination of flours for rye bread can be tricky. Thomas "Mac" McConnell took on the challenge last summer (the days made hotter by the eight-deck commercial oven he worked beside), experimenting day after day. All of his hard—and hot—work paid off in the delicious rye-bread recipe and variation that follow. In my opinion, Mac's combination of rye, white, and whole-wheat flours produces the correct proportion of rye to achieve terrific flavor in a loaf with an open crumb and a crunchy crust. A slightly "lighter" variation uses rye and white flour, eliminating the whole wheat. Try each to see which you prefer.

If you (like most individuals) don't already have a rye starter in your refrigerator, you can easily feed a regular sourdough starter with rye flour. After two feedings, the starter will "convert" from regular to rye sourdough starter.

Yield: 1 medium loaf

Day One
FEED STARTER (10 minutes)

1. In the morning, scale 50 grams (¼ cup) of the sourdough starter (toss out the rest) and add 100 grams (generous ¾ cup) rye flour and 100 grams (½ cup) of water to it. Blend everything together, place in container large enough to allow double or triple expansion, put a lid on the container, and place it in the refrigerator.

2. In the evening, repeat what you did in the morning—50 grams (¼ cup) of existing starter with an added 100 grams rye flour (generous ¾ cup) and 100 grams water (½ cup). Put the lid on the container and place it back in the refrigerator to sit overnight.

Day Two
SCALE AND MIX (5 minutes)

1. Scale 300 grams (1½ cup) water and the sourdough starter needed for the dough.

2. Break up the starter until the water and starter are blended.

3. Scale 70 grams of water (scant ½ cup) and the salt. Mix and set aside.

4. Scale the flours for the dough, add them to the water/starter mixture, and mix thoroughly.

5. Add the water/salt mixture and combine all of the ingredients.

KNEAD (10 minutes)

Knead the dough until it reaches the proper stage of gluten development.

FIRST PROOF (3 hours)

Place the dough in a proofing basket or greased bowl, cover it with a damp towel or plastic wrap, and allow it to proof in a warm location.

FOLD (5–10 minutes)

Perform two to three sets of letter folds (total of eight to twelve folds).

SECOND PROOF (3 hours)

Place the dough back in the proofing basket, cover it with a damp towel or plastic wrap, and allow it to proof again in a warm location.

SHAPE (10 minutes)

Shape the dough into a boule.

THIRD PROOF AND PREHEAT (1 hour)

6. Place the dough back in the proofing basket or greased bowl, cover it with a damp towel or plastic wrap, and allow it to proof in a warm location.

7. During the last 30 minutes of proofing, place your Dutch oven and lid in the oven and preheat to 450 degrees.

SCORE AND BAKE (50 minutes)

1. Score the dough with a simple pattern.
2. Take the Dutch oven and lid out of oven.
3. Sprinkle the bottom of the Dutch oven with cornmeal.
4. Transfer the dough to the Dutch oven, cover it, and bake at 450 degrees for 30 minutes.
5. Remove the lid and bake for another 15 minutes.

COOL (30 minutes)

Cool the bread completely on a wire rack before cutting it.

VARIATION

For a slightly lighter version of this rye bread, follow the same directions but use 375 grams (3¾ cups) of white flour and 125 grams (1¼ cups) of rye flour, eliminating the whole-wheat flour.

> ### SCHEDULE
>
> **Active Time**: 50 minutes
>
> **Total Time**: 21 hours
>
> **Day One**
> + Feed starter: 10 minutes
>
> **Day Two**
> + Scale and mix: 5 minutes
> + Knead: 10 minutes
> + First proof: 3 hours
> + Fold: 5–10 minutes
> + Second proof: 3 hours
> + Shape: 10 minutes
> + Third proof and preheat: 1 hour
> + Score and bake: 50 minutes
> + Cool: 30 minutes

Spelt Bread with Whole Spelt Berries and Sunflower Seeds

Ingredients:

Starter Feed:
+ Premade sourdough starter, 50 grams (¼ cup)
+ Spelt flour, 100 grams (heaping ¾ cup)
+ Water, 200 grams (1 cup)

Dough:
+ Spelt flour (whole if possible), 741 grams (6¼ cup)
+ Water, 549 grams (2¾ cups)
+ Sourdough starter, 50 grams (¼ cup)
+ Salt, 15 grams (1 tablespoon)
+ Spelt berries, 113 grams (½ cup)
+ Sunflower seeds, 111 grams (½ cup)

Equipment:
+ Scale or measuring cups and spoons
+ Medium bowl
+ Wooden spoon or Danish whisk (optional)
+ Lidded container
+ Saucepan
+ Proofing basket or bowl
+ Dishtowel
+ Bench scraper
+ 3 loaf pans made of porcelain or heavy metal (ideally Pullman pans with lids)
+ Rimless cookie sheet
+ 2 bricks or similarly heavy objects
+ Wire cooling rack

I try to accept that not everyone enjoys dense, thinly sliced breads baked for several hours at a low heat to create a dark brown color and moist texture, but I don't know why this bread isn't more wildly popular. When my children had one of their first Dutch breakfasts in the Netherlands, they immediately fell in love with the thinly sliced, dense Dutch breads served with cheese or ham. (More incredible to them was that the bread was even served with a hazelnut spread that had a hint of chocolate—chocolate for breakfast!).

Now, living in the Washington, DC, area, where the largest population of Ethiopians lives outside Ethiopia, I have made many Ethiopian friends. One day, I noticed that a friend's elderly mother was eating a Dutch-style spelt and rye bread, and my friend explained that her mother liked the bread for its "sour" taste, similar to the taste of their Ethiopian national bread, *injera*, which has a wild-yeast starter and is like, some people say, a "wet sponge." Imagine my surprise to find a culinary bond between Ethiopians and the Dutch—they both like their bread sour with a moist texture.

You will need one or two ceramic or heavy metal loaf pans to make this bread. The loaf pans must be thick enough to retain the dough's moisture while it bakes for 2½ hours at a low heat and then 30 minutes at a descending high-to-low heat. You can indulge in buying a Pullman pan with a sliding cover (which will last several generations), but I use a heavy-duty metal loaf pan with a cookie sheet (weighed down with bricks) as a cover to keep the dough from oozing over the edges of the pan. The goal is to bake a straight-sided rectangular loaf that can be sliced neatly into thin, identical pieces.

This bread lasts for a long time—first, because you slice it very thin and eat it in small quantities; second, because its moisture content preserves it. I hope that you love this bread too!

Yield: 3 loaves

Day One
FEED STARTER (10 minutes)

1. In the morning, scale 50 grams (¼ cup) of your existing sourdough starter (toss out the remainder) and add 100 grams (¾ cup) spelt flour and 100 grams (½ cup) water to it. Blend everything together, place it in a container large enough to allow double or triple expansion, put a lid on the container, and place it back in the refrigerator.

2. In the evening, repeat what you did in the morning—with the same ingredients and proportions. Put the lid on the container and place it back in the refrigerator to sit overnight.

PREPARE SPELT BERRIES (15 Minutes)

1. Put 113 grams (½ cup) spelt berries in a saucepan with approximately 150 grams (¾ cup) water, making sure that the water covers the berries completely.

2. Bring the water to a boil and then turn the heat down to simmer.
3. Cook until all of the water has evaporated.

PREPARE SUNFLOWER SEEDS (4 hours)

1. Amply cover the sunflower seeds with water and let them soak for 4 hours.
2. Drain and set the seeds aside.

Day Two

SCALE AND MIX (5 minutes)

1. Scale 500 grams (2½ cup) water with 50 grams (¼ cup) of sourdough spelt starter.
2. Break up the starter until the water and starter are well blended.
3. Scale and mix 50 grams (¼ cup) of water and 15 grams (1 tablespoon) of salt and set the mixture aside.
4. Scale the spelt flour and add it to the water/sourdough mixture. Mix until thoroughly blended.
5. Add the water/salt mixture that you set aside in step 3 and integrate it.

FOLD (10 minutes)

Perform three letter folds (total of twelve folds) until the dough appears to be developing gluten.

FIRST PROOF AND FOLD (65 minutes)

1. Place the dough in a proofing basket or greased bowl, cover it with a damp towel or plastic wrap, and allow it to proof in a warm location for 30 minutes.
2. After 30 minutes of proofing, perform one set of letter folds (total of four folds).
3. At the end of the proofing time (another 30 minutes), perform another set of letter folds (total of four folds).

DIVIDE AND SHAPE (10 Minutes)

Divide the dough into three equal pieces, shape those pieces into three log forms, and place them in Pullman pans or loaf pans.

SECOND PROOF AND PREHEAT (3 hours)

1. Cover the pans with a damp towel or plastic wrap and allow them to proof in a warm location for up to 3 hours.
2. Preheat the oven to 500 degrees during the last 30 minutes of proofing time.

PREPARE PANS AND BAKE (21/2 hours)

1. If you have Pullman pans, close the covers. If you are using heavy-duty loaf pans, lay a cookie sheet on top of the loaf pans and securely weigh them down with a couple of heavy objects, such as bricks.
2. Put the loaves in the oven. Over the next 30 minutes, gradually decrease the heat from 500 degrees to 300 degrees.
3. Bake for another 2 hours at 300 degrees.

COOL (30 minutes)

Allow the bread to cool completely on a wire rack before cutting it.

SCHEDULE

Active Time: 1 hour

Total Time: 20 hours

Day One
+ Feed starter: 10 minutes
+ Prepare spelt berries: 15 minutes
+ Prepare sunflower seeds: 4 hours

Day Two
+ Scale and mix: 5 minutes
+ Fold: 10 minutes
+ First proof and fold: 65 minutes
+ Divide and shape: 10 minutes
+ Second proof and preheat: 3 hours
+ Prepare pans and bake: 2½ hours
+ Cool: 30 minutes

Sunny Flax

Ingredients:

Starter Feed:
- Premade sourdough starter, 50 grams (¼ cup)
- White flour, 200 grams (2 cups)
- Water, 200 grams (1 cup)

Seed Soak:
- Flax seeds, 33 grams (heaping ¼ cup)
- Water, 66 grams (⅝ cup)

Preferment:
- White flour, 56 grams (heaping ½ cup)
- Water, 85 grams (¾ cup)
- Sourdough starter, 18 grams (⅛ cup)

Dough:
- Whole-wheat flour, 380 grams (3¼ cup)
- White flour, 22 grams (¼ cup)
- Water, 381 grams (1⅔ cup + 1 tablespoon)
- Sourdough starter, 18 grams (⅛ cup)
- Salt, 10 grams (2 teaspoons)
- Sunflower seeds, 50 grams (scant ½ cup)
- Coarse cornmeal, enough for dusting

Equipment:
- Scale or measuring cups and spoons
- Large mixing bowl
- 2 small mixing bowls
- Wooden spoon or Danish whisk (optional)
- Lidded container
- Proofing basket or bowl
- Dishtowel or plastic wrap
- Bench scraper (optional)
- Scoring tool
- Baking stone
- Rimless cookie sheet
- Parchment paper
- Steam-generating container
- Wire cooling rack

Sunny flax is the bestseller at Richard Bourdon's Berkshire Mountain Bakery; the combination of sunflower seeds and whole-wheat flour appeals to customers. In the food-conscious community of the Berkshires, consumers also appreciate flax for its nutty taste and the digestive benefits of its fiber. Richard has kindly shared this recipe with you in this book—its first publication ever.

Yield: 1 large or 2 medium bâtards

Day One
FEED STARTER (10 minutes)

1. In the morning, scale 50 grams (¼ cup) of your existing sourdough starter (toss out the rest) and add 100 grams (1 cup) white flour and 100 grams (½ cup) water to it. Blend everything together, put a lid on the container, and place it back in the refrigerator.

2. In the evening, repeat what you did in the morning—50 grams of existing starter with an added 100 grams each of flour and water. Put the lid on the container and place it back in the refrigerator to sit overnight. This amount of starter will give you enough for the recipe and some extra to store in the refrigerator for another baking.

MAKE PREFERMENT (5 minutes)

1. Scale and mix the ingredients for the preferment.

2. Place the mixture in a lidded container that is large enough to allow the preferment to double in size and place it in the refrigerator.

SOAK SEEDS (5 minutes)

Place the flax seeds in 66 (⅝ cup) grams of water and allow them to soak overnight. Pour off any excess water in the morning.

Day Two
SCALE AND MIX (5 minutes)

1. Scale 341 grams (2 cups) water and 18 grams (⅛ cup) sourdough and blend until the sourdough is the size of small peas.

2. Scale 40 grams (¼ cup) of water and add the salt. Set aside.

3. Add the whole-wheat flour and white flour to water and sourdough mixture.

REST (15 minutes)

1. Let the dough rest in the mixing bowl for 15 minutes.

2. Add the water/salt mixture that you set aside in step 2 and incorporate it into the dough mixture.

KNEAD (20 minutes)

Knead by hand using the pinching or bench-kneading method. Knead four times for 1 minute at a time; rest for 4 minutes between each kneading.

FIRST PROOF AND FOLD (2½ hours)

1. Place the dough in a proofing basket or greased bowl, cover it with a damp dishtowel or plastic wrap, and allow it to proof in a warm location for 1 hour.
2. Perform two sets of letter folds (total of eight folds) either in the bowl or on your work surface.
3. Recover the dough with a damp dishtowel or plastic wrap and allow it to proof again in a warm location for 1½ more hours.

PRESHAPE (5 minutes)

Leave the dough as one large piece or divide it into two pieces. Preshape the dough into one or two bâtard shapes.

SECOND PROOF (45 minutes)

Place the dough back in the proofing basket or greased bowl, cover it with a damp towel or plastic wrap, and allow it to proof in a warm location.

FINAL SHAPE (5 minutes)

1. Shape the dough into one or two bâtard shapes.
2. Place the dough seam-side up in one or two lightly floured proofing baskets.

THIRD PROOF AND PREHEAT (2 hours)

1. Cover a rimless cookie sheet with parchment paper, place the dough on it, cover it with a damp towel or plastic wrap, and allow it to proof in a warm location.
2. During the last 30 minutes of proofing time, put the baking stone and steam-generating container in the oven and preheat it to 450 degrees.

OPTIONAL: ADD GRAINS (5 minutes)

1. Prepare two shallow, wide dishes: one with a rough-napped towel moistened with water in the bottom and the other with a layer of sunflower seeds in the bottom. **Tip:** The towel should be damp, and there should be no standing water in the dish. You don't want the bread to get too wet, but you want the towel wet enough so that the dough won't stick to it.
2. Gently roll the dough on the damp towel and then in the seeds. You can add seeds all over the dough or just on the top.

SCORE AND BAKE (50 minutes)

1. Score the dough with a simple design.
2. Gently slide the bâtards and parchment paper from the cookie sheet onto the baking stone.
3. Bake at 450 degrees for 45 minutes until the desired golden color is achieved.

COOL (30 minutes)

Allow the bread to cool completely on a wire rack before slicing it.

SCHEDULE

Active Time: 50 minutes

Total Time: 20 hours

Day One
+ Feed starter: 10 minutes
+ Make preferment: 5 minutes
+ Soak seeds: 5 minutes

Day Two
+ Scale and mix: 5 minutes
+ Rest: 15 minutes
+ Knead: 20 minutes
+ First proof and fold: 2½ hours
+ Preshape: 5 minutes
+ Second proof: 45 minutes
+ Final shape: 5 minutes
+ Third proof and preheat: 2 hours
+ Add grains: 5 minutes (optional)
+ Score and bake: 50 minutes
+ Cool: 30 minutes

English Sunday Night Bread

Ingredients:

Starter Feed:
+ Premade sourdough starter, 50 grams (¼ cup)
+ Whole-wheat flour, 200 grams (1¾ cups)
+ Water, 200 grams (1 cup)

Dough:
+ White flour, 398 grams (4 cups)
+ Whole-wheat flour, 100 grams (1 cup)
+ Water, 363 grams (1¾ cups)
+ Sourdough starter, 124 grams (¾ cup)
+ Salt, 11 grams (2 teaspoons)
+ Coarse cornmeal, enough for dusting

Equipment:
+ Scale or measuring cups and spoons
+ Large mixing bowl
+ 2 small mixing bowls
+ Wooden spoon or Danish whisk (optional)
+ Lidded container
+ Proofing basket or bowl
+ Dishtowel or plastic wrap
+ Bench scraper (optional)
+ Scoring tool
+ Dutch oven with lid
+ Wire cooling rack

The name of this bread harks back to the days when the British grand houses had domestic staff who traditionally took Sundays as holidays, so the families ate humble meals for Sunday dinners. Even after domestic servants disappeared, families often ate simple meals of leftovers and bread on Sunday nights.

This bread is hearty enough to play a significant role in any meal. If you make it on Sunday, you can enjoy it for dinner with soup, a soufflé, or a salad and use it for sandwiches during the week. It is a terrific all-purpose bread that combines whole-wheat and white flours.

Yield: 2 medium boules

Day One
FEED SOURDOUGH STARTER (10 minutes)

1. In the morning, scale 50 grams (¼ cup) of your existing sourdough starter (toss out the rest) and add 100 grams (¾ cup) whole-wheat flour and 100 grams (½ cup) water to it. Blend everything together, put a lid on the container, and place it back in the refrigerator.

2. In the evening, repeat what you did in the morning—50 grams of existing starter with an added 100 grams each of flour and water. Put the lid on the container and place it back in the refrigerator to sit overnight. This amount of starter will give you enough for the recipe and some extra to store in the refrigerator for another baking.

Day Two
SCALE AND MIX (5 minutes)

1. cale the white and whole-wheat flours needed for the dough and mix them together.

2. Scale 63 grams (¼ cup) water with 11 grams (2 heaping teaspoons) salt. Mix and set aside.

3. Scale 124 grams (¾ cup) sourdough starter and 300 grams (1½ cups) of warm water and put them in a large bowl.

4. Break up the sourdough starter in the water until the two are well blended.

5. Pour the flours into the water/sourdough mixture and mix thoroughly.

6. Add the salt/water mixture from step 2 and integrate it into the dough.

KNEAD (10 minutes)

1. Knead the dough using the pinching or bench-kneading method until it becomes elastic.

2. Add the salt/water mixture that you had set aside and work it into the dough until it is integrated.

3. Continue to knead until the proper amount of gluten has developed.

FIRST PROOF (1 hour)

Place the dough in a proofing basket or greased bowl, cover it with a damp towel or plastic wrap, and allow it to proof in a warm location.

FOLD (5 minutes)

Perform two sets of letter folds (eight total folds).

SECOND PROOF (1 hour)

Place the dough back in the proofing basket or greased bowl, cover it with a damp towel or plastic wrap, and allow it to proof in a warm location.

PRESHAPE (5 minutes)

Divide the dough into two pieces and gently preshape them into boules.

THIRD PROOF (20 minutes)

Place the dough in two proofing baskets or greased bowls, cover them with damp towels or plastic wrap, and allow them to proof in a warm location.

FINAL SHAPE (5 minutes)

Give the dough its final boule shape.

FOURTH PROOF AND PREHEAT (45–60 minutes)

1. Place the dough back in the proofing baskets or greased bowls, cover them with damp towels or plastic wrap, and allow them to proof in a warm location.
2. During the last 30 minutes of proofing time, put the Dutch oven and lid in the oven and preheat to 500 degrees.

SCORE AND BAKE (35–45 minutes)

1. Score the dough with a design appropriate to the boule shape.
2. Remove the Dutch oven from the oven.
3. Sprinkle the bottom of the Dutch oven with coarse cornmeal.
4. Transfer the dough from the proofing form into the Dutch oven.
5. Replace the lid on the Dutch oven and bake at 500 degrees for 30 to 40 minutes. Repeat the process with the second loaf.

COOL (30 minutes)

Allow the bread to cool completely on a wire rack before cutting it.

SCHEDULE

Active Time: 45 minutes

Total Time: 17 hours

Day One
+ Feed starter: 10 minutes

Day Two
+ Scale and mix: 5 minutes
+ Knead: 10 minutes
+ First proof: 1 hour
+ Fold: 5 minutes
+ Second proof: 1 hour
+ Preshape: 5 minutes
+ Third proof: 20 minutes
+ Final shape: 5 minutes
+ Fourth proof and preheat: 45–60 minutes
+ Score and bake: 35–45 minutes
+ Cool: 30 minutes

CHAPTER 9

Flatbreads

Flatbreads are ubiquitous. In the melting pot of America, we are familiar with many flatbreads: the Mexican soft flour tortilla; the Indian naan, dosa, roti, and chapati; the French crepe; the Ethiopian injera, used as both a serving plate and a utensil; and the Vietnamese banh trang (dried rice-flour circles), which are rehydrated for spring rolls. Many of us in America are introduced to the different types of flatbread when we eat in restaurants featuring the food from these countries. With so many flatbread varieties, I've tried to select those that are different or particularly fun to make at home.

Tunisian Grilled Bread

Ingredients:
Dough:
+ White flour, 625 grams (5 cups)
+ Water, 474 grams (2 cups)
+ Olive oil, 12 grams (1 tablespoon)
+ Instant dry yeast, 7 grams (2¼ teaspoons)
+ Sea salt, 18 grams (1 tablespoon)
+ Tabil spice, 6 grams (1 tablespoon)
+ Additional salt and pepper, to taste

Tabil spice:
+ Coriander, 12 grams (3 tablespoons)
+ Cumin seeds, 12 grams (1½ tablespoons)
+ Caraway seeds, 9 grams (1 tablespoon)
+ Crushed red pepper flakes, 2 grams (½ tablespoon)

Equipment:
+ Scale or measuring cups and spoons
+ Electric grinder or mortar and pestle
+ Large mixing bowl
+ Wooden spoon or Danish whisk (optional)
+ Proofing basket or bowl
+ Dishtowel or plastic wrap
+ Bench scraper
+ 2 or 3 cookie sheets
+ Pastry brush
+ Grill
+ Wire cooling rack

Hot-climate countries in northern Africa and the Middle East are home to flatbreads that can be baked quickly to avoid generating additional heat from the oven for several hours. Living near Washington, DC, where the summers are hot and muggy, I can fully appreciate this tradition. When I want to make bread without having to blast the air conditioning, I turn to flatbreads that can be grilled outside.

My California friend and chef extraordinaire Gabriel Tiradani shared this recipe with me. The Tunisian spice will probably be a new taste to you and those to whom you serve this bread, but you will find that it goes well with vegetables, such as peppers, onions, and tomatoes, or meat, such as ground lamb.

You can also use this flatbread without the spices, topped with your favorite vegetables or cheese, and turn them into mini pizzas.

Yield: 8 rounds

MAKE TABIL SPICE (5 minutes)

Put all of the spice ingredients in a small electric grinder (or use a mortar and pestle) and blend. These amounts make 36 grams (6 tablespoons) of spice; you'll need 6 grams (1 tablespoon) for this recipe. You can save the rest.

SCALE AND MIX (5 minutes)

1. Place the water (warmed to between 95 and 110 degrees) and yeast into a large bowl.
2. Add the olive oil.
3. Add the flour, 125 grams (1 cup) at a time, and the sea salt.
4. Stir until the dough forms a ball.

KNEAD (10 minutes)

Knead the dough, keeping it as wet as possible.

PROOF AND PREPARE GRILL (1 hour)

1. Place the dough in a proofing basket or greased bowl, cover it with a damp towel or plastic wrap, and allow it to proof in a warm location until it doubles in volume, about 1 hour.
2. During the proofing time, prepare the grill's fire. If using coals, they'll need to be red hot. If using a gas grill, you'll want the heat very strong.

DIVIDE (5 minutes)

1. Transfer the dough onto a floured work surface and divide it into eight pieces.
2. Roll each piece into a ball and place the pieces on a platter or cookie sheet, at least 2 inches apart to prevent them from sticking together as they expand.

PROOF (15 minutes)

Allow the dough to rest for 15 minutes.

SHAPE (10 minutes)

1. Flatten each ball of dough using the heel of your hand.
2. Roll out each piece until it has a 9-inch diameter.

GRILL (15 minutes)

1. Brush each flatbread with olive oil and sprinkle the tops with tabil spice, salt, and pepper.
2. Place the flatbreads on oiled cookie sheets.
3. When the grill is ready, brush it with olive oil.
4. Grill each flatbread for 1½ minutes per side.
5. Transfer the flatbreads to a platter and cut them into wedges.

COOL (20 minutes)

Allow your bread to cool on a wire rack before cutting it.

SCHEDULE

Active Time: 1 hour
Total Time: 2 hours and 30 minutes

+ Make tabil spice: 5 minutes
+ Scale and mix: 5 minutes
+ Knead: 10 minutes
+ Proof and prepare grill: 1 hour
+ Divide: 5 minutes
+ Proof: 15 minutes
+ Shape: 10 minutes
+ Grill: 15 minutes
+ Cool: 20 minutes

Lefse

Ingredients:
- White flour, 250 grams (2 cups)
- Buttermilk, 44 grams (3 tablespoons)
- Butter, 36 grams (3 tablespoons)
- Russet potatoes, 600 grams (4 cups)
- Salt, 1 dash
- Sugar, 1 dash

Equipment:
- Saucepan (large enough for potatoes)
- Large mixing bowl
- Potato ricer or masher
- Rolling pin or traditional lefse roller
- Wide, flat, heavy-duty pan or griddle
- Long, thin spatula
- 6 dishtowels or plastic wrap

Lefse is a Norwegian flatbread that is often spread with butter and brown sugar or eaten with lingonberry jam. When I lived in Sweden, I used lefse as wraps for tuna or egg-salad sandwiches or as Scandinavian burritos with cheese and egg filling (one of my children's favorite breakfast foods).

During those wonderful midnight-sun summer evenings, when the sun would be up almost all night, friends would drop over for drinks and I would serve dip with lefse. The Scandinavians seemed surprised that I used lefse in this way, but I think everyone appreciated my American twist. Because lefse freeze well, you can make a big batch at one time and then pull out sections when you need them.

Yield: 12 rounds

PREPARE DOUGH (30 minutes)

1. Peel the potatoes and then boil them until they are soft enough to pierce with a knife (don't overboil).
2. Drain the potatoes and place them in a large bowl.
3. Add the butter, buttermilk, sugar, and salt.
4. Mix in the flour until all of the ingredients are thoroughly blended.

COOL (1 hour)

Put the dough in a tightly covered container and place it in the refrigerator until it is cool, approximately 1 hour. **Tip:** The dough will not roll well if it is warm. If you are in a hurry, put the mixture in the freezer until it gets cold (but don't let it freeze). You can also make the dough and refrigerate it overnight to guarantee that it will be cold.

DIVIDE AND PRESHAPE (5 minutes)

1. Divide the dough into 12 pieces and shape them into balls.
2. Form a flat, round, biscuit-shaped patty from each ball. **Tip:** If the lefse tear while you are handling them, they may be too tender, so you can add a bit more flour. Be careful not to add too much, though; the extra flour can make the lefse dry and tough. Make sure that the edges of the patties are smooth. If they are uneven and broken, it will be harder to roll them out. If it is a hot day, place the dough patties in the refrigerator and take them out one at a time to roll and bake.

PREHEAT AND ROLL (10–15 minutes)

1. Preheat your baking surface to reach about 500 degrees.
2. Flour a canvas cloth or your work surface.

3. Starting in the center of each patty, rolling toward the edges, roll the dough as thin as possible. **Tip:** Roll lefse as you would roll a pie crust. Don't be afraid to patch the dough if you make a little hole, or just leave the hole. I make mine about 10 inches in diameter.

BAKE (15 minutes)

1. Heat the pan over low heat until the pan is very hot and a drop of oil bounces on the pan's surface.
2. Place the dough disk in the pan and cook quickly for 1 to 2 minutes on one side, then flip it over and cook it on the other side.
3. As soon as brown spots appear on one side (about a minute), flip the lefse over with the long spatula and cook until brown spots appear on this side (another minute).
4. Remove the lefse from the pan and place it on a dishtowel.

COOL (20 minutes)

Cover each lefse with a piece of plastic wrap or another dishtowel to prevent them from sticking together and let the batch cool for 15 minutes. **Tip:** Use what you need that day and freeze the remainder. Fold the lefse in quarters for storing in containers or wrap them in aluminum foil, stack them, and place them in a freezer bag.

SCHEDULE

Active Time: 1 hour

Total Time: 2 hours and 30 minutes

- Prepare dough: 30 minutes
- Cool: 1 hour
- Divide and preshape: 5 minutes
- Preheat and roll: 10–15 minutes
- Bake: 15 minutes
- Cool: 20 minutes

Moroccan Flatbread

Ingredients:

+ White flour, 375–500 grams (3–4 cups)
+ Whole-wheat flour, 240 grams (2 cups)
+ Semolina (as used for pasta, not semolina flour), 162 grams (1 cup)
+ Water, 711 grams (3 cups)
+ Instant dry yeast, 4 grams (2 teaspoons)
+ Salt, 18 grams (1 tablespoon)
+ Anise seeds, 39 grams (1 teaspoon)
+ Coarse cornmeal, enough for dusting

Equipment:

+ Large mixing bowl
+ Small mixing bowl
+ Wooden spoon or Danish whisk (optional)
+ Proofing basket or bowl
+ Dishtowel or plastic wrap
+ Baker's peel or rimless cookie sheet covered with parchment paper
+ Bench scraper (optional)
+ Wire cooling rack

The cuisine of northern Africa, especially Morocco, has become a trendy, and several excellent Moroccan cookbooks have been published. When I was fortunate enough to visit relatives who were working and living in Morocco, they gave me a personal introduction to various parts of the country and its cuisine. We visited a Moroccan family in the seaside city of Esoria—think white structures with blue or green doors bathed in sunshine—where an eighty-two-year-old grandmother shared her family's flatbread recipe, which her son translated. I couldn't wait to convert the measurements and test it. Now, many miles later, this recipe has made its way to you. When you make this bread for guests, you can go all-out and make a Moroccan chicken or lamb dish in a tagine, but I have been known to serve it with vegetarian or meat chili, French stew, or seasonal soup.

You will need a device for transferring the dough into the oven. If you have a baker's peel, you are one of the lucky ones. Otherwise, you can proof the dough on parchment paper resting on a rimless cookie sheet and, when it's time, slide the dough and the parchment paper into the oven.

Yield: 4 medium loaves

SCALE AND MIX (5 minutes)

1. Add the whole-wheat flour and yeast to 521grams (2½ cups) of warm water.
2. Add the semolina and stir for 1 to 2 minutes until a fine batter develops.

FIRST PROOF (30 minutes)

Place the dough in a proofing basket or greased bowl, cover it with a damp towel or plastic wrap, and allow it to proof in a warm location for approximately 30 minutes.

SCALE AND MIX (5 minutes)

1. Combine the salt with 119 grams (½ cup) of water. Add the anise seeds.
2. Add this mixture to the water/flour mixture.
3. Add 375 to 500 grams (3 to 4 cups) of white flour slowly to the dough until it is firm enough to knead.

KNEAD (5–10 minutes)

Knead the dough on your work surface or in the bowl until the gluten fully develops.

SCHEDULE

Active time: 40 minutes

Total Time: 4 hours and 15 minutes

❖ Scale and mix: 5 minutes

❖ First proof: 30 minutes

❖ Scale and mix: 5 minutes

❖ Knead: 5–10 minutes

❖ Second proof: 1–2 hours

❖ Shape: 5 minutes

❖ Third proof and preheat: 30–45 minutes

❖ Bake: 15 minutes

❖ Cool: 20 minutes

SECOND PROOF (1–2 hours)

Place the dough back in the proofing basket or greased bowl, cover it with a damp towel or plastic wrap, and allow it to proof in a warm location for 1 to 2 hours.

SHAPE (5 minutes)

1. Prepare the space where your loaves will proof—either a countertop or a parchment-paper-covered rimless cookie sheet—by sprinkling the surface with coarse cornmeal.
2. Cut the dough into four pieces and roll each into a ball.
3. Flatten the balls using the heel of your hand.
4. With your fingers, working from the center to the edges, shape a piece of dough into a 6-inch circle.
5. Set the dough circle on your prepared proofing area.
6. Repeat steps 4 and 5 with the remaining pieces of dough.

THIRD PROOF AND PREHEAT (30–45 minutes)

1. Allow the dough pieces to proof in a warm location until they have puffed up, about 30 to 45 minutes.
2. During the last 30 minutes of proofing time, preheat the oven to 450 degrees.

   Tip: To imitate the traditional brick floors of Moroccan ovens, line the lower shelf of your oven with tiles, bricks, or one or more baking stones.

BAKE (15 minutes)

1. Slide the dough circles into the oven with your long-handled device or rimless cookie sheet.
2. Bake at 450 degrees until the bread is a golden color, about 12 to 15 minutes.
3. Remove the loaves from the oven and cover them with a dry dishtowel to keep them soft.

COOL (20 minutes)

Allow the bread to cool completely on a wire rack before cutting into wedges to serve.

One-Hour Pita Bread

Ingredients:
+ White flour, 250 grams (2½ cups)
+ Whole-wheat flour, 60 grams (½ cup)
+ Water, 237 grams (1 cup)
+ Salt, 12 grams (2 teaspoons)
+ Sugar, 13 grams (1 tablespoon)
+ Instant dry yeast, 4 grams (2 teaspoons)
+ Olive oil, 24 grams (2 tablespoons)

Equipment:
+ Large mixing bowl
+ Wooden spoon or Danish whisk
+ Bench scraper (optional)
+ 1 or 2 dishtowels
+ Aluminum foil
+ Plastic wrap

A few years ago, when I traveled to Syria, with all of its wonderful food, my only disappointment was the rather dry pita bread sealed in plastic and served in restaurants (for the sake of "cleanliness" for foreign visitors). The best pita I had there was offered to me in a narrow alleyway. My daughter and I could smell fresh bread, and we noticed a man carrying a stack of it. Our eyes must have betrayed our desire, because he handed each of us a small, warm, whole-wheat pita pocket.

We can buy pita bread at almost every grocery store, but it doesn't compare to the home-baked version. Think of the difference between a store-bought tomato and a homegrown tomato—it's like a whole different food, and the same can be said for pita bread. I suggest that you learn to bake your own pita. Pita bread has many uses—as an accompaniment to meals, as a pocket for fillings, as a scoop for dips, as a snack food unto itself when dried and sprinkled with spices, and as an appetizer or small meal when toppings are added.

I made an interesting discovery when reading Bernard Clayton's pita-bread recipe. (My dear French friend Jacqueline put her favorite Clayton bread books on the bedside table when I visited her in New York City last year.) It was enlightening to discover Clayton's secret for producing a soft, puffy pita—the trick to creating the pocket in pita bread is not the yeast in the dough, but the steam. He recommends baking the pita on aluminum foil, which keeps the dough soft and releases steam more slowly, giving the dough time to puff up and form its pocket. Before the Clayton revelation, I had always baked my pita on bricks, which can make the crust a bit hard.

Yield: 8 pitas

SCALE AND MIX (5 minutes)

1. Put 125 grams (1 cup) of white flour and the salt, sugar, and yeast in a large bowl.
2. Add the oil and water (heat the water to between 105 and 110 degrees).
3. Beat the mixture with a wooden spoon or Danish whisk for several minutes.
4. Add the rest of the flour (125 grams white and 60 grams whole wheat) 125 grams (½ cup) at a time, until the dough forms a ball in the center of the bowl. **Note:** The dough will be "shaggy" and a bit moist.

KNEAD (5–10 minutes)

1. Turn the dough out onto a lightly floured work surface
2. Knead for 5 to 10 minutes, adding more flour only if necessary.

DIVIDE, PROOF, AND PREHEAT (35 minutes)

1. Divide the dough into eight pieces and roll them into balls.
2. Lightly sprinkle the tops of the balls with flour and cover them with a damp dishtowel or plastic wrap.
3. Allow the dough to proof for 30 minutes in a warm location.
4. At the beginning of the proofing time, preheat the oven to 500 degrees.

SHAPE (5 minutes)

1. Flatten each ball using the palm of your hand.
2. Stretch each piece of dough into a circle, or roll the pieces out using a rolling pin, working from the center to the edges. Each circle should be about 6 inches in diameter and less than ¼ inch thick.

SCHEDULE

Active Time: 40 minutes

Total Time: 1 hour and 30 minutes

✤ Scale and mix: 5 minutes

✤ Knead: 5–10 minutes

✤ Divide, proof, and preheat: 35 minutes

✤ Shape: 5 minutes

✤ Bake: 15 minutes

✤ Cool: 20 minutes

BAKE (15 minutes)

1. Place each round on a square of foil.
2. Put several rounds into the oven on a middle rack.
3. Bake until the dough puffs up, approximately 5 to 8 minutes.
4. Remove the pitas from the oven and stack them on top of each other topped by a dry dishtowel to cover them in order to retain heat and keep them soft.
   Note: The baked pitas will collapse, but the pocket remains in the middle.
5. Repeat steps 2 through 4 until all of the dough has been baked.

COOL (20 minutes)

Allow your bread to cool completely on a wire rack before cutting it. **Tip:** To store the pitas in the freezer, wrap each piece tightly in aluminum foil and then in plastic wrap. To thaw, remove the pitas from the freezer and unwrap them; they will thaw in about 5 minutes. To heat them, wrap each one in foil and warm them in the oven at 350 degrees for 10 to 15 minutes.

Pita-Bread Variations

Use your imagination and try your own variations of the One-Hour Pita Bread recipe. Here are two of my ideas to jump-start your creativity.

Pita Chips

Bake the dough rounds in a 400-degree oven until they become crisp, between 5 and 15 minutes. Remove them from the oven, brush them with olive oil, and then sprinkle them with grated Pecorino Romano cheese and a little sea salt. An olive-oil coating with coarse ground pepper, cumin, and a dash of paprika is great too. I also love them with poppy and sesame seeds.

Mini Pizzas

So…what do you like on your pizza? Pesto, cheese, and chopped tomatoes? Potato and chopped sage? I adore mushrooms, but I don't buy them often because I feel as if the flavor gets lost in many of the vegetarian dishes I make. However, pita bread with a thin layer of tomato sauce, some soft melted cheese, and a lot of mushrooms really features their taste. If you're tired and hungry, just defrost a couple of pita breads and top them with cheese and whatever vegetables you have around the kitchen or in the fridge. With a salad and glass of wine, pita mini pizzas make a nice quick meal.

Syrian Flatbreads (Lachmanjun)

In the spring of 2010, my adult children, my brother, my sister-in-law, and I took a sentimental journey to trace some of my father's travels in the Middle East in the 1930s. Soon after graduating from college, my father traveled by ocean liner to Istanbul and then journeyed across land to Aleppo, Syria, where he taught for three years at Aleppo College, with its coeducational, ecumenical curriculum and student body: Muslims, Jews, and Christians, among them many Armenians who had escaped genocide.

We were fortunate to have my father's correspondence from these years, including a map of Aleppo that he drew in 1932. The city hadn't changed much in the almost eight decades that had passed since my father lived there, and we were able to find the site of the original college buildings where my father had taught. Pure luck put us in the hands of an extraordinary man, a graduate of the college who knew many of the same people my father had known. In addition to helping us connect to my father's past, the man introduced us to the wonderful flavors of Syrian cooking, particularly lamb kebabs with tart cherries from Aleppo and little flatbreads topped with spices and pine nuts. As soon as I returned from Syria, I made Syrian flatbreads part of my repertoire, and I hope that you will too.

Traditionally, Syrian flatbreads accompany meals the same way that the French serve baguettes with meals. If you wish to venture into nontraditional uses, you can utilize the flatbread as a wrap for sandwich fillings or as a canvas for your own masterpiece by adding toppings from sliced tomatoes and sautéed fennel to prosciutto and cheese. Because America is a melting pot of numerous nationalities, with spices and ingredients from many countries available in our grocery stores, be adventuresome and design your own fusion flatbreads.

Ingredients:
- White flour, 375 grams (3 cups)
- Whole-wheat flour, 120 grams (1 cup)
- Water, 474 grams (2 cups)
- Salt, 2 grams (¼ teaspoon)
- Olive oil, 12 grams (1 tablespoon)
- Instant dry yeast, 2 grams (1 teaspoon)

Equipment:
- Large mixing bowl
- Wooden spoon or Danish whisk
- Proofing basket or bowl
- Dishtowel or plastic wrap
- Bench scraper (optional)
- Small frying pan
- Pastry brush
- Greased cookie sheet (optional)

Yield: 10 loaves

SCALE AND MIX (5 minutes)

Mix the whole-wheat flour and 127 grams (1 cup) of white flour with very warm water and yeast. Stir the mixture using a wooden spoon or Danish whisk.

REST (10 minutes)

Let the mixture rest for 10 minutes in a warm location, covered with a damp towel or plastic wrap.

SCALE AND MIX (5 minutes)

1. Measure the salt and olive oil and add them to the flour/water/yeast mixture.
2. Gradually add the remaining white flour until the dough becomes stiff.

KNEAD (10 minutes)

Knead the dough using the pinching or bench-kneading method for 5 to 8 minutes until the dough is smooth and elastic and gluten has developed.

PROOF (2–4 hours)

Place the dough in a proofing basket or greased bowl, cover it with a damp towel or plastic wrap, and allow it to proof in a warm location until the dough has doubled in size.

DIVIDE AND SHAPE (10 minutes)

1. Place the dough on your work surface and divide it into ten equal pieces.
2. Shape one of the pieces into a ball and cover the rest with a damp dishtowel or plastic wrap.
3. Press into the center of the dough ball with the floured palms of your hands to flatten it out a bit.
4. With the tips of your fingers, press gently against the edges of the ball to create an evenly shaped small 9-inch circle. Set it aside on a lightly floured work surface or on greased cookie sheet and cover it with a dry towel.
5. Repeat the steps with the rest of the dough pieces.

BAKE (15 minutes)

1. Heat the small frying pan over low heat until the pan is very hot and a drop of oil bounces on the pan's surface.

2. Place the dough disk in a frying pan and cook quickly for 1 to 2 minutes on one side, then flip it over and cook it on the other side.

   Tip: You do not want the dough to brown too much; the dough needs to cook yet remain soft.

   Note: The first bread is the hardest to cook because if the pan is too hot, the bread will become stiff. It will still taste fine, but it will break when you try to roll it. Your goal is to bake the dough while still keeping it soft enough to roll up.

3. Brush the top of the cooked flatbread with olive oil and set it aside, covering it with a dishtowel. **Tip:** Do not stack these flatbreads as you cook them. Cover them and separate them with dishtowels to keep them warm and prevent them from sticking together.

COOL (15 minutes)

Cool for 15 minutes and serve with a meal, or put some favorite toppings on the flatbreads to create mini pizzas.

SCHEDULE

Active Time: 45 minutes
Total Time: 6 hours

+ Scale and mix: 5 minutes

+ Rest: 10 minutes

+ Scale and mix: 5 minutes

+ Knead: 10 minutes

+ Proof: 2–4 hours

+ Divide and shape: 10 minutes

+ Bake: 15 minutes

+ Cool: 15 minutes

PART III:

The Bakers

CHAPTER 10

Meet Our Testers

The bread recipes in this book were not created and tested in a vacuum. Professional and home bakers alike came together to help me provide you with the healthiest and most flavorful breads in an easy-to-follow format. Diane Abrams, former book editor of *Gourmet* cookbooks, shared with me (while I drooled) descriptions of the magnificent test kitchens and large cooking staff who tested each cookbook recipe for any book published under the *Gourmet* imprint. Diane talked about the difficulty of writing a clear and accurate recipe—a comment I fully underestimated until I tried to make recipes consistent and accurate for this book. My solution to competing with *Gourmet's* resources was to recruit a wide variety of home bakers—from historians to international education experts—to test the recipes. They were generous and devoted. As you bake, give thanks to each of them for ensuring that your bread will be delicious. I've included here a bit about each of the testers I recruited to help bring this book to life. Perhaps getting to know them will bolster your baking confidence and inspire you to have fun with bread making.

Virginia Rice

Ginny is the only home baker I spoke with who has a claim to professional culinary experience. "Many years ago I graduated from the two-year chef's training program at the Culinary Institute of America (CIA), but since bread baking wasn't a significant part of the curriculum," Ginny declares, "I am just another amateur baker like the other bread testers." Although Ginny also tested the recipes for fougasse and whole-wheat bread with hazelnut and currant, her most important assignment was to test master baker Ned Atwater's spelt-bread recipe. She was in the fortunate position to be able to buy and taste Ned's spelt bread because she lives fairly close to his bakery and farmers' market outlets. Ginny was pleased to be able to replicate Ned's recipe so closely that her blind tests at home proved her bread was indistinguishable from the original. (I hope you will have the same success as Ginny when you try Ned's spelt bread!)

"It's remarkable to see how much—in the field of food—has changed in the past couple decades," states Ginny. She admits that her personal conversion from Wonder Bread (crusts cut off) with egg salad to "real" bread didn't occur until she was in her late twenties, when she finally tried to bake bread using whole-wheat flour and whole-wheat berries. "Those whole-wheat berries could crack your teeth if they weren't soaked long enough," says Ginny, "but the bread was delicious, and I made that bread once a week for a long time."

Although she's busy these days, Ginny still tries to make time for bread. "My favorite activity is to take a day off and to be able to spend a Sunday afternoon at home baking. While the bread is rising, I can take time to read the Sunday paper or sew. It is such a luxury to relax and then to have bread for dinner that night." She is particularly amazed at how baking bread in a Dutch oven dramatically changed the quality of her bread: "What an amazing crust! Nibbling the crunchy crumbs and ends of the bread is divine. The Dutch oven makes really good bread. Course," chuckles Ginny, "when I began to bake bread, it wasn't done as an act of trying to live sustainably. My first loaf cost me $75 if I count my investment in the Dutch oven! But it was a worthy purchase since the Dutch oven will last the rest of my life and be passed on to my daughter and granddaughter. And it is providing us all with great bread right now. My husband likes a nice whole-wheat with an even crumb while my daughter prefers anything with a crunchy texture."

As someone with professional culinary training, Ginny is able to offer this comparison and advice to new bakers: "Baking is different from cooking. Cooking is more flexible, but with baking you need to follow directions and weigh your ingredients. Once you conquer the basics, though, you can begin to be create in a distinctive way—not with baking methods, but by experimenting with different flours and preferments. I am so glad I learned to bake truly wonderful bread, and I hope all the readers of this book will try Ned's spelt bread."

Louis Hutchins

Louis Hutchins claims he is an amateur baker, but his credentials include informally assisting the Smithsonian Institution's Museum of American History (where Julia Child's kitchen resides) with a Julia Child baguette recipe on a blog launched in connection with the book and movie *Julie and Julia*. Given his Boston location and expertise as a baker, I enthusiastically asked Louis if he would test a recipe graciously offered by the owners of Clear Flour Bakery in Boston. Louis tested (several times) the commercial version of the Paris Night bread formula (which I had scaled down for this book— see chapter 8) and ultimately produced versions of it that impressed the Clear Flour owners.

Louis's longtime interest in a great baguette inspired him to create an easy baguette recipe using a sourdough starter and a slow-fermenting process that eliminates the long proofing times of most sourdough recipes. The recipe is called Louis's Overnight Easy Baguette.

Louis also invented a brilliant method for creating oven steam to give the baguettes a deliciously crusty exterior. First, he preheats the oven, which is outfitted with bricks (or a pizza stone) on the middle rack. Louis places a large cast-iron pan on the floor of the oven as well as an old-fashioned iron made of cast iron. When the oven, pan, and iron are fully preheated, he slides the baguettes—and the parchment paper on which they have been proofing—directly onto the pizza stone (or bricks). Then, Louis removes the iron with tongs, pours some water in the large cast iron pan, and replaces the iron in the water, which creates a powerful blast of steam. After ten minutes, he removes the pan and iron from the oven and continues to bake the baguettes until they are done. Try his method and see what you think!

Julie Johnson

Julie tested Solveig Tofte's Farm Girl Beer Bread for this book. She baked it twice and reported that she had to bake her second loaf 10 minutes longer than her first because it was such a humid day and

the dough seemed to be moister as a result. Not just a fan of the recipe itself, Julie is eager to meet Solveig in person and visit her bakery café, Sun Street Breads (although she admits that it's a bit intimidating to replicate the bread of a baker who was on the US baking team for the Coupe du Monde competition and a member of the Bread Bakers Guild of America).

Julie admits that, when she was younger, she was afraid to vary a recipe. But now she enjoys introducing some of her own ideas. For example, she plans to bake two more loaves of the Farm Girl Beer Bread soon, each using a different type of Saison beer to determine the impact of their different flavors. Julie also mused whether she might add rosemary and thyme to the recipe and how the spices would interact with the beer flavor. This tester gives us a perfect example of how we can make our own delicious concoctions and start unique traditions by experimenting with home baking.

Nanci Edwards

Nanci Edwards has baked more than a few baguettes—most notably, perhaps, following a challenging recipe by Julia Child. In a contribution to a Julia Child blog, Nanci detailed her attempt to execute the great chef's twenty-two-page baguette recipe. Nanci was one of three female staffers who affectionately refer to themselves as "The Julias" and were responsible for overseeing the transfer of Julia Child's kitchen from Julia's Cambridge, Massachusetts, home to a Smithsonian museum in Washington, DC. Ten years later, anticipating the revival of interest in Julia Child following the release of the film *Julie & Julia*, the museum launched a blog inviting the public to bake and share experiences with Julia's recipes. The Julias decided they, after their intimate involvement with Julia's kitchen, should really "step up to the plate and try Julia's baguette recipe."

When the women met on a winter weekend to bake the baguettes, the air was cold and the dough was not rising properly. Nanci decided to take the bread home, keeping it warm using her heated car seats, and then on top of the television cabinet, until the dough proofed perfectly. Nanci reports that the Julias have "laughed themselves silly many times over that story about helping Julia's baguettes along."

The Julia project revived Nanci's interest in baking, which was fortuitous for me (and you) because she agreed to put her baking skills to use for this book by testing the ciabatta and Moroccan flatbread recipes. Nanci admits to using the wrong percentages of flours on her first try with the Moroccan flatbreads, but she took both the "wrong" and the "right" breads for a gathering of family at her parents' home. "I provided a dish of olive oil for dipping wedges and both breads disappeared immediately." Nanci commented that, in her opinion, "one of the major benefits of the artisanal bread movement is not just sharing bread with family but producing handmade bread with organic ingredients and being introduced to authentic regional and ethnic breads, which enhances our food experience."

By coincidence, while Nanci vacationed in Maine nearly every summer for the past 10 years, she always stopped at Borealis Bakery in Portland (see Jim Amaral's profile on page 200) to buy bread. The world of artisanal bread baking is both big and small.

Mac McConnell

Mac and I met during his second year as head baker at Berkshire Mountain Bakery, and we immediately shared a bond in our enthusiasm for artisanal bread. One weekend, we set off to visit some of the other artisanal bakers around New England. Our first stop was in Portland, Maine, where we met Jim Amaral, and suddenly the conversation was all about locally grown wheat.

At the time, Mac was beginning his fascination with heritage grains—to such an extent that he was trying to persuade his father to grow local grain on the family's West Virginia farm. Mac thought his father, a director of the Small Farm Center at the University of West Virginia, would be able to convince West Virginia farmers that there was a special niche for heritage grains that could be a great revenue producer for them. It turned out that Mac and Jim had a lot in common as they discussed local wheat.

"Once upon a time" is how Mac refers to his past as a mechanical engineer. Mac says that "for some unidentified reason" he began to "fool around" with baking bread with sourdough starter. There was nothing in Mac's background that would cause him to become particularly interested in bread. He didn't come from a family of bakers, nor had he been exposed to much artisanal bread when he was growing up. His bread memories consisted of his grandmother's sweet Portuguese bread, his mother's white-flour dinner rolls, and his father's baked *stollen* (a German bread) each Christmas.

With roots in West Virginia, Mac comes from farmers and teachers. Mac's mother's family owned 350 acres next to Mac's father's family's land. Marriage joined the land into one large farm, called Terra Alta ("high earth"), where they raise cattle and sheep and grow hay for feed. Mac and his two sisters were raised on the farm, and, although they know how to farm, their parents expected them to secure both college- and postgraduate-level educations, which they did.

Mac's path to becoming a bread-baking instructor took a couple of years. After Mac asked for a two-week leave of absence from his Chicago-based engineering job and enrolled in two artisanal baking courses at the San Francisco Baking Institute (SFBI), he was hooked. He really loved baking bread.

Over the next few months, while Mac continued his engineering work, he researched bakeries in the Chicago area. He visited the owners and asked questions. He watched nighttime wholesale baking operations because he had to be at work during the day. Mac tried to stay focused on mechanical engineering, but he was increasingly drawn to the lively world of bread baking.

Mac shared his conundrum with his family and, while they were supportive of his exploring a baking career, they cautioned him to contemplate the career change for a while before making any rash decisions. At this point, Mac was baking through the night and, he says, "...paying way more attention to bread baking than I was to my work."

Mac stayed in his engineering position for another four months before starting the five-month professional baking program in artisanal breads at SFBI. Mac says that being at SFBI solidified his decision. "I knew this was the right career path for me. I loved what I was doing. Baking excited and challenged me."

After graduation, Mac worked at a few small bakeries in Northern California and gained experience with wood-burning ovens. Richard Bourdon, founder, owner, and master baker of Berkshire Mountain Bakery in Massachusetts, heard about Mac through SFBI's director, Michael Souz, who praised Mac as "one of the best talents to come through the baking school in ages." Richard was curious to know if this young baker had "fire in the belly" and wondered if he might have discovered, in Mac, someone else with an endless passion for bread. Richard sent Mac a plane ticket to come from California and "work on the bench" with Richard for a few days.

Richard immediately sensed that Mac possessed the same "crazy drive" as he did. Richard perceptively recognized Mac's dual talents—his precise and technical approach suited the scientific aspects of baking, and he had a creative nature that helped him cope with variables such as fire, moisture, and wild yeast. Richard offered Mac a job, and Mac became an important part of Berkshire Mountain Bakery. As a bonus, the bakery wasn't too far from "the Gunks," one of the best rock-climbing locations in the United States, and Mac traveled there on his free time to climb alone or with friends.

The Berkshires, a rural area with a community of generations of farmers, also attracted individuals interested in the arts and education, and it reminded Mac of his home near Morgantown, West Virginia. His grandparents and his parents labored on the land, and the nearby university provided an avenue for intellectual pursuits. Mac has a strong sense of his roots and a deeply ingrained work ethic. As Richard watched Mac bake, he was pleased. "There aren't many young people around like Mac these days—ones who can work with their head, heart, and hands."

Mac stayed at Berkshire Mountain Bakery for two years until he was lured away to SFBI, where he was given the honor—at the age of 30—of being made the main instructor for the artisanal bread-baking courses; he also works as an SFBI consultant in places such as Mexico City. Mac is a superb baker and an encouraging and patient teacher who is quickly gaining an excellent reputation at the Institute. His advice to new bakers is, "When in doubt, ferment longer and become confident in your own touch."

Mac muses: "I know baking bread will be a lifelong learning experience for me. I get enormous pleasure from each new discovery. Now I am able to trust my sense of touch rather than the recipe and rely on my senses of feel, smell, and vision."

In fact, it's these senses that Mac uses when he slices open a loaf of bread, holds it up to his nose to inhale its scent, and examines the crumb. Mac's approach is authentic—there is absolutely nothing contrived about his understanding and appreciation of a loaf of bread. He has high standards, and he pursues his dedication to bread with a deep passion. By smelling and tasting his creations, Mac studies his bread and strives to make each loaf better than the last.

Mac's plan is simple: within five years, he wants to own and operate his own bakery, which he hopes will be able to utilize some locally grown and milled flours, similar to Jim Amaral's Borealis Breads in Maine. Mac suspects that he will return to West Virginia to establish his bakery, but wherever it is located, he knows that "the bakery will be."

Judy Gradwohl

Judy Gradwohl is a superlative bread tester, and I credit much of her talent in testing the bread recipes to her training and experience as a scientist. Judy carefully measured and recorded each step for every recipe. She conducted experiments with the recipes by keeping some ingredients constant while varying others, such as withholding a percentage of water, and testing different styles of Dutch ovens until she succeeded in achieving the outcomes she desired. Judy discovered the concept of placing a smaller bowl inside a Dutch oven (because most individuals own 4- to 6-quart Dutch ovens) based on her findings that bread will rise better in a bowl matched to its volume.

Judy tested a significant number of recipes in this book and seemed to thrive on the challenge of conquering a new recipe. Although my wet-dough philosophy was unfamiliar to her, and she struggled a bit at first, Judy persisted until her baked goods were on par with those of a professional baker. She is proof that it is possible for a home baker, with a bit of trial and error, to bake superior loaves of artisanal bread.

Testing the bread recipes allowed Judy to try new breads, which she always enjoys. She takes special requests from her children and bakes their favorite breads, including enough bread to make sandwiches for the family's lunches. The multigrain, olive, rye, and cherry-pecan breads in this book are among her family's favorites, and Natalie likes the Anadama bread especially for peanut butter and Nutella sandwiches.

Judy's advice to new bakers is that they should persevere. She admits to some "spectacular disasters," but she has become a more confident home baker. In fact, Judy says that she now feels comfortable altering a recipe rather than simply following directions because she has developed a "feel" for dough, particularly the wet dough.

Aaron Stuvland

It was a distinct advantage to have an individual of Norwegian heritage test the lefse recipe in chapter 9. I met Aaron when he took one of my bread-baking classes, and I was delighted when he agreed to test the recipe when he returned to his family's Idaho home during his summer break from graduate school. Although it is perfectly easy to make lefse without any special tools, Aaron's family still possesses an authentic lefse tool that creates narrow parallel indentations in the surface of the bread. Aaron's family usually prepares lefse during the Christmas holidays, but they loved making it with Aaron in August, and they gained a new appreciation for the bread as an all-purpose wrap for sandwiches. Aaron praises this lefse recipe and says, "Lefse are as easy to make as crepes, just lesser known."

Aaron grew up in northern Idaho, part of a family of six in a home where eating healthy foods was a way of life, as was raising milk goats and chickens and tending a serious vegetable garden. Aaron, with a touch of pride, comments, "I like to say that my mother started the organic-food movement in Idaho—a claim that is wildly exaggerated, of course—but for our small northern Idaho town, she was certainly one of kind. As kids, my siblings and I were 'subjected' to whole grains and good homemade bread as a family tradition. We tasted my mother's occasionally successful—but also unsuccessful—experiments that she conducted with local wheat from a wheat supplier not far from our house. My mother ground her own grain (even Saturday mornings, at 6 a.m., for buckwheat waffles), improvised recipes when some ingredients weren't available, and always took great care in educating us about the virtue of using *all* of the wheat kernel."

Aaron acknowledges, "It wasn't until leaving home for college that the uniqueness and novelty of our upbringing became apparent for my siblings and me. Suddenly we were *proud* of our nutritious childhood diet—whole grains and beyond—and not *ashamed* of it. In fact, I seemed to have had an abiding love of cooking since I was a child, partly because we were required to cook one meal a week for our large family."

Once Aaron went off to college, he began to invest time in learning to make great breads because he recognized that "bread making was an integral part of any self-described amateur chef." He explains, "Bread is very basic, and partly because of this, people rarely find the time or the energy to make it on their own. Because it is a staple across many cultures and histories, people often take the creation of it for granted, settling to buy it rather than involving themselves in the process of making it…. In fact, the process of bread making can be either complex or surprisingly simple but always very fulfilling. Admittedly, making your own bread is a mark of distinction. This, and the chance to be more closely tied to what I eat, are both motivating factors in my bread-making efforts."

Aaron moved to Washington, DC, to pursue graduate studies in political science, work for a small nonprofit that provides study-abroad opportunities to undergraduate students, and widen his culinary horizons. He is an enthusiastic baker: "I love to bake good healthy bread and use locally grown ingredients so that I can contribute to an economy that is both socially and environmentally responsible. I make baking a priority because I love to see (and taste) the product of my labor as well as share that experience with people I love. Making artisanal bread connects me to thousands of years of what it means to *be* human and to understanding that the relatively recent industrialization of food and foodstuffs is more of an aberration than the norm."

Because Aaron lists two of his best characteristics as patience and flexibility—traits that happily coincide with those needed for the art of bread baking—it is easy to foresee a great future for him as he travels the world to learn new bread recipes, always coming home to his Scandinavian roots.

CHAPTER 11

Profiles in Baking

As I have moved through the world of bread and baking, I have met some extraordinary and committed "master bakers." I define these bakers as individuals who use only the best and most authentic ingredients, who are personally involved—hands on—in the daily baking process, and who adhere to the highest standards for their products. I have included the stories of some of these remarkable and talented bakers in hopes of inspiring home bakers to appreciate the best bread and baking methods in the field. You'll also find a few of these bakers at the back of the book in the list of artisanal bakeries, which is a guide to finding great artisanal bread near you. After all, few things motivate a home baker more than fresh, delicious artisanal bread from a local bakery!

Christy Timon and Abram Faber

Owners, Clear Flour Bakery

Brookline, Massachusetts

www.clearflourbread.com

Clear Flour is a tiny bakery that has had a big impact—both on its local Boston-area customers and on artisanal bread baking in America. Two reasons for this impact, aside from the bakery's splendid bread, are the leadership role of co-owners Christy Timon (chief baker) and Abe

Faber (finance and business manager) in the nationwide artisanal bread-baking movement and their constant quest to experiment with new breads and pastries.

When Christy Timon first arrived in Boston in 1980 as a recent graduate of the University of Wisconsin, her aspirations were to pursue a dance career. But, like all starving artists, she had to get a day job, and she and a friend started a catering business. Delighted by her bread, customers began to request special orders. Next, a North End Italian bakery owner named Al Capone (real name) asked for a weekly standing order. Christy's breads were soon warming the tables of restaurants and the shelves of gourmet food stores. When Christy and her business partner amicably decided to split the business, her partner took the catering line while Christy kept the wholesale customers who had come to love her baked goods. She kept on baking, having decided that this was the life for her.

Christy had chosen baking over dancing, but she couldn't seem to choose an official name for her bakery. Then, one day, when yet another customer asked what her business was called, Christy happened to glance over at a bag of flour that was labeled "clear flour." Something clicked, and Christy responded, "The bakery is named Clear Flour."

At last it was done, as simply as that. Yet the name isn't simple at all. A milling term for the flour from the part of the endosperm closest to the bran in a wheat kernel, clear flour is graded *fancy*, *first clear*, or *second clear*, in a manner similar to how each press of olive oil is given a designation from *extra-virgin* to *regular*. Bakers use these various grades of flour—by themselves or combined—to achieve their desired blend for bread or pastries. Thus, the name Clear Flour represents the level of sophistication and expertise that Christy applies to her baking. For those who understand the language of artisanal bread, it is an indication that Christy is a serious scholar of baking. She is also hard working and talented, with a focus on perfecting the quality of the sumptuous goods that come out of Clear Flour's ovens.

Abe came to work for Clear Flour during its first year of operation, when Christy hired him to make a screen door for the back of the bakery (the door is still there) and deliver bread. Before long, they married and became partners in life and in the bakery business. Christy laughs about their early trials: "We didn't think it would be easy for me to bake and have a child, but we never anticipated that I might become pregnant with twins. That was a shocker—to be raising two at the same time instead of just one." Their daughters, their family, and their bakery are all flourishing.

Christy is responsible for every aspect of bread and pastry production, particularly the research and development of new products. She tests each formula over and over, breaking it down into phases that her staff can successfully conquer. Occasionally, she has canceled or withdrawn a product that doesn't pass her high standards of quality control. Abe's role is to handle the business operations, from hiring to managing the bakery's finances, plus purchasing and maintaining equipment, which is critical to production—especially for a bakery open seven days a week, all year long.

When Christy and Abe started Clear Flour Bakery, Abe admits, "We were stabbing in the dark...struggling to learn and implement." They visited with other bakers and went to Europe. "There were ten of us around the country," Abe recounts, "like Carol Field and Steve Sullivan of Acme and a few others who were all paving the path for artisanal bread baking in America. We are still learning and experimenting, but those first ten years were the most intense. Today, we can shoot off an email to a colleague or do research on the Internet. Answers and help are more accessible and available."

Now, Christy and Abe generously share what they have learned with the next generation of bakers. They are founding members of the Bread Bakers Guild of America, and Abe served on the board for eleven years. They boast, "Bread Bakers Guild of America's membership has gone from 100 members in our first years to more than 1,300 members today. We are really proud of the guild's work to advance the artisan baking profession in America through education."

In addition to their national presence, Christy and Abe are always encouraging and mentoring the many bakers who come to work at Clear Flour. Among the dozens of young bakers Christy and Abe have trained, quite a few have gone on to start their own bakeries, including Alison Pray and Matt James of Standard Baking Co. in Portland, Maine; Andrea Colognese of Jamestown, Rhode Island, whose Village Hearth bakery has a wood-fired oven; and Adam Gidlow, founder of On the Rise bakery in Cleveland Heights, Ohio. Two environmental technicians, Marsha Durgin and Paul Rizzon, quit their jobs and went through an apprenticeship at Clear Flour. Today, they own and operate a successful bakery called Crossroads in Doylestown, Pennsylvania, outside Philadelphia.

"Though it is painful each time a baker leaves," Abe admits, "it is a happy time, too, because that person will go forward to cultivate a community of people who begin to recognize the taste of good bread and become the future customers to support the growing American artisanal bread movement."

Clear Flour Bakery is still located in a small space in Brookline, Massachusetts, a diverse

community of various ethnic groups and college students and professors who are knowledgeable consumers and appreciate excellence. Clear Flour's baking area is squeezed into 1,300 square feet, and, because the retail area is only 150 square feet, customers usually stand in a line that winds down the sidewalk. Most customers are locals, but some drive an hour to get there.

Clear Flour Bakery is making a deliberate decision to stay small. Seventy percent of its revenue is generated by retail sales, and the bakery limits its wholesale and farmers' market sales to within a circumference of 15 miles from the bakery. "We simply don't have the space or the bakers to produce all of the breads and pastries our customers want," admits Christy. In fact, Clear Flour Bakery calls their cinnamon buns "morning buns" to remind customers that they will be gone well before the clock strikes noon.

Clear Flour Bakery has a broad base of traditional European breads and ever-changing specialty breads and pastries, reflecting Christy's endless curiosity about experimenting and trying new offerings. Although she could design a simpler bakery menu, she thrives on the challenge of developing new breads and nurturing her customers' palettes.

Currently, Christy envisions two new directions for the bakery: first, to offer more German-style breads and, second, to explore more *viennoiserie* (laminated dough) options to increase Clear Flour's repertoire. As always, Christy and Abe are encouraging to new bakers. Their words of advice to the home baker are, "It is enormously satisfying to make bread. It will require patience, but it is fun. The mark of a successful baker should be to make breads that make sense for you. Think of the rhythm of your life and then design your bread baking around a reasonable schedule for yourself."

Jim Amaral

Owner

❖ Borealis Bakery and Bistro, Portland, Maine

❖ Borealis Breads Store, Wells, Maine

❖ Borealis Breads Store, Waldoboro, Maine

www.borealisbreads.com

I discovered Jim Amaral of Borealis Breads in my daughter's Bates College alumni magazine, in an article about graduates involved in Maine's local-food movement. I drove to Maine to meet Jim and immediately recognized him by his signature handlebar mustache.

As the article indicated and I discovered in my own interview, the most outstanding characteristic of Borealis Breads is its dedication to Maine-grown wheat. Although featuring Maine wheat certainly has a marketing appeal that helps distinguish Borealis Breads from its competitors, Jim's use of local wheat is about personal beliefs and commitments, and he has provided critical leadership in Maine's local-wheat movement.

In 1999, Jim formed a partnership with Matthew Williams, a farmer located "way up" in Aroostook County, who is equally dedicated to the production and use of organic Maine wheat. Williams had bought an old potato farm in the county renowned for its potatoes and, after trying some experimental crops, started to grow wheat and sell it to Jim.

Initially, however, the wheat couldn't go directly to Jim to use at Borealis Breads because it had to be milled first. There weren't any millers in Maine who could handle the wheat, so it had to be shipped out of state for milling. Williams found this not only ridiculous but also contrary to one of the main purposes of growing and using local wheat. Williams decided to invest a quarter of a million dollars into milling equipment, despite concerns that there wouldn't be enough demand for his milled product to justify the cost. "The whole Maine-grown thing wasn't going to work if we didn't build some infrastructure," Williams says. "No one else would do it, so I did it."

The risk paid off. Williams's Aurora Mill and Farm is the only mill in the state of Maine with storing, cleaning, and milling capacity, and the mill is so busy now that Williams can't meet the demand for his locally grown and milled wheat. He sells at least two tons of Aurora Wheat each month to Borealis Breads. "We wouldn't be in the milling business without Borealis," Williams says. "They were our first customer, and, for a while, they were our only customer."

Jim's use of Maine wheat may be the most visible sign of his commitment to local food, but he uses other Maine ingredients in his bread too. Blueberries and potatoes are obvious choices, but I was intrigued with Jim's addition of sea vegetables to his dough. Jim secures kelp, a form of brown algae, from Maine Coast Sea Vegetables. Another favorite locally harvested ingredient is a red algae called *dulse*, which is popular in Iceland, where it has been used as a source of fiber for centuries. Kelp and dulse contain high levels of minerals, vitamins, and protein. Jim adds these "sea lettuces," dried and chopped, to his breads for extra flavor and health benefits.

Jim may have gone to a Maine college, but he spent his early adult years on the West Coast. He was a professional winemaker for five years, and then he joined the Seattle baking enterprise Grand Central Bakery a few years after it opened to rave reviews. A headline in the *Seattle Times* encouraged readers to "Run, Don't Loaf" to the Grand Central. Jim worked there with head baker Leslie Mackie, and they both went on to start their own bakeries.

Jim's first baking effort in Maine was located in the basement of a restaurant, where unused baking equipment had sat idle for years. With $10,000 borrowed from friends and family, he launched his first bakery, Bodacious Breads (later Borealis Breads), with twelve wholesale accounts and a production of 125 loaves a day. His next move was to a Wells, Maine, facility where he still bakes bread and also offers sandwiches and soups for takeout.

From 2001 to 2007, Borealis operated in a section of one of the largest New England grocery chains, Hannaford. It was a convenient partnership because it gave Jim another location where he could bake and sell Borealis bread. When the partnership ended, Jim used the change as an opportunity to open a bakery-bistro in a 2,700-square-foot building in Portland. In 2009, the new store opened with seating for about thirty-five people and serving breakfast, lunch, and early dinner.

Borealis's business is divided fairly equally between wholesale and retail. Jim describes his role as "strategic planner, director of marketing and sales, and a prophet who spreads the gospel of good bread and Maine-grown wheat." He also continues to develop all of Borealis's new formulas and test all of the products.

Most people know Jim for his leadership in the Maine-wheat and local-food movement (see chapter 1). The exorbitant costs of fuel and the demands of an export market have driven up the cost of wheat, igniting a growing movement throughout New England in which farmers are experimenting with various types of wheat under mostly organic conditions. Jim is often asked to work with bakers and farmers around New England and beyond. Currently, he is involved with a federally funded project in the states of Vermont and Maine to identify and grow wheat strains that will flourish in the harsh New England climate.

Jim takes his message everywhere. He is active in encouraging Maine schools to serve healthy foods and is especially involved in Farm to School, a nonprofit whose major goals include: 1) educating students about good nutrition and the role of local farms in promoting healthy, sustainable communities and 2) promoting and facilitating farm-to-institution purchasing. Jim has earned the respect of people in Maine for his impact on the food culture and communities.

Through Borealis Breads, Jim offers his retail and wholesale customers great bread. He also urges people to bake at home. He warns, "Don't get bogged down in the details. You don't even need a formula. Just get to know the flour and water. Experiment with local ingredients. Have fun, and bread will follow."

Ned Atwater

Owner

❖ Atwater's Naturally Leavened Bread Bakery and Café, Catonsville, Maryland

❖ Atwater's at The Shops at Kenilworth, Towson, Maryland

❖ Atwater's at the Belvedere Square Market, Baltimore, Maryland

❖ Atwater's Ploughboy Kitchen, Baltimore, Maryland

❖ Atwater's Falls Road, Baltimore, Maryland

http://atwaters.biz

Ned Atwater has established one of the most popular purveyors of naturally leavened bread in the Washington, DC, region. Coincidentally, like Chad Robertson of Tartine fame and Mac McConnell, artisanal bread instructor at the San Francisco Baking Institute, Ned traces his bread-baking education to Richard Bourdon, the founder and master baker at Berkshire Mountain Bakery in western Massachusetts.

As soon as he graduated from high school, Ned began a seven-year apprenticeship with French chef Michel Beaupin, who trained him in the classic French style. This stint was followed by another four years under European chefs Roland Jeannier and Bernard Lagarde. During the next fifteen years, Ned rose from head chef to owner or co-owner of restaurants in the Baltimore, Maryland, and Minneapolis, Minnesota, regions. Ned's restaurant guests included US presidents Bill Clinton and George H. W. Bush.

Although caught up in the whirlwind of restaurant life, Ned says that, at a certain point, he "needed a new challenge." He also recognized that the huge demands of being a chef and a restaurant owner were interfering with the quality of his family life. Of course, Ned admits that switching careers from chef to baker might be merely a case of "out of the frying pan and into the fire," but he decided to take a chance. Says Ned, "And I got the challenges I was looking for!"

Ned laughs when he recalls how Richard Bourdon spent three days trying to discourage him from becoming a baker and opening a bakery. Yet, according to Ned, "The moment Richard was convinced that I was solidly committed, [he] was most generous with his advice and assistance." Richard may have been skeptical of Ned's decision to leave his career as a chef and restaurant owner to focus on baking and opening cafés, but Ned knew it was the right decision.

After convincing Richard Bourdon of his serious intentions, Ned studied with him at the Berkshire Mountain Bakery. In the winter of 1999, with just one employee, Ned began a wholesale bakery operation based in a large warehouse space in Baltimore. Richard arrived to transition Ned through those first days and weeks of operating his bakery. Ned began to supply breads to restaurants, health-food stores, and farmers' markets. The irregularities of the wholesale business—the ever-changing quantities of each order and the loss or acquisition of contracts, among other things—were factors that Ned had to cope with to maintain a steady economic base.

Ned longed for an affordable retail/baking space and was delighted when, five years into his wholesale bakery operation, he was invited to establish a bakery café in a historic Baltimore neighborhood that was being restored and revitalized and is now a popular commercial and entertainment district. Ned's café offered sandwiches made with his breads and homemade soups. Seven years later, Ned expanded by establishing several new venues based on his classic model. Each of his cafés offers sandwiches and at least one soup each in the categories of vegetarian (sometimes vegan), meat, and fish. The inspiration and flavors come from cultures around the world.

Ned is thrilled to have moved his entire bread- and pastry-making operation into a restored 2,000-square-foot townhouse in Catonsville, Maryland, just outside Baltimore. The space also includes a retail area and café. Ned rattles off the statistics: "It takes a staff of about forty-five people, including sixteen bakers and pastry chefs, and a fleet of trucks to keep everything going smoothly."

Currently, Ned offers his wonderful artisanal bread to Baltimore and its surroundings in five different locations. In addition, he sends breads and pastries to fourteen farmers' markets in the greater Washington, DC, area.

Recognizing how important farmers' markets are to his own business as well as to the health and vitality of the area, Ned serves on the board of FRESHFARM Markets (FFM), a nonprofit that promotes and helps coordinate farmers' markets in the Capital Region. Ned is proud of FFM's innovative programs. For example, the group is experimenting with a special currency that allows food-stamp recipients to receive 25 percent extra value on purchases at farmers'-markets, where costs can be higher than those at grocery stores. FoodPrints, another cutting-edge FFM project, integrates food education into elementary-school science and social studies curricula. The students grow and cook their own vegetables, a process that has helped them embrace vegetables as part of their diets.

Although Ned experiments and likes change, he is dedicated to crafting his breads by hand in the traditional way. He comments, "Food should have integrity, and you should be able to identify the foods and flavors that you are eating. I am devoted to helping bring the naturally leavened sourdough bread tradition to as many people as possible."

Ned uses only stone-ground organic flour and bread formulas that create unusually wet dough, allowing him to ferment for long periods of time. Currently, he is exploring a flour source, a historic 1790 mill in Anville, Pennsylvania, with a gravity-fed system that drops the grains onto slowly moving steel plates that "smear" the grains in a cold-milling process. Ned describes the result as "a silkier and smoother flour, with greater flavor than anything else I have ever tasted."

Ned is also tuned in to how he can buy more local wheat. One farmer, who started with a small handful of heritage grain, has increased his yield to 60 acres, and Ned hopes to soon buy some of this heritage grain for Atwater's.

Ned speculates that any future growth will be about adding new products, such as artisanal cheeses or homemade ice creams, rather than more expansion, and he's already started to explore cheese making to "challenge himself." He attended cheese-making courses in Shelburne, Vermont, and at the University of Wisconsin and has also begun making and selling jams with one of his staff, Gabriel Tiradani, who studied with June Taylor, the famed English jelly-jam guru. The fruits come directly from local organic farmers, and the jams have been snatched up by customers.

As for the breads, 70 percent of Atwater's breads are sourdough, with the remainder, such as the popular Celtic Struan bread and the spelt-bread recipe included in this book, baked with yeast. Ned's advice to home bakers is to "just keep at it and you will have a lifetime of happy fulfillment. I courted my wife with home-baked loaves. Now, thirty years later, I can look back with satisfaction at a life with my wife and three daughters supported by selling bread at farmers' markets and in my store. Give bread-baking a try. Even if you don't make bread baking your profession the way I have, you will have a product to enjoy."

Richard Bourdon

Founder and Master Baker, Berkshire Mountain Bakery

Housatonic, Massachusetts

www.berkshiremountainbakery.com

It's hard to not fall in love with everything about Berkshire Mountain Bakery. Located on a curve of the Housatonic River, the bakery occupies a 7,000-square-foot nineteenth-century brick factory building that formerly operated as a paper mill. Stepping inside the old brick building, with its high ceilings and huge wooden beams, you find

yourself immediately seduced by the smell of baking bread and the sight of racks of deep-golden crusty loaves. The man behind the counter, master baker Richard Bourdon, who greets you in a voice still faintly laced with the accent of his birthplace, Quebec, is passionate about authentic artisanal bread.

Twenty-five years after establishing Berkshire Mountain Bakery, Richard still researches each ingredient he uses, how it is grown, and its health benefits. As a result of the care and concern that Richard puts into every step of the process, the bakery's customers can almost taste the passion and energy with which Richard produces his breads. He is happiest at "the bench," shaping breads, and vigilantly watching over each phase of the bread baking in other parts of the bakery.

Where did all of this dedication to authentic breads and baked goods start? "My appreciation for good food and authentic flavor derived from the foods I ate as a child," says Richard, who grew up on a farm in Ville-Marie in northwestern Quebec, one of eight children—little wonder the family produced and made their own foods! "Our food was truly local," says Richard.

Richard initially wanted to see the world and play music, and he studied the French horn at the Royal Conservatory of The Hague in Holland. At age twenty, he decided to leave the conservatory and pursue a career in food. Not quite sure which direction to take, he ran a newspaper ad stating that he was "interested in food production with either a farmer or a baker" —and a baker called first.

Over the next few years, Richard apprenticed and studied with bakers throughout the Netherlands, France, and elsewhere in Europe. By then, Richard had married a Dutch musician, and the couple returned to the Netherlands, where Richard operated a bakery for six years and worked on reviving the traditional Dutch bread-baking process that used wild yeast and long fermentation times. For his successful efforts, he received a medal from the Dutch government.

In 1985, Richard met the founders of the Kushi Institute (the leading macrobiotics educational center), Michio and Aveline Kushi, who invited the master baker to teach and bake at their center in the Berkshire Mountains. With only $300 in his pocket, Richard says, he, his wife, and their three children moved across the Atlantic to bring his knowledge of traditionally made, natural, and long-fermented breads from Europe to the Berkshires.

His first efforts at reproducing his breads were not so successful. As he discovered, the most basic ingredient, wheat, did not ferment the same way as it had in Europe—different continents, different strains of wheat. With a scientific bent and baker's passion, he experimented for a while and soon was producing breads that the Berkshire community still loves. Richard established Berkshire Mountain Bakery in 1986 and by 1987 was producing 8,000 loaves a week. That's when he moved his operation into the large former paper mill.

Richard has a loyal following of locals, weekend visitors, and those who own second homes in the Berkshires. They buy his breads at the bakery's retail outlet, local stores, and farmers' markets. From time to time, depending on the staff he has working for him, the bakery has produced some pastries, but sourdough bread is definitely Berkshire Mountain Bakery's raison d'être.

Richard is the only baker I interviewed who uses a "cold" method of slowly stone-grinding all of his whole grains on-site. Years ago, Richard brought grinding stones from Canada and set them up in his bakery to grind fresh grain, believing no one would argue that "fresher is better." Fresh grains provide more nutrients than grains that have been stored for a period of time, so Richard continues the tradition of stone-grinding grains even though the process has been abandoned by almost all other bakers.

A bit of a guru, Richard has generously welcomed and taught many of the great bakers, such as Ned Atwater and Chad Robinson, who now run their own bakeries. Chad wrote about the two years he spent apprenticing to Richard in his book *Tartine*, and he praised Richard's bread. Mac McConnell, another rising star, worked and studied with Richard for a year before being invited to become an artisanal bread-baking instructor at the San Francisco Baking Institute.

Richard can be credited with contributing to the revival of hydrated dough and sourdough breads within the American artisanal bread-baking movement. If you ask him what his mission is, he will respond, "To bring good food to the world." He certainly has accomplished that at Berkshire Mountain Bakery.

Solveig Tofte

Owner, Sun Street Breads

Minneapolis, Minnesota

www.sunstreetbreads.com

In March 2011, baker Solveig Tofte and her husband, Martin Ouimet, opened Sun Street Breads in Minneapolis, Minnesota. This collaboration was born from a discussion during a long car trip. Martin talked about the lack of "meaning" in his current work and suggested that they open their own bakery/café together. A celebrity baker, Solveig had been content to leave everything but the baking to someone else. Now her husband was offering to be the business manager and "front-of-the-house" guy. She was startled, but by the end of the car ride a plan was in place. They had even mentally designed a little desk for their daughter, where she could read and do homework when she wasn't helping in the bakery. A successful family operation was born.

Sun Street Breads occupies a 2,200-square-foot space, with enough room for retail and forty-eight seats for customers to enjoy the café's "simple foods," as Solveig says: "Good meat, cheeses, soups, salad, and my breads." Windows on three sides and an open layout allow customers and passersby the opportunity to watch Solveig in action. She feels that affording the customers the chance to learn more about the baking process builds a positive relationship and a sense of community between them and the bakers.

The importance of community and strengthening it through baking is a theme that runs through Solveig's career. Long an integral part of local farmers' markets, Solveig spent a decade as master baker and bread-baking instructor at Turtle Bread Company in Minneapolis. At the end of one farmers' market season, she wrote on her website, "I've always agreed that getting involved in your community is great, worthwhile, rewarding. But until I started this gig I never really understood what that meant. It's all those things and a million more. . . . We live here, our daughter attends school with a bunch of your kids, our neighbors helped unpack my wagon, I made breads for your birthdays, parties, and Sunday dinners. . . . Let me just say it's a privilege to be involved with you all, and thanks so much for doing what you do."

Community also applies to her fellow artisanal bread bakers in this country and around the world. Solveig sits on the board of the Bread Bakers Guild of America (BBGA), the most important educational and membership organization in the field of artisanal bread baking. After a 2010 event in which the BBGA's Team USA won a spot in the Coupe du Monde de la Boulangerie (the World Cup of baking finals) she wrote on her website, "Once again I fell in love with the artisan baking community of the world....The whole goal of this thing is to foster international camaraderie and to inspire bakers everywhere to be the best they can be. It's definitely worked for me—and all the guys I met last week are all fired up to go home and get to the absolute top of their game. Thankfully, baking is a lifelong learning process."

As a member of the BBGA's Team USA 2008, Solveig set herself up for some intense training, and she approached training the way she approaches everything she undertakes—passionately. During the two years of training leading up to the Coupe du Monde, she estimates that she baked 6,000 baguettes and traveled 20,000 miles. She says, "[I] jotted down notes beside my bed when ideas occurred to me, when I was waking or sleeping."

The United States team came in fourth in the competition, and the experience strengthened Solveig's skills and helped establish her in the national and international community of artisanal bread bakers. So how did it all start—her love for artisanal bread baking and her desire to use it to help strengthen communities on local, national, and international levels? You could say it all started with a little-known fruit called the olallieberry and the fine art of procrastination. When Solveig left her home state of Minnesota to attend the University of California at Santa Cruz, she, like many students, found interesting ways to avoid her assignments.

"Baking was a major procrastination tool," she says. And then there was the olallieberry, a cross between a loganberry and a youngberry, which is primarily grown in California. "I'd never even heard of an olallieberry in Minnesota, so being in California and baking with olallieberries felt exotic and so cool."

After baking her way through college (and graduating in spite of it), Solveig settled in the San Francisco area, where she "took about 10,000 jobs to pay the rent" before landing an interview at Sconehenge, where owner Harvey McLain saw her potential. Today, McLain says that Solveig's "combination of brains and personality has made one of the best bread bakers in the country." Solveig eventually decided to attend the California Culinary Academy. After she graduated in 1999, she and her husband, Martin, moved to Minneapolis, where the Turtle Bread Company hired her.

Solveig loves encouraging bakers of all ages and offering them some basic advice. "You can learn so much from how the dough feels. That's something instructors don't always touch on with new bakers…. The recipes always say to let it rise until it doubles in size. Sometimes, that's not going to happen—you didn't knead, the gluten didn't develop, crazy flour—there are too many factors to rely on a visual. So, you make bread over and over, you learn to feel when it's kneaded enough, when it's ready to go in oven. You make it until it is awesome, then you branch out."

GLOSSARY

all-purpose flour: Usually a blend of soft and hard wheat with a lower protein (gluten) percentage of 10 to 12 percent.

baker's peel: A tool comprised of a flat wooden square attached to a long handle used for transferring loaves to and removing them from the oven.

baking stone: A porous stone on which you bake bread in the oven to draw moisture from the dough and create a crisp crust.

baguette: Thin, long French bread traditionally made of white flour, water, salt, and yeast with a crunchy exterior and soft interior full of air holes.

banneton: The French term for a woven-reed basket used to support dough during proofing phases.

bâtard: Bread shaped into an oval form.

biga: The Italian term for a preferment mixture.

boule: Bread shaped into a round form.

bread flour: White unbleached flour made of hard red spring wheat with a high percentage (12 to 14 percent) of protein (gluten), which is what creates the texture in bread and helps it rise.

brotform: The German term for *banneton*.

cake flour: A finely milled flour used for cakes and pastries that blends well with sugar and butter because it has the lowest percentage of protein (gluten) at 8 to 10 percent.

circle folds: A method for degassing and kneading bread by picking up portions of the dough in a circular pattern, moving in quartered segments.

couche: A piece of linen fabric on which dough is placed during the proofing stage; most commonly used for baguettes. The coarse fabric accumulates flour into its texture, preventing the dough from sticking.

crumb: The texture of the bread, particularly the spacing of the air holes.

Danish whisk: A strong wire curled into two concentric circles and attached to a wooden handle; used for mixing dough.

degas: To remove gas or air bubbles from the bread.

divide: Portion the dough into a number of pieces that will be shaped into individual loaves.

dust: To sprinkle lightly with flour.

épi de blé: The basic baguette shape transformed through a scoring technique to resemble the shape of a shaft of wheat, with its kernels alternating to each side.

fermentation: When yeast and bacteria cause a chemical reaction to occur, forming carbon dioxide gas, which helps the dough expand.

ficelle: A thinner, smaller version of the baguette.

khorasan wheat: An ancient grain with origins thousands of years ago in the Near East that is now marketed in the United States under the trademarked name KAMUT. The grain has a nutty flavor and bakes to a slightly yellow-brown mustard shade.

kneading: The process of strengthening the dough by creating gluten, which gives bread its texture and is integral to the bread's rising.

lame: A curved blade set into a handle; used to score dough.

letter fold: The technique of folding the dough in three motions, in a pattern similar to the fold of a business letter, to degas it.

leavening agent: A substance—commercially made or natural—causes dough to produce gas and aeration.

lift: Refers to how well bread rises. Achieving a "good lift" is a criterion for creating a superior loaf of bread.

locavor: An individual who tries to eat foods grown in his or her local area. Some restrict the term to food grown within a 100-mile radius; others suggest that supporting local famers' markets, even if some of the produce comes from farther afield, still defines a person as a locavor.

mise en place: French term meaning "everything in its place," especially used in restaurants and culinary schools to signify that one has all necessary ingredients and equipment at hand.

misting: The process of spraying thin streams of water into an oven to generate steam to help the dough rise.

no-till (or zero-tilled) farming: A sustainable method of farming that aims to cause less soil disturbance by using a machine that pokes small holes in the ground into which the seed is released instead of using large machinery to cut a deep continuous channel into the earth.

mother starter: A batch of sourdough starter saved to create future batches of starter for use in recipes.

parchment paper: Specially treated paper used to line baking sheets. It will not burn in oven.

preferment: Mixtures (mainly flour and water) that are made prior to mixing the main dough and allowed to ferment for a certain period of time (often overnight) before being blended into the dough. Preferments add a complexity of taste to bread.

preshape: To round or roll the dough into a preliminary shape.

proofing: Proofing is the process of leaving the bread undisturbed to ferment or rise.

proofing basket: A container with round sides used to support dough while the bread is proofing/rising; it can be made of traditional woven reeds or materials such as plastic or silicone. See also *banneton*.

retard: A process used to slow down the rising of dough and allow flavors to increase.

scaling: Using a scale to calculate the weight of ingredients; the most effective and efficient method for measuring.

scoring: Cutting the dough with a sharp instrument; this allows the dough to expand through these areas, creating a pleasant aesthetic.

slow-fermenting bread: Bread created by allowing the yeast and bacteria to proof several times to enhance its texture and taste, and to release nutrients in the grains.

spelt: An ancient grain, probably 8,000 years old, that originated in the Middle East as a hybrid of wheat and a wild goat grass.

sponge: A preferment made with instant active dry yeast that adds complexity of taste to the bread.

starter: See *preferment*.

sourdough starter: A natural leavening agent—a living symbiotic culture of yeast and bacteria—usually made with a mixture of flour and water and then allowed to ferment.

stone grinding: A process in which two stone wheels slowly grind whole grains between them, preserving valuable nutrients that are lost in conventional high-speed high-heat milling methods.

thumbing: A technique used mainly in shaping baguettes, named because the method utilizes both thumbs.

wild yeast: Spores that exist everywhere in our environment and in substances such as flour that can be activated to create sourdough starter.

whole grains: Grains that are milled in their entirety—germ, endosperm, and bran coating—providing more nutrients and fiber.

RESOURCES

ARTISANAL BAKERIES IN AMERICA

While this list of artisanal bakeries isn't comprehensive, it is extensive. You may even recognize some of the bakers' names from book jackets and awards.

A&J King
Andy and Jackie King
Salem, MA
www.ajkingbakery.com

Acme Bread Company
Steve and Susie Sullivan
Berkley and San Francisco, CA

Albemarle Baking Company
Gerry Newman and Millie Carson
Charlottesville, VA
www.albemarlebakingco.com

Amy's Bread
Amy Scherber
New York, NY
www.amysbread.com

Anjou Bakery
Heather and Kevin Knight
Cashmere, WA
www.anjoubakery.com

Applegate Valley Artisan Breads
Dennis and Pat Larson
Williams, OR
www.applegatevalleyartisanbreads.com

Alon's Bakery
Alon and Janine Balshan
Atlanta, GA
www.alons.geomerx.com

Baker & Spice
Julie Richardson and Matt Kappler
Portland, OR
www.bakerandspicebakery.com

Baker Street Bread
Tom Ivory
Philadelphia, PA
www.bakerstreetbread.com

Beach Pea Baking Co.
Mariah and Tom Roberts
Kittery, ME
www.beachpeabaking.com

Berkshire Mountain Bakery
Richard Bourdon
Housatonic, MA
www.berkshiremountainbakery.com

Borealis Breads
Jim Amaral
Portland, ME
www.borealisbreads.com

Bracken Mountain Bakery
Bill and Deborah Tellman
Brevard, NC
www.brackenmountainbakery.com

Bread Alone Bakery
Dan Leader
Boiceville, NY
www.breadalone.com

Bread Farm
Scott Mangold and Renee Bourgault
Bow, WA
www.breadfarm.com

The Bread Shack
Dara Reimers
Auburn, ME
www.thebreadshack.com

Brother Moon
Polly and Alex Glover
Landrum, SC
http://brothermoonbread.com

Carter's Creekside Bakery
Charles and Jeanette Carter
Williamsport, PA
www.carterscreeksidebakery.com

Clear Flour
Christy Timon and Abe Farber
Brookline, MA
www.clearflourbread.com

Della Fattoria
Edmund, Kathleen, and Aaron Weber
Petaluma, CA
www.dellafattoria.com

Denver Bread Company
Gregory Bortz
Denver, CO
www.thedenverbreadcompany.com

Elmore Mountain Bread
Andrew Heyn and Blair Marvin
Elmore, VT
www.elmoremountainbread.com

Evergrain Bread Company
Douglas Rae
Chestertown, MD
www.evergrainbreadco.com

French Meadow Bakery
Lynn Gordon
Sold nationally
www.frenchmeadow.com

Grand Central Bakery
Gwen Bassetti and Ben and Piper Davis
Portland, OR and Seattle, WA
www.grandcentralbakery.com

H & F Bread Co.
Atlanta, GA
www.hfbreadco.com

Hillside Bakery
Knoxville, TN
www.hillside-bakery.com

Hot Bread Kitchen
Jessamyn Waldman
New York, NY
www.hotbreadkitchen.org

Jeff's Breads
Jeff Kessler
Lewisburg, WV
www.mountainsavvy.com/jeffsbreads

King Arthur Flour Store and Café
Norwich, VT
www.kingarthurflour.com/visit

little t american baker
Tim Healea
Portland, OR
www.littletbaker.com

Macrina Bakery
Leslie Mackie
Seattle, WA
www.macrinabakery.com

Madison Sourdough Co.
Andrew Hutchison and David Lohrentz
Madison, WI
http://madisonsourdough.com

Magnolia Bread Company
Dianne Reinhardt
White, GA
www.magnoliabakery.com

Manderfield's
The Manderfield Family
Menasha and Appleton, WI
www.manderfieldsbakery.com

Metropolitan Bakery
Wendy Smith Born and James Barrett
Philadelphia, PA
www.metropolitanbakery.com

Mrs. London's Bakery and Café
Wendy and Michael London
Saratoga Springs, NY
www.mrslondons.com

Nouveau Bakery
William Leaman
Seattle, WA
www.bakerynouveau.com

Neidlov's Breadworks
John and Angela Sweet
Chattanooga,TN
http://niedlovs.com

O Bread
Chuck Conway
Shelburne, VT
www.obread.com

One Acre Garden and Bakery
Richard Miscovich
Beaufort, NC

Orchard Hill Breadworks
Noah Elbers
East Alstead, NH
www.orchardhillbreadworks.com

Pure Grain Bakery
Michael Miethe and Holger Seibert
Vacaville, CA
www.puregrainbakery.com

Red Hen Baking Co.
Liza Cain and Randy George
Middlesex, VT
www.redhenbaking.com

Ross' Bread
Ross Schneiderman
Ridgefield, CT
www.rossbread.com

Ryus Ave Bakery
Adrienne Berkun and Mary Backiel
La Veta, CO
www.ryusavebakery.com

Seven Stars Bakery
Lynn and Jim Williams
Providence, RI
www.sevenstarsbakery.com

Serenity Farm Bread
David Lower
Leslie, AR
www.serenityfarmbread.us

SoNo Bakery
John Barricelli
South Norwalk, CT
www.sonobaking.com

Standard Bakery
Matt James and Alison Pray
Portland, ME

Sullivan Street Bakery
Jim Leahy
New York, NY
www.sullivanstreetbakery.com

Sun Street Breads
Solveig Tofte
Minneapolis, MN
www.sunstreetbreads.com

Tartine
Chad Robertson and Elisabeth Prueitt
San Francisco, CA
www.tartinebakery.com

The Village Hearth Bakery
Andrea and Doriana Carella
Jamestown, RI
www.villagehearthbakerycafe.com

Wild Flour Bread
Jed Wallach
Freestone, CA
www.wildflourbread.com

FLOUR, SUPPLIES, AND SUCH

Arrowhead Mills
800-858-4308
www.arrowheadmills.com
This Texas company manufactures flours such as spelt and kamut and grains such as amaranth and quinoa.

Bob's Red Mill
800-349-2173
www.bobsredmill.com
This is an excellent source for a variety of all-natural, organic, and gluten-free flours, many stone milled. Bob's Red Mill is an employee-owned company, and tours of the mill are available.

The Fresh Loaf
www.thefreshloaf.com
This site is an online community for artisan bakers and bread enthusiasts.

Giusto Specialty Foods
888-884-1940
http://giustos.com
Giusto is a second-generation family-run business that produces superior flour used by some of the best artisanal bakeries.

Heartland Mill
800-232-8533
www.heartlandmilll.com
Another great resource for organic flour.

Hodgson Mill
800-525-0177
www.hodgsonmill.com
This company manufactures a good selection of flours, many stone ground. Their products are available in major grocery stores.

King Arthur Flour
800-827-6836
www.kingarthurflour.com
King Arthur's is America's oldest flour company. It is employee owned, features a baker's hotline and live chat, and sells both flour and baking supplies. The KAF Baking Education Center in Vermont offers special short educational courses for both the homebaker and the aspiring commercial baker.

Old Will Knott Scales
www.oldwillknottscales.com
This site specializes in scales and boasts a wide variety of food scales.

San Francisco Baking Institute
www.sfbi.com
SFBI is the only culinary school in the country where you can focus on artisanal bread baking. They offer specialized courses, such as German Breads, as well as an eighteen-week in-depth bread and pastry course. SFBI also sells baking supplies and books.

Wheat Montana
800-535-2798
www.wheatmontana.com
Wheat Montana carries some flours grown with the no-tilled method.

INDEX

PHOTO CREDITS

Jane Barton Griffith

Jane Barton Griffith is an author, professional baking instructor, and consultant to bakeries, most recently at Berkshire Mountain Bakery in western Massachusetts, which was selected as "one of the top 10 bakeries in America" in 2011 by *Bon Appetit* magazine. Jane is currently working on a cookbook on recipes and food producers from the Berkshires and Hudson Valley region. Before settling down on a Maryland farm, Jane worked and lived in Europe and Southeast Asia and traveled to 50 counties where she tasted breads and pastries to improve her baking expertise.

In addition to her baking career, Jane, who is fluent in Vietnamese, worked for three years as director of Quaker humanitarian projects in Vietnam during the height of the war and wrote articles about it for various newspapers in several countries. More recently, Random House sent her back to Vietnam in connection with the publication *Last Night I Dreamed of Peace: The Diary of Dang Thuy Tram* to find the location where the diarist had been killed and to conduct research for 300 footnotes documenting the diary. Jane also served as historic preservation director, fundraiser, and communications specialist for federal and state historic landmark buildings and held several senior positions at various nonprofits.